Prisons in America

Prisons in America

Marilyn D. McShane

LFB Scholarly Publishing LLC
New York   2008

Copyright © 2008 by LFB Scholarly Publishing LLC

All rights reserved.

Library of Congress Cataloging-in-Publication Data

McShane, Marilyn D., 1956-
Prisons in America / Marilyn D. McShane.
  p. cm.
Includes bibliographical references and index.
ISBN 978-1-59332-295-3 (alk. paper)
 1. Prisons--United States. 2. Corrections--United States. 3. Imprisonment--United States. 4. Punishment--United States. 5. Prisoners--United States. 6. Prisoners--Legal status, laws, etc.--United States. I. Title.
 HV9471.M47 2008
 365'.973--dc22

2008004164

ISBN 978-1-59332-295-3 (paperback)

Printed on acid-free 250-year-life paper.

Manufactured in the United States of America.

Dedication

This book is dedicated to all who strive to make the prison a place of humane rehabilitation.

Table of Contents

Chapter Title	Page
Acknowledgments	ix
Preface	xi
01 Punishment and Rehabilitation	1
02 A History of Incarceration in the United States	19
03 Prison Leasing, Prison Industry and the Work Ethic	39
04 The Corrections System Today	57
05 Prison Management and The Role of the Correctional Officer	77
06 Classification and Programming	101
07 Prisonization, Rules and Discipline	123
08 Prison Violence	149
09 Issues in Medical Care	175
10 Legal Issues in Corrections	197
11 Recreation, Privileges, Visitation and Family Relations	221
12 Overcrowding, New Construction and Privatization	239
Index	267

Acknowledgments

This book would not have come to fruition without the stalwart support of my publisher, Leo Balk, who has renewed my faith in the academic press. My husband and formatting guru, Trey Williams, offered continuous encouragement and his patience with this project, as with so many other things, is greatly appreciated.

Preface

The prison is a very dynamic environment. Policies, legislation, staffing demographics, the law and other outside influences evolve and are continuously reinterpreted. In communities across the country, prisons blend local history and ancient suffering with the politics of contemporary bipartisanship. Still, there is no doubt that even though the architecture and technology changes and the demographics of the inmate population shift, there is great similarity between the first American prison and the institutions we encounter today.

Prisons rarely enter the news unless there is some type of scandal, escape, or violent event thus they are misunderstood and often maligned. Day after day, dedicated employees struggle to maintain the health and safety of those incarcerated even though they are overruled and micromanaged by forces with much less knowledge about how prisons can function effectively. The failure to allow experts in corrections to manage corrections is a perennial complaint and one that has perhaps kept prisons from fulfilling their rehabilitative potential.

This textbook strives to present a very basic picture of the framework of institutional corrections so that the forces that shape its character are evident to the beginning student of criminal justice. To understand the functions of the prisons of the past as well as those today, it is important to appreciate the context in which they operate. As any scholar of prisons will tell you, it's not really about the inmates after all.

CHAPTER 1
Punishment and Rehabilitation

INTRODUCTION: THE UTILITY OF PUNISHMENT

A philosophical discussion of punishment often asks what value or utility there is to a particular course of action. By examining our rationale or motive for punishment, we can better evaluate whether or not a specific response is effective. We should also determine what makes a punishment effective, and how important is it how the offender subsequently feels or acts or how we feel in the end. How we react to crime tells us a great deal about ourselves and about our society. As views change on what is acceptable or appropriate punishments, so then, should our responses.

RATIONALES FOR PUNISHMENT

Vengeance

Vengeance is perhaps the earliest rationale for punishing and is frequently described as *revenge*. In early societies, when one was harmed by another, the harmed party (or his/her family, clan, or tribe) had a right to vengeance by personally doing harm to the offender. The old adage "an eye for an eye" is another way of expressing this philosophy, although the adage connotes a presumed right to exact *equal* punishment rather than any punishment the victim deemed proper. While this historically has often seemed practical ("you kill my goat, I take your goat"), an actual eye could never "replace" another eye. Thus, maiming, as in the Biblical "cut off the offending limb" appears to be more symbolic than useful. While this would seem to produce a sense of "making things right," the actual practice of vengeance resulted in problems of perception of what was "right." The offended party's actions to punish the offender were often perceived differently by the offender. Thus, the offender perceived him/ herself as a new "victim" and set out to take vengeance on the (old) offended party, now the new "offender."

The practice of vengeance, then, frequently resulted in an escalating series of "punishments" with entire groups of people (relatives, clans or tribes) wiped out. Such an undesirable situation probably produced the first laws—designed to prevent harmful escalation of vengeance-based punishment. In all likelihood, the first solutions (no-one was around to know for sure…) were based on the intervention of a socially-authorized third party who acted as judge and punisher; thus, preventing the punishment from being viewed as a personal and self-interested act of the victim. The third-party person and the creation of rules governing the amount of allowed punishment were a product of a simple form of government, for instance, a family elder acting as a "leader." An important distinction here is the adaptation of punishment from an individual right to a "governmental" function done on behalf of "society." Of course, it should be obvious, that for this application of punishment to be seen as legitimate, the leader, the rules, and the third-party punisher had to be acknowledged by all concerned.

An example of modern vengeance can be seen in the case where an offender is given a prison sentence of 1200 years for a particularly heinous crime. It is, of course, unlikely that the offender will ever serve more than 60 or 70 years of that sentence before dying. Therefore, the sentence actually represents the emotional outrage of the community and satisfies the need for vengeance.

Retribution

The punishment rationale of retribution is often linked to revenge, but it is much less visceral and more philosophical. The major concept is that of *desert*—what the offender deserves as a product of his or her offense. A minimum of two factors are involved in the determination of desert: the proper amount of punishment and the lesson to be learned by the offender. The first factor, a proper amount of punishment, raises the difficult question of *justice*. Determining the level of punishment the offender has earned as product of his offense is no easy task.

Classical theorists who were otherwise espousing deterrence (ca. 1760–1820), such as Beccaria and Bentham, ultimately proposed a series of punishments that would exactly offset the offender's gain with an equal amount of pain. Of course, the exact nature of the original harm (the offender's gain) is virtually impossible to determine; thus, the amount of punishment remains inexact. Justice, then, becomes a combination of what offenders, victims, and society at large perceive as "proper" punishment for an offense. The 1970s saw the emergence of a form of retribution that denied the use of victims and society in determining punishments. This was David Fogel's (1975) sentencing theory of "just deserts," which expressly argued that the severity of a crime is the only proper element for determining a fair and just punishment.

Today, most proponents of capital punishment argue that a death is necessary to balance the life lost, the murder. While few, aside from those close to the victims, may feel the emotional satisfaction of vengeance, retribution is more of a balance for society and the way to show the offender that the rights of the individual who is wronged will be recognized. The state pursues justice on behalf of those victimized.

The second factor, the lesson to be learned by the offender, is a highly philosophical rationale for punishment. One well-known school of retributive theory was espoused by the German philosopher Immanuel Kant as the "categorical imperative." Kant argued that whenever a person acted, that person was, in effect, saying the act should be a law that others should follow. Thus, the person "deserved" having the same act committed on him or her to show the ramifications of the act being treated as a universal law (thus, the name "categorical imperative"). More modern philosophical positions have argued that by harming another, an offender has a right (actually some have called it a "demand") to be shown that the act is properly "wrong." In effect, these retributive theorists are saying that a failure to punish offenders denies their demand to be punished.

Modern versions of retribution expressly recognize that punishment is no longer the province of individual victims and instead the province of government. Legislative discussions of what sentence to apply to a particular crime are part and parcel of the retributive framework. Recent attempts to introduce *restitution* as a correctional staple can be viewed from a retributive rationale. Theoretically, the idea of restitution means that offenders are asked to compensate their victims either with actual materials, services or monetary payments. Restitution is thus viewed more as a "restorative" measure, a utilitarian effort to make a person or a community "whole" again, while pain and suffering are of dubious value and are certainly subjective in interpretation.

Incapacitation

Although incapacitation is often thought of as incarceration or imprisonment its meaning is actually much broader. Incapacitation is closely allied with the concept of prevention and refers to keeping an offender from committing further offenses, specifically by restricting them in such a way that committing further crime in the community is unlikely. From the Sixteenth to the Nineteenth Centuries, offenders were often banished from communities or transported to remote regions as a means of isolating or incapacitating them from committing further crimes in that jurisdiction. Today, a person may be restricted in movement by an electronic monitoring system that prevents them from leaving a designated area. The theory behind the technology is to make it impossible for the offender to commit certain types of crimes such as drinking and driving or shoplifting. Castration and chemical castration are both considered means of preventing or restricting certain types of sexual offenses. The purpose is to render the offender incapable of repeating the crime. As we have moved away from barbaric, corporal and even chemical punishments, it is more likely that incapacitation will be achieved through incarceration or house arrest.

There are two forms of incapacitation: collective and selective. ***Collective incapacitation*** treats all similar offenders equally, on the assumption that incapacitating all of them will reduce the crime rate. Under this approach, those who would never commit another crime are locked up as long as those who are high rate offenders, thus wasting prison space. More popular with politicians recently, ***selective incapacitation*** is designed to resolve this problem and provides for longer prison sentences for those who are predicted to be high rate offenders. The problem here is that we have yet to develop an accurate prediction scheme. An example of selective incapacitation is the recent "three-strikes" law.

The long term effects of incarceration have always been a concern to reformers and health professionals. While some cite the benefits of being in prison as the potential for exposure to education, vocational and rehabilitation programming including marginal levels of health care, exposure to reading and religion and simply maturing through some of the most dangerous and violent street crime years, most focus on the detrimental impact. Tonry and Petersilia (2000) list the six main collateral consequences as: the impact on one's later life through loss of income, employment opportunities, voting and citizenship practices as well as the possible break up of family relationships; the negative impact on a prisoner's physical and mental health; the problems caused for spouses, children, parents and other family members; the higher likelihood of future involvement in crime and recidivism; loss of role models and neighborhood support in certain demographic regions; and finally, the immediate risks of violence and harmful activities and relationships formed while in prison.

Deterrence

Deterrence is the attempt to prevent the recurrence of crime through a planned lesson in the relationship between crime and punishment. It should be noted that deterrence is a concept that is based entirely on *legal* sanctions, not informal or non-legal punishments. Ideally, as described by theorists of the Classical Era (1700s), punishment should exactly match the gain from a crime. Humans, being rational, will calculate the pleasure versus the pain, see that there is no "profit" and choose not to commit the crime—assuming that the crime would result in swift, certain and serious punishment.

There are two types of deterrence models. ***Specific deterrence*** refers to a person being discouraged from committing a second crime because he or she has been previously caught and punished for a first offense. This would mean that after having received a speeding ticket, a person now slows down when driving and obeys the posted speed limits in order to avoid another ticket. Because the perspective requires a rational person, it is assumed that the effect of the first punishment is enough to convince the first-time offender that another crime is not worth the effort. Therefore, the person has to *think* about the crime and punishment and *decide* not to commit another crime. The necessity of the decision making process insures that a person who is executed cannot benefit from specific deterrence. Specific deterrence cannot be created from capital punishment, because the person being executed has no opportunity after the execution to think about the gain/pain equation and decide not to commit such an act again. A person who is dead may be incapacitated, but they are not, by definition, deterred. Likewise, a person who is insane or seriously mentally ill is not rational and therefore, not engaged in the thought process that would allow them to benefit from deterrence.

For **general deterrence** to occur, a person would only need to see someone else being punished for a proscribed behavior to learn not to duplicate that action. This is often the case when we come upon a person pulled over by state troopers and immediately lower our speed. For general deterrence to take place, someone must be punished as an example in order for everyone else to benefit from that experience. Capital punishment is obviously a means to achieve general deterrence by public knowledge of an execution (although there is very little evidence to support this occurring). Modern examples of deterrence-based punishment are drunken-driving laws that send first-time offenders to jail, longer prison sentences for those in possession of weapons during an offense, and "enhanced" sentences for various "aggravated" crimes. Deterrence, as a correctional rationale, has been extremely popular with legislators since the mid-1970s.

Rehabilitation

According to Palmer (1992) the purpose of rehabilitation programs is to either change or modify offenders or to help them to modify themselves. More broadly, they are used to change or modify the life chances and social opportunities of offenders. Rehabilitation, as a correctional philosophy, arose from the work of late Nineteenth Century criminologists known as "positivists" (see especially the work of Lombroso, Garofalo, and Ferri) and continues today. Partly as a rebellion against the Classical concept of deterrence and equal treatment of all offenders before the court, positivists insisted that offenders differed from "normal" people. These "different" people could be made normal by experts who would determine the form and length of treatment needed to accomplish change. The positivists never referred to rehabilitation as punishment because it was designed not to punish, but rather to treat the offender for his or her own good. They also noted that treatment accomplished societal goals as well by returning reformed criminals to socially productive lives.

Rehabilitation is often linked to the medical model of corrections, arguing that offenders can be taught, trained or coerced into proper behavior. In one sense, the search has been for an "inoculation" that would prevent crime. Treatment programs are closely associated with rehabilitative goals attempting to address the perceived causes of crime. This notion of prevention is especially important to rehabilitation philosophy—if potential offenders can be identified and treated before their crimes occur, then we might be able to create a society free of crime. Rehabilitation became the most popular correctional philosophy in the United States from the 1930s until 1970.

Every year, more than 600,000 persons are released from state and federal prisons (Butterfield, 2001). Without meaningful programs that alter the occupational and lifestyle opportunities of ex-prisoners, the chances of one avoiding revocation and return to prison are slim. Estimates from 2005 are that at least 39 percent of discharged parolees were reincarcerated in prison or jail (Carroll, 2005).

Patricia Van Voohris (1996) uses the term "planned intervention" to describe the many educational, vocational, psychotherapeutic and substance abuse programs available in prison. She cites the most successful approaches as behavioral, cognitive behavioral, life skills and family intervention. Many social programs from the 1960s until today are rehabilitative in nature and designed to reduce crime. Examples are Head Start, the Comprehensive Employee Training Act (CETA), various self-concept and family-values programs, and parenting classes. Two of the problems associated with rehabilitation are that many have claimed that the programs do not work and that most criminals have never been "habilitated" in the first place. In regard to the first, the issue of efficacy, a major study in the mid 1970s (Martinson, 1974) was alleged to have proclaimed that "nothing works." While the study never actually said that, correctional managers and legislators assumed it was true and rejected rehabilitation in favor of retribution, deterrence and incapacitation. There is now a substantial amount of evidence that rehabilitation does work, but must be designed specifically for individuals (Palmer, 1992). On the second problem, some theorists argue that "re" habilitation assumes that the miscreant had the necessary social and life skills in the first place, while a better description of prison treatment programs is often "habilitation." Although this might seem like a minor point, it is true that many criminals have never had "normal" lives and therefore cannot be "returned" to normality—they must be taught such skills for the first time.

Current trends toward mandatory treatment for some offenders, particularly those convicted of domestic violence and sex offenses raises additional concerns about the nature of treatment. Some of the ethical considerations are whether we should compel people to change or whether they have the right to be who they are, regardless of how socially inappropriate we may deem them to be. Should limited resources be directed toward those who do not wish to participate in therapy? Legal issues involve constitutional questions about the right to refuse treatment, particularly if that course might come in conflict with religious beliefs. For example, In several cases, prisoners have argued that access to parole or early release, visitation or other benefits requires them to participate in Alcoholics Anonymous or Narcotics Anonymous which requires members to recognize and engage in a relationship with God which they argue violates the Establishment Clause (Calabro, 1998).

PUNISHMENT IN EARLY AMERICA

Though prisons were used in Europe as early as the twelfth and thirteenth centuries, they were not considered necessary by the founders of this country. Punishment for offenses in the colonies consisted largely of branding, whipping, and maiming. To a degree, attempts were made to make the punishment fit the crime: branding a scarlet letter on an adulteress, cutting out the tongue of a liar or the hand off a thief. Other punishments included fines, banishment, and humiliating devices like the stocks, pillory, and public cages which supposedly not only shamed the errant into never committing another crime, but deterred others as well.

Capital punishment, also practiced frequently during this time, attracted the criticism of European scholars of the eighteenth century. Writers focused on the arbitrary and capricious sentencing practices that favored the wealthy. This criticism grew from discontent with the legal traditions of corruption and class favoritism. Court officials were seen as "guilty" of arbitrary and capricious actions and demands were made for reform of penal codes that would make laws clear and punishments more temperate in form and in length. Influential classical-period writers such as Cesare Beccaria attacked the use of torture and death as crimes of the state. Such charges were instrumental in advancing a wave of enlightened thinking on more utilitarian punishments.

By the early 1800s, violent public executions and floggings were rare, and incarceration became the popular form of justice based on the notions of penance and reform. Corrections, as we know it today, began with a number of attempts at different types of institutions, such as the eighteenth-century almshouse and workhouse and the nineteenth-century penitentiary. The almshouse or poorhouse, according to Rothman (1971, p. 39), "lodged residents who were incapable of caring for themselves, were without relatives to assume the responsibility, and would have greatly inconvenienced a neighbor." In his description of the typical residents, "One-quarter of them were lame or blind, insane or idiotic; another quarter were not only very old but infirm, sickly, and weak—in all likelihood, senile and incapacitated. Some fifteen percent were young and parentless children—the orphaned and the deserted—who would remain until beginning an apprenticeship."

The almshouses, workhouses, and some of the first prisons built in the last few years of the 1700s resembled large two-story houses where men, women, and children—the sane and the insane—were all kept together. The almshouse had a different purpose from the workhouse where debts and fine were paid off by hard labor. Rothman posits that the intent of the workhouse was to put a harsh and deterrent punishment behind the laws that prohibited strangers from wandering into town. Also it "seemed an appropriate way to punish the petty criminal" (1971, p. 25). In Massachusetts, legislation enacting a workhouse in 1699 was entitled "Act for Suppressing and Punishing Rogues, Vagabonds, Common Beggars… And Also Setting the Poor to Work" (Rothman, 1971, p. 26).

Laws in the 1700s also dictated that offenders perform degrading work in the public streets where there were often fights, sympathetic crowds, and the availability of prohibited items. Humanitarian groups such as the Philadelphia Society for Alleviating the Miseries of Public Prisons, which probably evolved from the Quakers, sought to have laws passed that would put the offender into what they believed was a more private, protective, and reforming environment—solitary confinement. The group pressed for the establishment of a prison which would accomplish this goal and keep prisoners off the streets away from ridicule and negative influences (Takagi, 1975).

In 1790, such legislation passed. It directed that witnesses and debtors be separated from convicts, that prisoners be separated by sex and that cell blocks be erected in the Walnut Street Jail. The Philadelphia facility, which had previously been a jail with an adjacent workhouse, was now, officially, the first state prison ever used in this country (Takagi, 1975).

Early nineteenth-century approaches to the study of criminality had a biological orientation. Popular theory held that the criminal was physically and morally inferior, lacking in training and in proper sensibilities. It was believed however, that through proper instruction and reform, he could at least be influenced to adopt a meaningful work habit and Christian life-style. Indeterminate sentencing gave judges the discretion to tie the release of offenders to their ability to conform to the middle class (and Protestant Ethic) values of hard work, piety and sobriety. Over time, education and industrial/trade skills continued to be the hallmark of prison training programs.

Criminal justice scholars agree that rehabilitation programs appeared to be at their height of popularity during the 1950s. Francis Allen (1959, p. 226) wrote, "it is almost assumed that matters of treatment and reform of the offender are the only questions worth of serious attention in the whole field of criminal justice and corrections." Nonetheless, only about 5 percent of most state corrections budgets were set aside for the conduct of such functions (Clear and Cole, 1986).

THE QUALITIES OF PUNISHMENT

Philosophers will argue that although there are many views on acceptable and appropriate punishments and the rationale behind them, it is more important how and when punishment is delivered rather than what it consists of or why it is given. Three qualities have been cited as affecting the outcome of punishment, the certainty, the celerity or swiftness and the duration of the punishment.

Based on a behaviorist model one would argue that the certainty of being caught or being punished is always in the mind of offenders. If you were caught each and every time you committed a crime, you would soon be disabused of any value or benefit from that behavior. Rather, it is that offenders are so infrequently caught or convicted of crimes that sustain their perceptions of the benefit of crime.

The swiftness of the punishment is also believed to contribute to its deterrent value. The longer the time between the crime and the repercussions, the less likely the person is to connect the actions and consequences. Public criticisms of the long waits between arrests and trials or the years that elapse between a capital murder and the execution of the offender attest to our belief that the swiftness or celerity of punishment is an important deterrent.

Writing in the 1860s about the importance of swift justice in the early American frontier, Thomas Dimsdale (1866/1953, p. 13) argued that "swift and terrible retribution is the only preventive of crime, while society is organizing in the far West. The long delay of justice, the wearisome proceedings, the remembrance of old friendships, etc., create a sympathy for the offender so strong, as to cause a hatred of the avenging law, instead of inspiring a horror of the crime." This is similar to a recent controversy over the execution of former Crips gang founder Tookie Williams. The anger and outrage concerning the four murders he was convicted of seemed to diminish over time as supporters pointed to his disavowal of violence and attempts later in life to steer children from gangs as indications that he was rehabilitated and should be spared. Likewise, Carla Faye Tucker made headlines with her conversion to a life of religious contemplation which garnered her support from not only across Texas, but across the world as protesters seemed to outnumber her detractors at the time of her execution for a murder committed when she was a teen.

Finally, the amount or duration of a punishment should also be weighed. Theorists argue that some punishments, if carried out too long, would lose their benefit and drive the offender deeper into a criminal mindset. Others argue that punishments that are too short, do not allow the criminal adequate time to change or to benefit from treatment interventions. What is an appropriate length of time for a sentence or a meaningful fine or service period may need to be assessed on a case by case basis making it difficult to distribute equally and thus, constitutionally. More comparative research is needed on the success of interventions relative to their duration or seriousness.

RECENT DIRECTIONS IN CORRECTIONAL PHILOSOPHY

What Works?

Rehabilitation and reform strategies came under fire by 1960. Analyzing 100 reports of treatment programs and using a rigorous research evaluation process, Bailey (1966) concluded that there was little evidence that any of the treatments had successful outcomes. According to Bailey, there are several reasons that rehabilitation may not work in prison. One reason is the nature of prisons themselves; the punitive aspects, the deprivations, and the unnaturalness of the environment may be too oppressive to promote an improved self-image. He also suggested that treatment may be based on incorrect assumptions about offenders and their behavior and that the right treatment may be assigned to the wrong type of offender (Reid, 1981, p. 269).

Many writers suggest that at this time the mood of the country just happened to be right for condemning the reformist approach to correcting offenders. The most critical ammunition in this assault on rehabilitation was a study commissioned by the state of New York, now called the Martinson Report. The 1975 study by Martinson, Lipton and Wilks, called *The Effectiveness of Correctional Treatment*, reviewed 231 published evaluations of correctional programs during the period 1945–1967. The study concluded that treatment had been ineffective in reducing recidivism and that, although some forms of treatment may work, results were not measurable, or benefits had not been quantified at the time.

Even though Martinson entered the project late in its progress, he wrote the controversial preliminary article entitled, "What Works?—Questions and Answers About Prison Reform" (1974) that later became dubbed the "Nothing Works" article. This piece was seen as the impetus for an entire philosophical movement by the same name. Many critics of Martinson's work argue that he overstated his findings, that if more than 50 percent of the programs did not succeed for more than 50 percent of the clients, it was declared ineffective. In truth, 48 percent of the studies did, indeed, have positive or partly positive results. Critics have also argued that (1) Martinson et al. neglected a whole range of projects that would have shown higher success rates, (2) recidivism should not be the only measure of a program's success, and (3) Martinson did not consider the possibility that treatment might be immediately effective and then fade over time without some type of continued intervention. Even stronger criticism notes that Martinson was looking for a single program that would work for everyone, and when he did not find it, he declared the system bankrupt. Years later, analysis of the same literature seems to require the conclusion that some things might work for some people under some circumstances (Wilson, 1980; Palmer, 1992).

There is some controversy over the magnitude of effect such critical works as the Martinson Report have had on corrections. Patricia Van Voorhis (1987, p. 58) writes "Unfavorable evaluation reviews of the 1960s and early 1970s and their political aftermath have interrupted the implementation of several practices that were well-grounded in research and showed promise of greatly improving the efficacy of correctional treatment." According to Peak (1985), for the past fifteen years or more the "nothing works" attitude has continued to "bedevil and vex" the field of corrections. Looking at the federal prison system, one reporter commented that "without the medical model... most prison administrators have not known what kind of model to use" (Allen, 1989).

Today, the status of rehabilitation continues to be controversial. In a survey of policymakers and public attitudes, Gottfredson and Taylor (1984, p. 196) found that the policymakers, to an alarming extent, misinterpret what it is the public wants from the criminal justice system. "Although the attitudes of both the public and the policy group can be characterized as somewhat liberal, non-punitive, utilitarian, and reform-oriented, the policy sample attributed almost the reverse to the public." While public surveys seem to support the idea that prisons should be punitive, they also want to see rehabilitation programs in place (Cullen et al., 1990; McCorkle, 1993; Public Agenda Foundation, 1987). Indeed, surveys which have asked the public about the purposes of prisons have consistently shown that both punishment and rehabilitation are highly valued (Williams, 1987). Also overlooked is research that shows that correctional officers and administrators continue to support rehabilitation programming (McShane and Williams, 1989).

A study of federal prisoners by Van Voorhis et al. (1997) found that inmates viewed prison as a rehabilitative experience but also saw it as a deterrent, a just desserts consequence and an opportunity for reparation. Older, more criminally experienced, non-minority inmates as well as those employed at the time of arrest were more likely to say that no purpose was served by the experience. These distinctions were more pronounced among the maximum security inmates than those classified as minimum security.

Over time, researchers have assembled evidence that some strategies do appear to be successful in correctional interventions (Gendreau, 1996; Lipsey & Wilson, 1998, Andrews and Zinger, et al., 1990; Andrews & Bonta, 1994). These include matching an offender to services consistent with their needs, risks and personal characteristics (Levrant et al., 1999). Successful programs seem to include the following features:

- a social learning approach that assumes attitudes and behavior can change if noncriminal attitudes and behaviors are introduced and reinforced
- clear, consistent rules and sanctions to make legal sanctions certain and understandable
- illustration of and support for noncriminal attitudes and behaviors
- practical problem-solving skills
- positive links between community and program resources
- relationships between staff and offenders that are open, emphatic, warm, trusting, and encouraging of non criminal attitudes and behaviors
- advocacy for offenders and brokerage with appropriate community resources
- use of ex-offenders as positive role models
- offenders' involvement with the design of specific interventions
- occupy 40–70 percent of high risk offenders' time
- offender peer groups directed toward reinforcing prosocial and noncriminal behavior
- last at least 23 weeks
- multiple methods of intervention rather than reliance on narrowly-based interventions
- emphasis on relapse prevention and self-efficacy

Most correctional experts would argue that we must be realistic about what rehabilitation can really accomplish. With current recidivism rates ranging from 55 to 75 percent, any intervention that has even a marginal effect for some offenders would be worthwhile in terms of savings. We must also think practically about what constitutes success and what are expectations are. Many find that incremental improvements over time, shifts to less serious offenses, less frequent incidences of violations, or less harmful drugs, the ability to hold a job or adhere to most of the terms of probation or parole do constitute effects of rehabilitation and should not be entirely ignored. Rehabilitation, it seems, is a subjective concept.

SUMMARY

The rationales and purposes of correctional institutions have been broad and varied through the years. While each period has produced a dominant punishment philosophy, it would be incorrect to think of that philosophy as the only one in operation. Others continue to affect what we do and how we handle prisoners, but mostly in the background. Some punishment rationales have come, gone and returned again as dominant philosophies. Deterrence and retribution, for example, were mostly discredited by the 1870s—only to appear again a century later and become the dominant punishment rationales in the 1980s and 1990s. At this writing, it appears that rehabilitation, written off in the 1970s, may be making a comeback, particularly drug and alcohol treatment programs. The law in some states now requires certain offenders such as batterers and sex offenders to participate in programming specifically aimed at preventing relapse. The courts have upheld this mandatory treatment requirement even in terms of requiring successful completion as a prerequisite to release.

We now turn to a history of incarceration and the penitentiary, through which punishment philosophies have operated. As you will see, although prisons have often operated out of direct public view, the incarceration environment is extremely vulnerable to changing political, economic and social forces.

References

Allen, C. (1989, February 13). The success of authority in prison management. *Insight*, 8–19.

Allen, F. (1959). Legal values and the rehabilitative ideal. *Journal of Criminal Law, Criminology and Police Science, 50*, 226.

Bailey, W. (1966). Correctional outcome: An evaluation of 100 reports. *Journal of Criminal Law, Criminology, and Police Science, 57*, 153–60.

Butterfield, F. (2001, May 31). U. S. crime figures were stable in '00 after 8-year drop. *The New York Times*, A1–A14.

Calabro, R. F. (1998). Correction through coercion: Do state mandated alcohol and drug treatment programs in prisons violate the Establishment Clause? *De Paul Law Review, 47*, 565–613.

Carroll, R. (2005, November 3). Number in prison or on supervision nearly 7 million. *Houston Chronicle* (from Associated Press), A–12.

Clear, T., & Cole, G. (1986). *American corrections*. Belmont, CA: Wadsworth.

Cullen, F., Skovron, S., Scott, J., & Burton, V. (1990). Public support for correctional treatment: The tenacity of rehabilitative ideology. *Criminal Justice and Behavior, 17*, 1, 6–18.

Dimsdale, T. J. (1866/1953). *The vigilantes of Montana*. Norman: University of Oklahoma Press.

Fogel, D. (1975). *'We are the living proof...': The justice model for corrections*. Cincinnati, OH: Anderson.

Gottfredson, S., & Taylor, R. (1984). Public policy and prison populations: Measuring opinions about reform. *Judicature, 68*, 4/5, 190–201.

Levrant, S., Cullen, F., Fulton, B., & Wozniak, J. (1999). Reconsidering restorative justice: The corruption of benevolence revisited? *Crime and Delinquency, 45*, 3–27.

Martinson, R. (1974, Spring). What works?—Questions and answers about prison reform. *The Public Interest*, 22–54.

McCorkle, R. (1993). Research note: Punish or rehabilitate. *Crime and Delinquency, 39*, 240–252.

McShane, M., & Williams, F. P., III (1989). Running on empty: Creativity and the correctional agenda. *Crime and Delinquency, 35*, 562–575.

Palmer, T. (1992). *The re-emergence of correctional intervention.* Newbury Park, CA: Sage.

Peak, K. (1985). Correctional research in theory and praxis: Political and operational hindrances. *Criminal Justice Review, 10*, 2, 27–31.

Public Agenda Foundation (1987). *Crime and punishment: The public's view.* New York: Edna McConnell Clark Foundation.

Reid, S. (1981). *The correctional system.* New York: Holt, Rinehart & Winston.

Rothman, D. (1971). *The discovery of the asylum.* Boston: Little Brown.

Takagi, P. (1975). The Walnut Street Jail: A penal reform to centralize the powers of the state. *Federal Probation, 39*, 4, 18–25.

Van Voorhis, P. (1996). Rehabilitation programs. In M. McShane & F. P. Williams III (Eds.), *Encyclopedia of American Prisons,* pp. 391–399. New York: Garland.

Van Voorhis, P. (1987). Correctional effectiveness and the high cost of ignoring success. *Federal Probation,* 51(1), 56–62.

Van Voorhis, P. (1997). The meaning of punishment: Inmates' orientation to the prison experience. *The Prison Journal, 77*, 135–167.

Williams, F. P., III (1987). *Crime and victimization in Texas: A Texas crime poll report.* Huntsville, TX: Criminal Justice Center.

Wilson, J. Q. (1980). 'What works?' revisited: New findings on criminal rehabilitation. *Public Interest, 61*, 4–17.

Online Exercise

Go to the your library website and look up academic journals for which you have access (the full text, either in pdf or html) in your collection that would be good sources for articles about prisons, jails, and corrections.

Name five of those journals.

Questions for Thought and Discussion

1. What are the four basic rationales for punishment and which do you think are most practical and effective?

2. What is the difference between a strategy of collective incapacitation versus selective incapacitation, and what are the costs and benefits of each?

3. What are some of the characteristics of programs that seem to work for offenders and what are the barriers or difficulties in meeting these conditions?

4. What are some of the controversies surrounding the role of rehabilitation today? How would you defend the need for continued emphasis on rehabilitation efforts?

Books You May Want to Read:

Jacobo Timerman (1980) *Prisoner without a Name, Cell without a Number*. NY: Vintage.
David Von Drehle (1995) *Among the Lowest of the Dead*. NY: Times Books

Films You May Want to See:

The Big House
There was a Crooked Man

CHAPTER 2
A History of Incarceration in the United States

THE RISE OF INCARCERATION

The use of prisons and the popularity of an incarcerative model are tied to a broader movement in our society where the state is increasingly called upon to address community problems like crime, unemployment and disease. Local officials felt unqualified and financially unable to meet the demands of the care and treatment of the many special populations the scientific community was identifying—the mentally ill, the criminal and the handicapped. Workhouses and penitentiaries, asylums and almshouses were all developed to help the young nation deal with poverty, sickness, and sin.

The penitentiary as a model for punishing criminals was part of an international movement that dealt with the concerns of the nineteenth-century. Distaste for the violent and very public nature of sanctions such as branding, banishment, stocks and executions gave rise to a series of institutions that would better serve any evolving enlightened country. Increased scholarly understanding of the nature and behavior of man led to a new emphasis on the offender (not the system) as the deviant or guilty actor. A criminal lifestyle seemed to indicate that family and religious control or influence had broken down. A disciplined regime within the prison could restore some of the character deficiencies of the prisoner.

In his well-known book, *The State of Prisons in England and Wales*, John Howard suggested prisoners be classified according to their offenses and they be employed in useful labor. He went on to say the prisons should be tended by honest and humane gaolers (jailers), chaplains, and medical officers. Howard proposed that liquor sales to prisoners, who had the means to buy drink, be terminated. He advocated the separation of prisoners at night into small rooms or cabins and the removal of women and young offenders from the ranks of the hardened criminal (Hibbert, 1963).

The Histories of Prison Systems in America

There are two very basic assessments that can be made about the development of prison systems throughout America. The first is that most states developed in a similar fashion with the same types of financial, political, and management problems. They all suffered from incidents of scandal and corruption, they all were vulnerable to public and media censor and they all experienced doubts about the mission and goals of prisons that have led to crises in programming, operations and administration. The executive, legislative and judicial branches of government have all been overzealous regulators of the prison. Grabbing on various appendages of the corrections corpus they have tugged and torn it into a seemingly useless mass of civil service.

The second assessment is that the problems that plague prisons today are the same as they were in the very first prisons. Crowding, under funding, mismanagement, escape, violence, sexual assault, understaffing, inmate idleness, and recidivism are now, and always have been, fixtures in the institution regardless of whether it is run by the state, the federal government or private contractors. For example, in a report to the Colorado legislature in 1899, Warden C. P. Hoyt complained that there were 582 inmates in a prison built for 400 (Chapman, 1992). Keeping these ideas in mind, we can see the patterns and trends in the history of incarceration that lead us to wonder if there can be a solution to the problem that is the American prison.

The Purpose of Prison: The Pennsylvania and Auburn Systems

While there did not appear to be much debate about the need for penitentiaries in the late 1700s, the focus seemed to be on the search for the most efficient and effective method of incarceration. This resulted in the development of two contrasting styles of prison design and management. Differences between the two approaches addressed both the structure and the function of the penitentiary. The first was called the Pennsylvania (or solitary) system. Influenced by the Quakers, officials blended heavy stone architecture with a philosophy of solitary confinement. Inmates spent their entire incarceration without ever seeing another inmate. They entered and left with a head covering to insure that there was no contact between prisoners. Inmates ate, slept, and worked on individual piece production labor in their fortress-like cells. The items were basically handcrafted materials, and the quantity and quality of the goods produced were difficult to control. What officials were proudest of, however, was the routine that insured that no corruptive influence would be rendered by other inmates in this solitary rehabilitative process. "Efforts had to be made to conceal all pipes, and walls had to be a certain thickness to prevent any communication, spoken or in code, between prisoners" (Walker, 1988, p. 6). Even food was passed anonymously through a slot. By meditating on one's sins, repenting, and reading the Bible, the prisoner – reformers believed– could be saved and returned to a productive life in the community.

One of the first Pennsylvania designs was the **Eastern Penitentiary** at Cherry Hill designed by the famous architect **John Haviland**, whose work was influenced by prisons in England, Rome and Russia. Opened in 1829, the radial design of the building–with the foreboding and gloomy facade and the high, vaulted ceilings of the cells – became world famous (Miller, 1974). Haviland also built these extravagantly expensive prisons in New Jersey, Rhode Island, New York City (The Tombs), and Missouri.

The philosophy of the second type of prison system, initiated at **Auburn** prison in New York in 1819, was similar. Like in the **Pennsylvania** system, officials were deeply committed to keeping inmates from associating with one another and contaminating each other with negative ideas. The primary difference between the two, however, was that under the Auburn system inmates would work together during the day in a common area. This allowed goods to be mass-produced in an assembly-line fashion, although inmates were forbidden from communicating with each other. For this reason, this arrangement was referred to as the silent system (because they didn't talk) or the congregate system (since they worked together). After work, the inmates would return to solitary cells for the night. The cells at Auburn were eight feet long, seven feet high and three and half feet wide. Although there were over 1330 inmates in the institution, there was only contract work for 878. The contractors paid 40 to 50 cents per worker per day making shoes, collars, machinery and porcelain hollow ware (Steuben, 1879). One of the most famous Auburn-style prisons was opened in 1825 at **Ossining**, New York, and was referred to as Sing Sing. Of her visit there, reformer **Dorothy Dix** (1845) wrote,

> The officers at Sing Sing certainly deserve high praise for their efforts during the past year, at establishing and maintaining a mild form of discipline. Difficulties and serious obstacles present themselves continually... since the internal construction and arrangements of the prison prevent separation.

Though Dix clearly favored the Pennsylvania model and opposed business or profit-making motives in prison, the Auburn system boasted better work performance and lower construction as well as operating costs. This cultivated the politicians, and more facilities were built along the Auburn model. Reports also seemed to indicate that the solitary isolation in prisons, like the Eastern, drove many men mad. The debate between the Auburn and Pennsylvania systems was indeed one of the great correctional controversies of all times. Rothman (1971) relates that dignitaries from many foreign countries were drawn into the arguments, and scholars wrote editorials and rebuttals over the advantages and disadvantages of each. Today, penologists still debate some of the basic philosophical questions of reform, work, and the negative influences of other inmates.

By the late 1800s, both sides were coming to the realization that both approaches might be ineffective in reducing criminal tendencies. The desire to give different types of treatment to different categories of offenders, such as juveniles and nonviolent criminals, led to a search for more progressive designs.

The Reformatory—Elmira

A new model of incarceration built on the theme of rehabilitation, with an emphasis on the young offender, was the reformatory. The first reformatory, Elmira in New York, was opened in 1876 under the creative supervision of Zebulon Brockway. "Elmira's inmates were exposed to academic and vocational education, as well as programs of labor designed to teach skills and instill the Protestant work ethic. A carefully planned mark and classification system allowed inmates to earn their own release and promoted internal order" (Pisciotta, 1989). As Rothman (1980) explains, there were three classifications. "The inmate entered at grade two and if he behaved himself well (fulfilling work and school assignments and committing no disciplinary infractions), he could earn up to nine marks a month, thus, six months or fifty four marks later, he could win promotion to grade one—the only grade from which he could be released." Under this system, inmates were, for the first time in the United States, released on parole. There were also three ways the inmate could be demoted: crookedness, quarreling, and disregarding the rules (Rothman, 1980).

The tenure of Zebulon Brockway was not without its alleged abuses. On several occasions, Brockway and his staff were formally questioned over incidents of beatings, sexual improprieties and torture-like punishments dealt to the young men in his care. Details of these events are chronicled by Pisciotta (1994) in his work, *Benevolent Repression* which recounts not only the achievements of this period but the potential problems with overzealous disciplinarians that have haunted the correctional system.

Despite the controversies over Brockway's performance, over the next 25 years, a dozen other reformatories, based on this new penology, were opened. They included facilities in Michigan (1877), Massachusetts (1884), Pennsylvania (1889), Minnesota (1889), Colorado (1890), Illinois (1891), Kansas (1895), Ohio (1896), and Indiana (1897) (Pisciotta, 1989). As Miller (1974, p. 108) explains, the reformatory "served to siphon off the under-thirty prison population, and was an important regulating force in prison population growth." According to Reid (1981), the reformatory movement began to decline in 1910 primarily because funds were not appropriated for the necessary trained professionals to perform the original mission.

Progressive Designs in Old Institutions

The reformatory was not the only attempt to make prisons more rehabilitative and humane. Progressives of the early twentieth century sought to modernize prisons by abolishing the lockstep and striped uniforms, liberalizing correspondence and visitation policies, and burying once and for all the rules of silence (Rothman, 1980). One of the most important figures in this struggle was **Thomas Mott**

Osborne, a prison warden who anonymously spent a week as an inmate in the Auburn prison to gain insight into his problems. Certain that such a repressive environment caused deviance and brutality; he sought to create an environment where the inmate could be responsible for his own conduct (Rothman, 1980). Progressives such as Osborne and later Howard Gill sought to redesign the prison by creating communities with outdoor recreation, fund-raising events, and psychiatric services.

THE WESTWARD EXPANSION OF PRISONS

Unlike the controversy of siting prisons today, where no one seems to want a prison located "in their neighborhood," a state prison was a fiercely competitive undertaking in states and territories throughout the 1800s. The award of construction funds was sought by ambitious developers and political aspirations were tied to the belief that the location of a state prison would insure that a city would eventually become the new state's capital. In Missouri and California, for example, those bidding for the contract to build the first state prison were hoping that additional projects would come with the decision to place the state capital in the same location.

In Arizona, legislators even stooped to trickery to obtain the prison contract. In 1868 the legislature had approved prison construction in Phoenix but had failed to appropriate funds. When the issue came up again seven years later, "Jose Maria Redondo and R. B. Kelly, representatives from Yuma County, amended the bill by inserting the name Yuma where Phoenix had been. Quietly, the bill was brought before the legislature, and was signed by Governor Anson P. K. Safford" while the legislator from Phoenix, who had originally introduced the bill was outmaneuvered (Trafzer & George, 1978).

In the early 1830s, Missouri Governor John Miller proposed a site in Jefferson City for the state's first penitentiary that would strengthen the city's bid to be the state capitol (Schroeger, 1984). Designed by John Haviland, the castle-like structure operated under the Pennsylvania "solitary" system. The development of the state correctional system in Missouri was typical of many other states in that officials hoped the facility would be able to generate profits from industry and be self-supporting. The prison opened in 1836 with a forty-bed capacity and in two years was overcrowded with two inmates in each cell. The first guards employed in the system received no training. They worked 48 hours per week and were on call 24 hours a day, 7 days a week. There was no overtime, insurance, benefits or sick leave. The guards were paid $130 per year, and each person had to purchase their own whistle, club and blue serge suit. Uniforms were not adopted until 1955 (Schroeger, 1984).

The California Prison System

For the first five years of the American occupation of California, there were no fixed laws or prisons (Wilkins, 1918). There were six jails (San Francisco, San Jose, Los Angeles, Monterrey, San Diego and Santa Barbara) at the time California became a state. At the first legislative session in 1850 an extensive penal code was adopted and jails were declared to be state prisons until such time as a state prison could be built. Sheriffs were directed to work convicts on public accounts and if no work was available, they were to be transferred to a county where services were needed. However, jails at this time were flimsy and easy to escape from and serious offenders were thrown together with petty criminals. A variety of scandals ensued.

In 1851 the legislature decided to put an end to the debate over building a prison and ordered the state to lease out the convicts. Prisoners were leased to General Vallejo and General Estill after they posted a $100,000 bond supporting their promise to provide food, clothing, and shelter for their charges. The lessees would build a temporary shelter for housing and provide the tools and chains as well as the expense of the guards, wardens, etc. The Governor appointed Prison Inspectors, volunteers, who would make prison rules and enforce standards of care (Wilkins, 1918).

Women prisoners could not be employed with the men but they could work separately as they lived and ate separately. There were only three women incarcerated in the early 1850s; Scotch Mary, Dolores and Russian Kate) and all had children by high ranking guards in the system which caused a scandal. All three were discharged by 1854.

At this time, sheriffs received $1 per mile for transporting the convicted to prison and overestimating mileage was a well-known form of corruption. If prisoners escaped, the lessees would have to post the reward (up to $2500) for their safe return. Escapes were not uncommon as much of the work the prisoners performed was outside the prison, even outside the county. Once, four to five convicts were sent with a guard to prospect for a gold mine in Mariposa County. The guard returned alone. In addition, in 1851, all 25 prisoners escaped and General Vallejo used the opportunity to convert an old hulk into a prison boat to house the offenders. This was consistent with his plan to develop the north end of the bay where the Army Headquarters at Benicia and a port for Pacific Mail Steamships would be. He hoped that the town of Vallejo would be named the state capitol, and he would receive the contract to construct state buildings using inmate labor, but the legislature rejected this idea. Disappointed, General Vallejo withdrew from the deal and left Estill with the lease (Wilkins, 1918).

The framers of the 1851 Act never anticipated over 50 inmates at any one time. The lessees expected free labor from a small, compact body of men who would be easily guarded, cheaply fed and confined at night on a prison ship.

The legislature directed the prison inspectors and the commissioner of public buildings to spend $10,000 on a 20 acre prison site at Quentin Point. Named after an Indian Chief, historians believe the "San" was later added as Americans attached "San" or "Santa" to everything they believed was Spanish. On July 14, 1852, the hulk with 40-50 convicts was moored at San Quentin as the prisoners built temporary quarters and offices for staff and dug wells. Within one year, 100 inmates were crammed on the ship which grew to 150 as four men were placed in an 8 foot x 8 foot cell. Estill established a brick factory to build the prison with, but the state did not want to reimburse this expense and construction stalled (Wilkins, 1918).

Meanwhile disease was rampant on the ship. Reports criticized conditions, long overlooked and the state tried to terminate the lease on the offenders. Estill, who was now a state senator, fought back and all that seemed to change was that the Prison Inspectors were no longer allowed their $500 personal expenses. Estill moved the most trustworthy prisoners to temporary sleeping quarters on land.

There were 83 escapes in 1854, some alone, some in groups. The largest group of escaping inmates was 22. Some took boats from the nearby area, others escaped into the brush and woods of Marin County. Upset residents gave chase but the heavy fog in the area and the tendency for the moisture to clog muskets made pursuit difficult and dangerous. Often guards and inmates were killed in escapes and escape attempts. Concerned over lowered property values surrounding the prison, Governor Bigler called on the Prison Inspectors and Legislature to do a special investigative report. The findings were that the principle cause of escape was the trusty system where inmates were unsupervised, sometimes roaming around the county on errands or gone for days at a time. Rumors persisted about "bars" operating in prison areas and that guards were undisciplined, lazy and often drunk on duty. Investigators believed the number of escapes and deaths were actually higher than reported and called for the law to be modified to insure that inmates would only work on prison property (Wilkins, 1918).

At this same time, construction had begun on San Quentin which was now set to hold 300 inmates, far more than anyone ever imagined. Officers' quarters and administration offices were on the first floor with tiers of cells on the second, third and fourth floors. One of the oldest facilities still in use today, San Quentin has undergone significant renovations, but remains rich in historical presence.

MINING, TERRITORIES AND PRISONS FOR THE LAWLESS

Unlike the rapidly developing trade and industry states, territories like Utah, Arizona, Colorado, Montana and Alaska were just being settled when the need for prisons arose. Federal interests in having peaceful, orderly areas for families to ranch and mine, establish homes and contribute toward the young nation's powerful image had the government carefully monitoring the territories. Gold rushes and land fights, the vast wealth that changed hands daily, the flood of bars, brothels, and gun fights emphasized the dangerous lawlessness that pervaded the area. Officials feared that news accounts of scandals, vigilante justice, and bands of outlaws would curtail the westward migration of decent God-fearing families who would play a vital role in America's economic growth.

To insure order in the territories, weak law enforcers were quickly replaced and requests for territorial jails and prisons were funded expediently. In some instances, territories had prisons before statehood was sought or a state capital. Still, the politics of site selection and control of the prisons was as controversial as everywhere else. In Colorado, an ambitious newcomer, attorney Thomas Macon lobbied for the territory's prison to be at Canon City. As a member of the territorial legislature, he agreed to support his cronies' efforts to make Denver the future state capital in return for their votes for his penitentiary site. In 1867, the U.S. Congress authorized the Colorado Territory to use its entire fiscal revenue from 1866 to construct their penitentiary, which was the sum of $40,000. Although some of the territories' facilities were only small log cabins, the Colorado prison was an imposing two story, 40-cell stone structure (Chapman, 1992).

In 1871 the federal government authorized the building of Montana's territorial prison at Deer Lodge although it reverted to the state in 1889 when it was admitted to the union (Edgerton, 2004). As were the other territorial prisons in Utah, Arizona (Yuma) and Colorado, it was overcrowded soon after it was built. Alaska suffered through long periods of neglect from the government as a civil and judicial district even before it became a territory. An outbreak of smallpox in 1892 meant the makeshift jail would have to be abandoned and the weeks of delay in correspondence with Washington led U. S. Marshals to improvise inmate care including using a moored schooner and a rented house. It wasn't until after the Klondike gold rush that Alaska became a territory in 1912 and funds were set aside to build a jail. Unfortunately, no additional money was allocated to heat the facility and it sat unused for quite some time. The Federal Bureau of Prisons provided oversight of an Alaskan jail system until the territory became a state in 1959 (Keve, 1992).

THE 1930s–1940s: SOCIAL PROBLEMS AND PRISON RESPONSES

The 1930s and the Great Depression brought many socio-economic problems that changed the structure and function of American prisons. Nationwide, institutions suffered from economic and political neglect. Touring the Texas prisons in 1930, one legislator commented that they were "not fit for a dog" (Martin and Ekland-Olson, 1987). Attempts to make prisons profitable or at least self-sustaining meant that institutions were built on remote farms where crops and livestock were tended by inmates. Growing cities, particularly capitols, no longer wanted unsightly prison facilities within their boundaries.

The Depression also meant years of record high unemployment, and Prohibition meant bootlegging and organized crime. The FBI grew to be a powerful crime-fighting establishment under J. Edgar Hoover, and G-men rounded up "gangsters" considered the most dangerous in the country. Looking for the most secure facility possible, the government adopted a military prison at Alcatraz, California. This island prison off the coast of San Francisco was described by the Attorney General as

> ...the ultimate punishment society could inflict upon men short of killing them, the point of no return for multiple losers, the threat which harassed or malicious wardens could dangle over unruly charges, the one place in the American penal system that made not even a pretense at rehabilitation, whose one avowed aim was to confine and punish—the great garbage can of the San Francisco Bay into which the Feds dumped its most rotten apples.

Indeed, Alcatraz was equipped to be escape proof. It had automatic locking devices, a tear gas release system, and bars over all the sewer outlets. As time went on, however, incarceration without rehabilitation became unpopular, the cost of running Alcatraz became prohibitive, and two very highly publicized escape attempts made the institution less worthwhile; it was finally closed in 1963.

During the 1940s, all of the problems of limited resources, violence, and overcrowding were put on the back burner while the production of clothing for the war effort took priority. According to the Bureau of Justice Statistics, during WWII the country's prison population declined by nearly 50,000 in five years as most of the pool of potential offenders was drafted. By 1946, the incarceration rate had dropped to 99 per 100,000. This trend was seen again during the Vietnam Era when the prison population declined by 30,000 in the years 1961-68. The 1968 incarceration rate dropped to the lowest point since the late 1920s.

THE PRISON IMAGE PROBLEM

Prisons have historically been plagued by an unprofessional image. According to Carleton (1971), there are several reasons for this. First, the locations of the facilities were, especially across the South and Midwest, remote farms. Employees drawn from these rural sites were undereducated and unsophisticated. The culture conflict that developed between the city inmates and the country guards usually resulted in power struggles and brutality. Another related problem was that there was no systematic officer training taking place. Officers had little of no understanding of the broader goals of penology. The salaries, as shown in the case of Missouri and California, were exceptionally low. Likewise in Louisiana, a guard in 1945 made between $130 and $180 per month. However, one of the most serious problems in rural prisons was that few guards were even employed. At Angola prison in Louisiana in 1942 there were only 14 civilian employees whose duties were "purely custodial" (Carleton, 1971). In most instances, the toughest inmates were selected to supervise the others. Parker (1986) describes the Arkansas system:

> ...in the absence of sufficient free world employees, a hierarchy developed among the inmates. Long-line workers were called rankmen. Inmates who worked without armed supervision were called do-pops. These two groups lived together in the wooden barracks. The inmates in authority were called trustees, and lived apart from other inmates. Along with authority went special privileges, including being able to run money making enterprises. The long-line rider sold food and drinks in the field. The floorwalker sold beds and mattresses.

In evaluating the problems historically faced by prison officials in Louisiana, Carleton (1971) touches on factors common in most states during the period from 1900 to 1950. First, public opinion, the ultimate arbiter of policy formation, was not interested in the prison system. The public abandoned it, ignored it, and gave it no support. When this happens, the void represented by the citizens' lack of interest is filled by political control. Time and time again, efforts by a few dedicated reformers were subverted by the insurmountable costs accompanying improvements and the disfavor this incurred with politicians. Thirdly, the more contemporary penological goal of rehabilitation, perhaps because of its associated expenses, has been unable to overcome the farm-for-profit image that many officials and perhaps some of the public still maintain.

Finally, one of the most damaging policies in prison operations was the use of management positions as gifts of political patronage. In many states, jobs running prisons were given as rewards to political supporters or to family members and friends. Jacobs (1977, p. 20) describes circumstances in Illinois:

> Elmer Greene, for example, former sheriff of Lank County became the Stateville/Joliet warden in 1926. As Sheriff he had earned the indebtedness of Governor Len Small by helping the latter sway public opinion in Waukegan, where Small had been tried (and found innocent) of converting public funds to his own use.... As warden, Greene considered it a matter of course to require employees to contribute to the governor's political party and to the payment of the $650,000 judgment that had been entered against Small in a related civil suit.

One of the chief consequences of political ties is that wardens or prison superintendents have traditionally held office for very short periods of time. When the reformist warden of Sing Sing, Thomas Mott Osborne, resigned in 1916 after less than two years, he was the eighth man to leave that office in twelve years (Takagi, 1975). Theoretically, a short tenure disrupts prison operations, destabilizes other employees, and impedes the progress of planned reforms.

A study by Lunden (1957) examined 612 wardens who had held office in 43 states over a period of 50 years. He found that 37 percent of the officials served 2 years or less, 24 percent held office from 3 to 4 years and another 26 percent served between 5 and 9 years. This means that 87 percent were in office less than 10 years. The author explained that "In the 50 years from 1906 to 1955, the annual rate of turnover in wardenships varied from the lowest of 3.4 in 1930 to the highest of 35.6 percent in 1935" (p. 15). In Missouri, no warden served over four years in the period from 1880 to 1920 as they changed with each governor (Schroeger, 1984). The same happened in Arizona where the warden of the Yuma State Prison changed almost every two years. Another interesting phenomenon that Lunden (1957, p. 15) refers to is the in-and-out of power career. "Twenty-seven wardens were in and out of office twice, 5 three times, and 1 four times." He relates that "No facts are available to explain this revolving-door procedure, but in all probability political patronage played an important part in the changes."

The Civil Rights Revolution and Experiments in Treatment

The 1960s presented this country with human rights challenges that were met with reform legislation, innovative programs and court cases that changed the policies and practices of prisons nationwide. In 1963, Attorney General Robert Kennedy closed the Alcatraz prison, perhaps as a reflection of his combative relationship with FBI Director J. Edgar Hoover but most likely because of the awareness that image no longer trumped practical expenditures. The labeling perspective presented by criminologists created an awareness of the need to explore deinstitutionalization, due process, diversion and decriminalization. Experiments with shock probation placed many offenders in prison for only short periods of time and the *Prisoner Rehabilitation Act* and the *Narcotic Addict Rehabilitation Act* provided prison treatment initiatives. In 1964, the Supreme Court's decision in *Cooper v. Pate*, meant that prisoners could sue for violations of their constitutional rights, which mirrored the growing civil rights movement around the U.S.

The decade between the Attica riot of 1971 and the New Mexico riot of 1980 was one of political turmoil and a rapidly changing correction's landscape. Protests on the outside were *Furman v. Georgia* (1972) struck down the death penalty, converting death row offender's terms to life in prison. The *Vocational Rehabilitation Act* was passed at about the same time that most states were maximizing work release programs. Prison industries were revived under the *Prison Industry Enhancement Act* and *Dothard v. Rawlinson* cleared the way for more females to be hired as correctional officers. Despite many promising treatment initiatives, the optimism of a program friendly experimental movement was derailed by Robert Martinson's "Nothing Works" article published in 1974.

The dramatic increases in prison populations throughout the 1980s led many jurisdictions to search for meaningful alternative punishments. In 1982 Georgia began Intensive Supervision Probation which was soon copied by most other states. The first boot camps opened soon afterward as did electronic monitoring. Policymakers wanted to appear conservative and tough on crime, despite the need to save money in the face of ballooning correctional expenses. Private prisons were contracted as another way to potentially reduce costs while still appearing "tough on crime." Legislators believed, despite some evidence to the contrary that their constituents were dissatisfied with rehabilitation efforts, punitive and willing to spend whatever it would take to lock up offenders for ever-increasing periods of time.

Incarceration From the Jacksonian Era to the Drug War Era

Historians often label the early development of prisons as the Jacksonian Era 1825–1850. This period is dominated by the large fortress like institutions. Support for solitary confinement was eventually offset by the need to establish factory enterprises that would help make the prisons self-sustaining. In the south, large plantations produced crops and livestock for consumption as well as sale. Critics of the large scale warehousing and oppressive conditions were able to make piecemeal reforms toward more humane conditions and the implementation of some programs aimed at improving the future for inmates. The Progressive Era, 1850 to 1900 was characterized by a medical model of corrections that led to experiments with treatment facilities, inmate self-government and parole. Despite attempts to make prisons impressive fortresses that protected society and reformed the individual, problems of overcrowding, unhealthy conditions, understaffing and mismanagement were common.

The period from 1900 to 1940 is often referred to as a Bureaucratic or Business Era where leasing, farm work and road building crews, described in the next chapter, reflected the states' interest in finding alternative arrangements for funding incarceration. The Modern Era in corrections, from about 1940 to 1980 refers to a period where more emphasis was on efficient operations, the installation of technology to enhance security, and the professionalizing of the officer workforce. Finally, the Drug War Era, beginning in the early 1980s reflects the political emphasis on combating the sale and use of narcotics throughout the country. Waves of prison facility construction and tougher sentencing laws made this period infamous for its get-tough approach to addressing what was perceived to be a major social problem. Still, overcrowding and under funding has meant that there is pressure on officials to find more alternatives and cost-cutting measures to sustain the corrections network. Private prisons and upgraded "self-pay" jails like those in Santa Ana, California (Steinhauer, 2007) where low security inmates can pay anywhere from $75 to 127 per day to have clean, quiet, upscale facilities to serve their sentences in seem likely to continue debates about discrimination and differing levels of justice in this country.

References

Carleton, M. (1971). *Politics and punishment.* Baton Rouge, LA: Louisiana State University Press.

Chapman, J. (Ed.). (1992). *This is the prison: Colorado Penitentiary, Canon City* (3rd ed.) Canon City, CO: Colorado Territorial Prison Museum.

Clauss, F. J. (1981). *Alcatraz: Island of many mistakes.* Menlo Park, CA: Briarcliff Press.

Dix, D. (1845). *Remarks on prisons and prison discipline in the United States.* Montclair, NJ: Patterson Smith (reprinted 1967).

Edgerton, K. (2004). *Montana justice: Power, punishment and the penitentiary.* Spokane: University of Washington Press.

Hibbert, C. (1963). *The roots of evil.* Boston: Little, Brown.

Jacobs, J. (1977). *Stateville: The penitentiary in mass society.* Chicago: University of Chicago Press.

Keve, P. W. (1992, Winter). The BOP's Alaskan adventure. *Federal Prisons Journal,* 43–47, 55.

Lunden, W. A. (1957). The tenure and turnover of state prison wardens. *American Journal of Corrections, 19*, 6, 14.

Martin, S., & Ekland-Olson, S. (1987). *Texas prisons.* Austin, TX: Texas Monthly Press.

Miller, M. (1974). At hard labor: Rediscovering the 19th century prison. *Issues in Criminology, 9*, 1, 91–114.

Parker, M. L. (1986). *Judicial intervention in correctional institutions: The Arkansas odyssey.* Unpublished doctoral dissertation. Huntsville, TX: Sam Houston State University.

Pisciotta, A. (1994). *Benevolent repression: Social control and the American reformatory-prison movement.* NY: New York University Press.

Pisciotta, A. (1989). Eugenics, social control and the state: Progressive penology at the Indiana Reformatory, 1897–1923. Paper presented at the annual meeting of the Academy of Criminal Justice Sciences, Washington, DC.

Reid, S. (1981). *The correctional system.* New York: Holt, Rinehart & Winston.

Rothman, D. (1971). *The discovery of the asylum.* Boston: Little, Brown.

Rothman, D. (1980). *Conscience and convenience.* Boston: Little, Brown.

Schroeger, D. (1983–84). The course of corrections in Missouri, 1833–1983. *Manual of the State of Missouri.* Jefferson City: Office of the Secretary of State.

Steinhauer, J. (2007, April 29). Great deal: clean cell, nice neighbors. *Houston Chronicle,* A3.

Steuben. (1879, May 29). A visit to Auburn Prison. *New York Evangelist, 50,* 22. (APS Online)

Takagi, P. (1975). The Walnut Street Jail: A penal reform to centralize the powers of the state. *Federal Probation, 39,* 4, 18–25.

Trafzer, C., & George, S. (1978). *Prison centennial, 1876–1976.* Yuma, AZ: Rio Colorado Press.

Walker, D. (1988). *Penology for profit.* College Station, TX: Texas A&M University.

Wilkins, J. H. (1918). The evolution of a state prison: Historical narrative of the ten years from 1851 to 1861, during the period when the care and employment of convicts was turned over to lessees. *The Bulletin (San Francisco).* June 13 to July 10.

Online Exercise

Go to the website for corrections history (the URL is below) and find an article called "A Tale of the Tombs" about the New York City Department of Corrections infamous facility built in the late 1830s.
   http://www.correctionhistory.org/html/chronicl/nycdoc/html/histry3a.html

Read the short article and make notes about:
   1. the problems the facility encountered in its construction
   2. the executions that were conducted there
   3. the housing arrangements made for children and women

How do you think this period in the Tombs history compares to today's correctional approach?

Questions for Thought and Discussion

1. What were some of the reforms of the progressive era in prisons?

2. What themes and similarities seem to characterize the conditions of prisons throughout their development and even today?

3. Compare and contrast the Pennsylvania System and the Auburn systems and give examples of each.

4. Who were some of the contributors to and shapers of the developing prison system and how did they influence the nature of prisons and prison reform?

Books You May Want to Read

Rideau, W., & Wikberg, R. (1992). *Life sentences*, New York: Times Books

Hassine, Victor. (1996). *Life without parole: Living in prison today.* Los Angeles: Roxbury.

Movies You May Want to See

Brubaker
Cool Hand Luke

CHAPTER 3
Prison Leasing, Prison Industry and the Work Ethic

INTRODUCTION

Ever since the invention of the penitentiary, discipline and work have been the only consistent underlying themes of its operation. One of the very first prisons in this country was an administration building erected over a copper mine shaft in Symsbury, Connecticut. Because mining was considered to be one of the worst occupations, it was impossible to find employees to mine for the local smiths. Consequently, a legislative committee suggested that sentenced criminals be sent to the mines which appeared to have all the natural qualities of secure confinement. In late 1773, the first inmate descended into the mine, renamed New-Gate Prison and lived in a "lodging room" 25 feet below the surface (Dean, 1979).

Prophetic of the experiences to come, the first inmate in the Symsbury mine escaped after only 18 days. It is also historically significant that the first prison riot also took place here. New-Gate also served as a military prison and today, is a museum.

Sentences of work were originally used as a punishment as well as a deterrent. Prior to the establishment of the Walnut Street Jail, statutes called for inmates to perform hard labor around the city streets and country highways. Citizens were to observe the backbreaking efforts and be deterred from crime. Prisoners had their heads shaved, and they wore "conspicuous multi-colored garb and were chained to their wheelbarrow." According to Teeters (1937)

> some of these degraded persons expressed a preference for hanging rather than to continue to work and exist little better than cattle. Not only was the work onerous and humiliating,

but the convicts were the butt of ridicule by the idle and course members of the city who followed them about, sometimes hurling garbage and stones.

Nineteenth-century reformers soon introduced various factories and mill works within the prison confines as the way to rehabilitate the undisciplined and unsavory character of the offender. Work was used as a tool to mold a proper, obedient, productive citizen. As Miller (1974) explains, prison practices and the legislation which affected management—the controls and incentives of 'good time' law, parole, and the indeterminate sentence—all become understandable within the context of convict labor.

Providing both control and organization, military-like models were often used not only to reform the prisoner but also to run an efficient industry. According to Rothman (1971, p. 93), however, "Convicts worked slowly and sloppily, shirking whatever tasks they could. Lacking incentive and close supervision, they were neither reliable nor efficient." Also, Rothman concludes, prison officials did not have the ability to manage factory operations. "They lacked experience in bulk purchasing of raw materials and in marketing procedures." Consequently (Rothman, 1971, p. 93),

> prison labor never brought great returns and in many instances was unable to meet the daily expenses of operation, let alone cover the costs of construction. Some of the first prisons did claim a profit in their annual reports, but often the figures were more testimony to the jugglings of the warden than to actual returns.

Because labor was not profitably successful, many rationalized its purpose as punitive and, subsequently, some of the most menial and exhausting forms of work were reintroduced.

The inability of prisons to make a profit at the various industries, the mounting costs of maintaining the prisons, and the rapid growth of inmate populations led officials to turn to the private sector for help. Private businessmen would employ or lease convict labor in two ways. One way was for the prisoners to be sent out to work in industries or fields. In Texas, the laws allowed less serious offenders to work on public utility projects such as building railroads, mining, and improving the navigation of waterways (Walker, 1988).

Another method of inmate work was to set up shops inside the prison managed by private owners. This was called the contract system and is not unlike some of the prison industry models used today. Sometimes the manufacturer just supplied the raw materials, and state prison officials worked the inmates at producing the goods. Because the private company then bought the products back at an agreed upon price per piece, this was called the piece price system.

The Leasing Experience

The frustration of state officials at the seeming inability of the prisons to make a profit and the increasing expenses of prisoner care led to the decision to give up control of the prison entirely. The policy of leasing entire prison systems to private businessmen was widely adopted throughout the United States. It began in Kentucky in 1825, and Michigan, Missouri, Louisiana, Alabama, Indiana, Illinois, California, Nebraska, Montana, Wyoming and Oregon soon followed (McAfee, 1987, p. 853). In almost every state, the period of leasing included the following similar events.

1. Leasing was determined a failure; the state took back the prison system but, within a short time, resorted to leasing again. For example, California took the prison system back after a disastrous four years of leasing and vowed never to allow prison management out of the state's hands again. After only one year, the state was again leasing out the inmates. In both periods of leasing, the state did not enact provisions for getting the system back should the terms of the contract be broken and the result was years of costly litigation (McAfee, 1987).
2. The lessees took advantage of the state, failed to abide by their contracts, and did not make agreed upon payments to the state.
3. The inmates were abused, brutalized, overworked and improperly fed, clothed, and sheltered. Abusive treatment generated great public concern. People realized that, because of the profit motive, inmates were beaten, neglected and driven beyond human endurance. Many religious and social service organizations effectively protested the harsh treatment.
4. Businesses did not maintain state facilities when they used them, and conditions deteriorated and became uninhabitable. Despite

some initial construction and improvements when they first leased, most businesses left the prisons in horrible condition when they terminated. Equipment and buildings were returned to the state in total disrepair.
5. Public anger was roused by the frequency of escapes. For example in Missouri, the typical escape meant that bells rang, and all the townspeople felt compelled to join in the search, brandishing whatever guns, knives, and clubs they possessed and taking to the countryside on horseback and on foot. In a twenty-month period between 1843–1844, 28 percent of the total inmate population escaped (Schroeger, 1984).

The Missouri system was leased out in 1839 to contractors who paid the state $30,000 to use the prisoners in various businesses including enterprises on the prison property. This included a brickyard, a smithy, a ropewalk, a cooper shop, and a carpentry shop. Inmates worked dawn to dusk producing wagons, plows, drays, harnesses, singletrees, chairs, bureaus, bedsteads, tables as well as boots, shoes, bricks, cigars, bacon and lards. Outside services included grounds keeping, blacksmithing, mining, house and sign painting, and "buildings of any kind at a moments notice" as the newspaper ads claimed (Schroeger, 1984).

The Louisiana prison system was leased by a cotton plantation owner from 1870 to 1901 who also worked the inmates building railroads and the Mississippi River levee system. Stories of the cruel treatment of inmates angered the public and legislative hearings resulted. One report indicated that 216 inmates had died in 1896 alone. One prisoner had worked outdoors with no shoes in the winter and suffered frostbite. One gangrenous foot was amputated with a pen knife, the other simply rotted off. The inmate was serving five years for a five-dollar theft (Carleton, 1971).

In Texas, contracts were given to a railroad company that agreed to pay $12.50 per inmate per month. However, many inmates escaped or were allegedly killed attempting to escape, and the company failed to make regular payments. Though the state cancelled existing leases, they still did not want to pay for repairs to the institution to upgrade equipment, expand facilities or improve sanitation and medical services so three years later in 1871, the system was released. Although the lessees made physical improvements and hired a chaplain and doctor, the positive steps were short lived. Contractors failed to make transportation payments, prisoners who transferred to other states related the horrors of the real conditions inside, and stories appearing in the New Orleans newspapers embarrassed Texas. Conditions included lack of food or spoiled food, inadequate clothing, seven-day work weeks, regardless of the weather, and beatings and cursings (Walker, 1988).

Despite having to terminate the 15 year lease after only 6 years, the prison was again leased to a different company in 1877. This time, on a five-year lease, the company—with a saw mill, a sugar and cotton plantation, a wood-chopping operation, as well as railroad crews— operated smoothly and brought the state substantial profits. Ironically, it was the few periods of productivity and profits that always seemed to encourage states to terminate leasing and try running the operation themselves. As did other states, Arkansas abandoned the practice of leasing inmates in the early 1900s but continued to hire out the workers on public and private property up through the 1960s (Parker, 1986).

Labor Protection Legislation and the Demise of Prison Industry

When prison officials took back the prisons and proceeded to farm and develop industries, some met with success. Many had learned from their previous experiences with manufacturing and leasing and were able to maintain better facilities. California reported that in the years after leasing, (1860–1880), the state was able to provide almost half of its own support through profits realized with private entrepreneurs operating within the prison confines (McAfee, 1990).

The prisons' attempts to make a profit at a variety of industries were cut short by the protests of outside businesses. In Louisiana, minority leaders grew to disfavor the leases because it was their constituents who were put out of work by the inexpensive inmate products. In all states, craftsmen could not compete with inmate production and were driven out of business. Community leaders joined together and pressured legislatures for relief from what they saw as unfair competition.

In 1897 Pennsylvania passed the ***Muehlbronner Act*** stipulating that no more than ten percent of an institution's inmates could be producing goods for sale on the outside (Johnston, 1994). With the loss of profitable work, inmates fell idle and this trend spread, mostly across the eastern United States. By the 1920s, there were several factors operating on the side of prison industry opponents. For one thing, outside labor was becoming more organized and labor leaders carried significant political clout. Manufacturers were also losing business to the prisons and joined laborers in their opposition (Hawkins and Alpert, 1989). Sentiment against the inexpensively-produced inmate goods ran even higher during the Depression when so many Americans were poor and out of work.

In 1929, Congress responded by passing the ***Hawes-Cooper Act*** which allowed each state to decide whether or not it wanted to prohibit the sale within their borders of articles manufactured by prison labor. Over the next few years, every state had passed their own legislation prohibiting the sale of prison-made goods (Clear & Cole, 1990). With the ***Ashurst-Summers Act*** in 1935, Congress also banned the movement and sale of prison goods in interstate commerce. This meant that one state could not try to sell their prison-made goods in another state. Because prison industries could no longer participate in the open market, all hopes of operating a profit-oriented, or even a self-sustaining system, seemed to die. It appeared that prisons would be totally dependent on the state to support their operations.

All that was left for prison industries was the production of goods that could be internally consumed or bought up by other state agencies. Thus a highly restrictive market was developed and the manufacture of license plates, institutional uniforms, brooms, soaps, mattresses, desks and road signs began. Inmates also repaired state vehicles and raised livestock and produce for institutional use. Contemporary critics of these sheltered market industries point out that these jobs often lack transferable or marketable skills.

During World Wars I and II, prison industries sprang to life and many necessary military products were produced. According to McAffe (1990) California led all other states in the volume of war related goods.

> San Quentin received production orders for Red Cross garments, air-raid sirens, submarine nets, and Navy commando boats... convicts addressed a half billion dollars worth of ration books to the public. Convicts fought wartime forest fires with a minimal guard, and prisoners manned "harvest camps" to insure that needed food production did not

slacken due to manpower shortages.... Eleanor Roosevelt came to San Quentin and specifically praised the war work of the inmates. Morale was high; the general society valued convict labor.

Chain Gangs

The era of the automobile created a new use for inmate labor—the improvement of public roads. Although in 1923 all states except Rhode Island had specific laws allowing county convicts to be worked on public highways, chain gangs were used mostly in the South. Bureaucratic structures were altered to accommodate the need, and manpower was allocated to fill it. In fact, at a time when North Carolina had over fifty county chain gangs, the legislature transferred the control of all prisoners sentenced to thirty days or less to the State Highway and Public Works Commission (McShane, 1996).

The assignment of prisoners to chain gangs spans a period of time from 1910 to 1945. Sentences on a chain gang ranged from a few weeks to ten years. There are accounts of drunkards, hitchhikers and travelers being arrested and forced into labor. Besides constructing roads and bridges, the gangs filled potholes, cleared land, and repaired buildings. Convicts were transported between work sites in caged wagons where they also slept at night. The cages were usually eight feet in width and eighteen feet long. Eighteen men were typically bunked in the cage with a night bucket, a pail of drinking water, and a stove. Most remained chained at night. As any movement would rattle the chains, a prisoner would have to yell "Gettin up" to the guard and receive permission before rising from the floor to use the bucket. The wagons were stuffy and dark with tarpaulins covering the sides in bad weather. Prisoners were likely to remain in the cages from noon Saturday until work resumed on Monday morning.

As one survivor of a Georgia chain gang explained, every meal was the same: a square of corn pone, three slices of fried pig fat, and a dose of sorghum. The only variation was that on holidays there were only two meals instead of three.

Prisoners usually wore striped uniforms and were supervised by poorly paid and often sadistic armed guards. In some areas, inmates were promoted to trusties and given the task of tracking escaped prisoners. With the promise of reward money, the trusties shot as many "escapees" as they could. In some instances, escapes were fabricated and unsuspecting convicts were shot for the bounty.

Most chain gang work was done with a pick and shovel. In some instances prisoners were connected by an ankle iron to a chain attached to a belt. Others had both ankles clamped with steel bands with a twenty inch chain between them. At night the chains could all be connected to a steel rod running the length of the sleeping area.

Flies and mosquitoes transmitted disease, as did pits of open sewage and communal wash basins, towels and bedding. Punishments for not working hard enough included flogging with a heavy leather whip, the sweatbox (a coffin like box with a single small air hole) and a diet of bread and water. Some inmates were fitted with iron collars or were forced to torture or beat fellow prisoners (McShane, 1996).

The work available for chain gangs diminished when soldiers returning from war needed civil service, construction, and maintenance jobs to provide for their families. Some chain gangs were settled in permanent camps where work was ongoing. In some jurisdictions, inmate crews from minimum-security camps continued to work on road maintenance through the late 1960s.

Today, some "get tough" sheriffs and wardens claim to have created old fashioned chain gangs to work public projects. However, the high cost of supervising such crews outside and the provision of the necessary work and health related resources make these ventures impractical and little more than a political show. Only a small number of inmates have been involved in these demonstrations. In reality, by returning to well-maintained prisons at the end of a regular 8 hour shift each day, and escorted by officers whose contracts would forbid the harsh conditions of the old road camps, these inmates have little in common with the chain gangs of the past. With constitutionally enforced standards of care, the modern work crew is in no way representative of the true brutality of the early 1900s chain gang.

Prison Industry Today

A number of factors have contributed to a resurgence of interest in prison industries. Legislatures are concerned about the growing cost of facilities and shrinking fiscal budgets appropriated to operate them. Officials are also aware of the problems caused by inmates being idle, underemployed, and employed in meaningless activities. Many prisons were offering outdated vocational programs in industries that were not related to today's markets. In addition, a growing number of inmates have been ordered by the courts to make restitution to their victims and, without any earning power, these orders were most often unfulfilled.

During in-processing, offenders are often screened for work experience and skills. Considering age and physical health, appropriate job assignments are made. Some jobs within the prison must be applied for and are awarded on a competitive basis. Care must also be taken when assigning inmates to potentially hazardous employment such as asbestos removal or firefighting. Wages from prison jobs allow inmates to pay for their own personal supplies, send money to loved ones, save for release and make payments on restitution, court costs and attorney's fees. As part of the "get tough" philosophy many states passed legislation requiring inmates to work and even to help defray the costs of their incarceration.

In Oregon, *The Prison Reform and Inmate Work Act of 1994* explains that inmates:

> should work as hard as the taxpayers who provide for their upkeep; and... be fully engaged in productive activity if they are to successfully re-enter society with practical skills and a viable work ethic.

The Oregon legislation requires that inmates work a 40 hour week and only 20 of those hours can be replaced by education or treatment programs. Those classified as unable to work are exempt. States mandating full time work for their entire inmate population face the responsibility for finding enough jobs and supervision staff.

In Colorado the Department of Corrections is about to launch a special work initiative to compensate for the loss of migrant workers in the agriculture sector. Tough immigration enforcement endeavors have limited the usual supply of field workers that the fruit and vegetable farmers depend on each season. Inmates will be contracted out to more than a dozen farms to pick melons, pumpkins, onions, and peppers as the growers struggle to meet harvest demands (Riccardi, 2007). Correctional officers will oversee the operation where low security inmates will be paid sixty cents per day for their labor. When associated costs supporting the program are tallied, farmers complain they will have spent more for this less attractive option that they say raises safety concerns for them and their families.

PRIVATE INDUSTRY GOES TO PRISON... AGAIN

Beginning in 1979, many states eased restrictive legislation to encourage the private sector to become involved in prison work programs. The federal government also provided exemptions through the ***Justice System Improvement Act*** (Percy Amendment) allowing for prison industry projects to be certified as exempt from federal restrictions on inmate made goods in interstate commerce (Hawkins & Alpert, 1989). To ward off private business protests, special conditions were established guaranteeing that inmates would be paid wages comparable to those prevailing on the outside, "in order to reduce the competitive advantage of less expensively produced prison goods" (Mullen et al., 1985, p. 13). By 2007, the Prison Industry Enhancement Certification Program (PIECP) involved 37 states and 4 county-based industry initiatives that manage more than 175 business partnerships with private industry. Approximately 2,500 inmates per year participate in the program which uses strict criteria and selection procedures. Manufacturing includes aluminum screens and windows, circuit boards, street sweeper brushes, gloves and corrugated boxes. Other projects pack papaya, process potatoes, build boats and refurbish automobiles. The key to the program is to provide realistic job experiences that better mirror potential opportunities on the outside than prisons had been able to offer in the past (Moses and Smith, 2007). From 1995 to 2005, the Bureau of Justice Assistance reports that PIECP programs generated $33 million for victims' programs, $21 million for inmate family support, $97 million for prisoner room and board expenses and over $46 million in state and federal taxes. Evaluation reports also estimate that inmates completing PIECP programs were more successful following release than inmates working in other industry programs or engaged in activities other than work. That is the PIECP inmates found work faster, held it longer, earned more and higher wages and were rearrested, reconvicted and reincarcerated at much slower rates than other inmates (Moses & Smith, 2007).

Another reason that attitudes may be changing toward prison industry is the realization that our large corporations are already going to other countries such as Mexico and India in order to secure inexpensive labor. Rather than lose these companies and potential wages for Americans, inmates may represent a better alternative in the eyes of labor organizers. Many manufacturers realize that maintaining an oversees plant and increased shipping and supervising costs could be avoided in prison programs here (Clear & Cole, 1990).

When PRIDE, a private, non profit organization took over prison industries in 1981 in Florida, they accomplished three tasks. First, they got rid of unprofitable industries. Second, they revamped the structure and management of those industries with promise. Third, they brought in new ventures that they believed would be successful. Currently operating in 21 correctional institutions, their products include full service printing, computer services, furniture and textile manufacturing, as well as medical products, and vehicle renovation. They also produce and sell beef products, quick drying paint, cardboard boxes and dental prosthetics.

By 1985, at least half of the states and the federal prison system had ventured into private sector enterprises. There are four commonly used models for setting up programs.

Under the **employer model**, a private company owns and operates a business that uses inmate labor to produce goods or services. The business has control of hiring, firing and supervision of the inmate labor force. A good example of this is a telemarketing firm that trains and employs inmates to do telephone surveys for them. With the **investor model,** the private sector capitalizes or funds a business that the state correctional agency will operate. Aside from the financing, the business will play no other role. Like the investor model, the **customer model** represents a limited role for the private sector. Here, the outside company purchases a significant percentage of the output of a state owned and operated business which is located within the prison. Finally, under the **manager model**, the private sector simply manages a business owned by the correctional agency. The company does not supply any material or funding, nor does it purchase any of the products. The business simply provides the manpower with technical industry expertise, which is not usually found in the civil service system. This is a personnel-supplying model, which provides managers, supervisors, and technicians.

The Federal Bureau of Prisons operates its own self-sustaining enterprise, **UNICOR**. Begun in 1924, the system produces furniture, electronics, brooms and brushes, eyewear, military gear, mattresses, kiosks, signs, mousepads, and clothing and textiles including law enforcement apparel. They also do graphics printing and a variety of other services such as recycling, data management, and vehicle retrofitting (Roberts, 2007).

The California Prison Inmate Work Initiative

In 1990 California voters passed the ***Prison Inmate Work Initiative*** (Proposition 139) which allowed private industry back into state prisons. A number of employers applied, competing for the limited factory/business space available in eleven institutions across the state. Projects are accepted after careful review of a company's financial records and plans and, so far, fourteen have been given contracts that guarantee a specified number of inmates will be employed. By mid-1999, 288 inmates were working in jobs ranging from sewing t-shirts for CMT Blues to making wine vats for Pub Brewery. The Donovan Unit has a recycling plant operated by Quantum Group and On Display Inc. manufactures merchandising fixtures (Ballon, 1999).

Employers claim that the workers are motivated and conscientious. Good service at the prisons has allowed these manufacturers to move operations from Mexico back to this country and to put "Made in America" labels on their products. Still, critics, particularly activists who see the expanding prison industry complex as an exploitive mechanism of the state, argue that young minority men should be earning money for their families and not assisting prisons in becoming self-sustaining, or even profit making. Reporting on civil rights concerns, Huling (1999) argues that private industries in prison pay nothing into overtime, vacation, sick time, unemployment insurance or workers' compensation. According to Huling, private prison authorities at Wackenhut recoups 80 percent of what the inmates earn in a minimum wage job that was converted to inmate jobs after a plant in Austin, Texas was closed, laying off civilian employees.

Most inmates earn minimum wage and keep 20 percent for everyday use in prison stores. The rest is divided between savings accounts, a designated family member, the state (which charges room and board) and a victim's compensation fund. This is in contrast to regular prison chores that only pay 13 to 90 cents per hour (Ballon, 1999).

EVALUATING WORK PROGRAMS

Work programs, like any other intervention strategy or daily operation, should be continually evaluated. Some states, such as Illinois, have laws requiring that data such as recidivism rates for work program participants be reported. Prison officials should critically examine their industries and any training opportunities to improve and update them as necessary. Five areas worthy of exploration are listed below.

How Much Time Does Work Involve?

This measures the level of activity over time. Are there full time jobs, or part time? How many hours per day are spent working and how many days per week? In some systems there are not enough jobs to go around and many inmates are unemployed or underemployed.

What Proportion of Inmates are Involved?

Programs should be able to include a significant number of inmates as well as an appropriate number of hours. While some operations are small and require special training, they also may not take up a significant amount of space. It would be important to know what percent of the inmate population, capable of work and available for work, have jobs. While the specific types of businesses and industries will vary from facility to facility, some facilities will have less industry as is the case with a medical unit or reception or processing center. It is also important to determine whether there is equity between male and female work opportunities.

Does the Inmate Self-Improve?

This facet of the evaluation asks questions about the effects of the job on inmate attitudes and self-image related to work. Does the inmate have the same type of job he or she might be able to realistically get on the outside? Are the skills transferable? It is discouraging if inmates face significant barriers to obtaining the same type of job they do well while incarcerated, once they are released. Are there licensing or bonding requirements on the outside?

Are Special Inmate Populations Involved?

Over time, prisons have made more attempts to include special populations in the work routine. In Texas, special work programs have been developed at the unit for physically-challenged inmates. For some, schedules and assignments have been approved by a doctor who specializes in paraplegic care. Also, across the country, more systems are including work assignments for Death Row inmates as well as elderly and developmentally-disabled offenders. In Texas, roughly one third of the 454 inmates on death row work, either as custodians or in the unit's garment factory (Langford, 1998). However, changes in the work program were made after seven death row inmates attempted escape. Although only one made it over the fence, he was found drowned a week later near prison property. Inmate work routines, which extended access to the recreation yard were blamed for the security lapse (Lyman, 1998).

Are the Goals of the Work Program Realistic?

Not all prison programs are going to make money, even if inmate wages are being used for family and criminal justice system expenses. For example, Illinois reports that the Correctional Industries programs there lost $899,000 in fiscal year 1996, 534,000 in FY 1995 and $1,275,000 in FY 94. Overall, 14 industries lost over $8.6 million during a five year period (Corrections Journal, 1997).

Also, a vocational program or work opportunity cannot be expected to reduce recidivism all by itself, and it would be unrealistic to expect as much. While successful employment is related to successful community reintegration, offenders are all different, as are job experiences, so there is no magic solution. It is more appropriate to think of job programs as beneficial if they instill an appreciation of work, contribute to a positive outlook, and motivate inmates to control their behavior while participating in the work experience. An inmate's ability to accumulate job skills and promotions are extra achievements that seem to characterize the better work programs.

SUMMARY

Employment in prisons has always been tied to the outside economy. Low unemployment and competition for workers means that low-wage prison labor is tolerated and even encouraged. In 1885, 90 percent of inmates worked in prison industries but by the 1930s that number was only 50 percent. By 1980 only 10 percent of prisoners were employed in agency industries and less than one percent were utilized in private sector programs (Grey & Meyer, 1996). Today, the Correctional Industries Association strives to provide meaningful and competitive work skills in private industry projects that also provide revenue for victims, offenders' families and the state. Even the best programs however, serve only a small portion of the number of inmates incarcerated and more work opportunities are needed. Although we have moved from leasing entire prison systems to limited industry programs, the value of work for keeping inmates occupied and instilling positive values and marketable skills continues unchallenged.

References

Ballon, M. (1999, September 22). Captive work force filling labor gaps. *Los Angeles Times*, C1, C12.

Carleton, M. (1971). *Politics and punishment*. Baton Rouge, LA: Louisiana State University Press.

Clear, T., & Cole, G. (1990). *American corrections*. Belmont, CA: Wadsworth.

Corrections Journal. (1997, April 7). Illinois Audit Criticizes State's Correctional Industries Program, p. 3. Washington, DC: Pace Publications.

Dean, C. (1979). The story of New-Gate. *Federal Probation, 43*, 2, 8–13.

Gray, T., & Meyer, J. (1996). Expanding prison industries through privatization. In G. L. Mays & T. Gray (Eds.), *Privatization and* the provision of correctional services: Context and consequences (pp. 125–133). Cincinnati, OH: Anderson.

Hawkins, R., & Alpert, G. (1989). *American prison systems.* Englewood Cliffs, NJ: Prentice Hall.

Huling, T. (1999, April). Prisons as a growth industry in rural America: An exploratory discussion of the effects on young African American men in the inner cities. Paper presented to the United States Commission on Civil Rights. Retrieved November 22, 2007 from www.prisonpolicy.org/scans/prisons_as_rural_growth.shtml

Johnston, N. (1994). *Eastern State Penitentiary: Crucible of good intentions.* Philadelphia: Philadelphia Museum of Art.

Langford, T. (1998, November 29). Texas escapee from death row eludes manhunt. *Arizona Republic,* A8.

Lyman, R. (1998, December 4). Death row escapee found dead. *Arizona Republic*, A16.

McAffe, W. (1987). Tennessee's *Private Prison Act of 1986*: A historical perspective with special attention to California's experience." *Vanderbilt Law Review, 40,* 4, 851–865.

McAffe, W. (1990). A history of convict labor in California." *Southern California Quarterly, 72,* 1, 19–37.

McShane, M. (1996). Chain gangs. In M. McShane & F. P. Williams III (Eds.), *Encyclopedia of American Prisons,* pp. 71–73. New York: Garland.

Miller, M. (1974). At hard labor: Rediscovering the 19th century prison. *Issues in Criminology, 9,* 1, 91–114.

Moses, M. C. & Smith, C. (2007, June). Factories behind fences: Do prison 'real work' programs work? *NIJ Journal, 257.*

Mullen, J., Chabotar, K., & Carrow, D. (1985). *The privatization of corrections.* Washington, DC: National Institute of Justice.

Parker, M. (1986). *Judicial intervention in correctional institutions: The Arkansas odyssey.* Unpublished doctoral dissertation. Huntsville, TX: Sam Houston State University.

Riccardi, N. (2007, March 1). Colorado to use inmates to fill migrant shortage. *Los Angeles Times* Retrieved March 1, 2007 from www.latimes.com/news/nationworld.

Roberts, J. (n.d.). Work, education, and public safety: A brief history of federal prison industries. Retrieved June 21, 2007 from www.UNICOR.gov/about/organization/history/overview_of-_fpi.cfm.

Rothman, D. (1971). *The discovery of the asylum*. Boston: Little, Brown.

Schroeger, D. (1983–84). *The course of corrections in Missouri, 1833-1983*. Manual of the State of Missouri. Jefferson City, MO: Office of the Secretary of State.

Teeters, N. K. (1937). *They were in prison: A history of the Pennsylvania Prison Society, 1787–1937*. Chicago: John Winston.

Walker, D. 1988. *Penology for profit*. College Station, TX: Texas A&M University.

Online Exercise

Go to the website for Eastern Kentucky University's Correctional Photo Archives (www.cpa.eku.edu/about.htm) and browse through the menu for photos of prisoners at work in the photo collections for construction, farming and industry. What types of industries existed in the various state institutions and what types of vocational education were available?

Questions for Thought and Discussion

1. Discuss the lease system used in many correctional systems. What were its advantages and disadvantages?

2. What are some of the problems in developing fair and effective work programs in prison today? What would you do to address these problems if you could?

3. Describe some of the legislation that influenced the nature of work in prisons over the course of correctional history in the United States.

4. What are some of the current models used for private industry in prison and how have they been evaluated?

Books You May Want to Read

Oshinsky, D. (1996). *Worse than slavery: Parchman farm and the ordeal of Jim Crow justice.* New York: The Free Press
Carleton, M. (1971). *Politics and Punishment: The History of the Louisiana State Penal System.* Baton Rouge, LA: LSU Press.

Movies You May Want to See

Pappillion
Murder in the First

CHAPTER 4
The Corrections System Today

Crime, like the economy, health, education, (and) defense... is a matter of grave concern to our society and people have the right and the necessity to know not only of the incidence of crime but of the effectiveness of the system designed to control it.
                                    Justice William Douglas in *Pell v. Procunier*

In the past, prisons operated as closed systems. It is characteristic of closed systems to promote leaders from within the ranks, to surrender very little information to the outside concerning daily operations and events, and to avoid the scrutiny of persons not in their immediate line of authority. This meant that scandals, problems and suspicious incidents never came to the attention of the public. Today, corrections programs are viewed more as open systems with continuous interaction with a number of external influences. These influences are diagramed in Figure 1 below. As you can see, the success of our current model of prisons is dependent upon positive relations with many outside groups.

INFLUENCES ON MODERN CORRECTIONAL SYSTEMS

There are a number of reasons that correctional departments made the transition from a closed to an open system. First, there were many scandals during the years from 1930–1960 that drew public attention and interest to the daily operations of the prison. Alarming incidents such as deaths, maimings, riots, escapes, reports of graft, corruption, political favors, and abuse of authority inspired the perception that the administration needed watching and monitoring. Suspiciously motivated activities throughout the state and federal government caught our attention and created the impression of citizen vulnerability. As a result, many watchdog groups have formed, and in corrections, appointed boards have assumed the responsibility of overseeing daily operations.

Figure 1. External Influences on Prison Staff

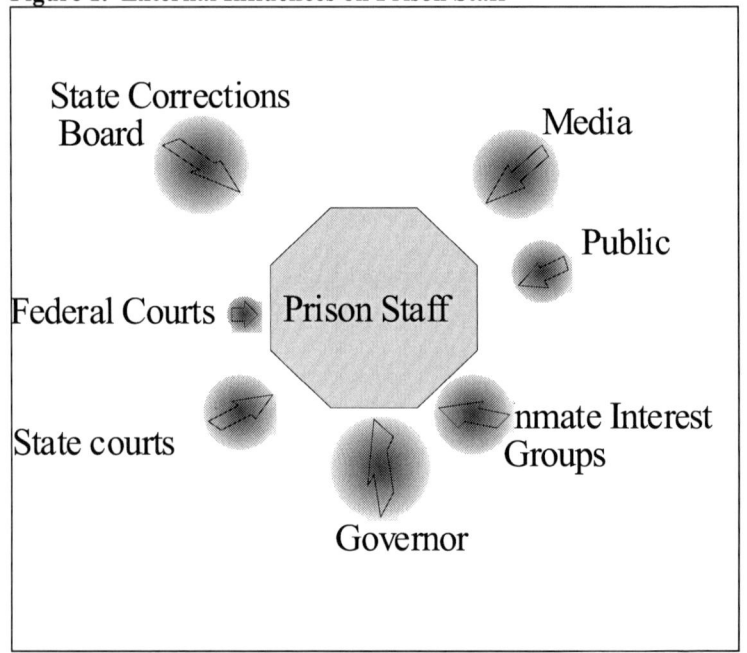

A second reason that the prison system is considered open is because of a special public awareness and interest in the corrections process. The passage of the *Freedom of Information Act* has allowed ordinary citizens as well as media representatives access to a wealth of data on prison activities in a number of areas like management, rehabilitation, and population characteristics. The human rights movements of the 1960s made many people aware of the oppressive and unhealthy conditions existing within our prisons. As social consciousness grows, academics and concerned groups become involved in prison issues. As publicity grows, we are reminded of our right to pertinent information and to be part of the decision-making process.

In the past, prison officials only gave out the information they chose to. As Jacobs (1977, p. 36) wrote about Stateville Prison during the period 1931–1961 when it was run by authoritarian Joe Ragen,

> There were almost no interactions between outside groups concerned about prison conditions and Stateville.... Ragen's Stateville was an autonomous institution accountable neither to other public agencies nor to the public at large.

In Texas, each yearly report showed that all inmates who had died, had died of "natural causes," something the prison could claim with no concern of challenge.

Another reason for the openness of prisons today is the fact that budgeting and funding today are now tied to a complex reporting process that requires extensive disclosure and justification of expenses. The competition for limited resources means that much public debate and accountability is involved in the budgeting process, which we often see debated on the front page of the newspaper. Along that line, corrections systems are now competing for precious state monies which means that they are actively campaigning publicly on their needs and concerns. In order to get money, officials today are more likely to bring their problems to the media and to the legislature in hopes of getting a bigger share of the budget.

A fourth reason that prisons are more open today is the evolution of constitutional rights for prisoners and for the media. A series of cases on correspondence privileges have opened lines of communication for inmates and members of the public that were once tightly controlled and censored by prison authorities. Other prison rights cases have put the court in a position of intervening in all aspects of prison management. The trial transcripts, which are matters of public record, give us insight into the history and current operation of our institutions. Any conflicts between testimony taken under oath and the official reports of the past can now be resolved by an informed interpretation.

Also, as suburban and rural areas develop and urban populations shift out to undeveloped areas, isolated prisons are no longer so. Once hidden in sprawling farmlands, prisons are now virtually all built in somebody's "back yard." Proximity to large population bases insures a public accountability as workers bring information about the prison and its operations to their surrounding community. Concerns about potential negative impacts from prisons on housing values in an area has also spurred states into transforming prisons into "greener" more eco-friendly environments.

Finally, open systems have become a popular approach to public administration. Studying the success of private business, the public sector incorporated many similar principles. A view of the past structure of a prison system would give us a simple management hierarchy like the one in Figure 2 below.

Figure 2. Past Organizational Structure of Prisons.

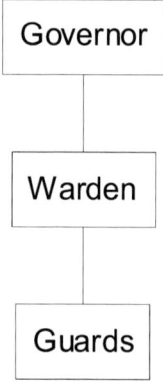

Today's prison organizational structure looks more like the one outlined in Figure 3.

Oversight of the prison system comes from many sources. Some forms are internally generated, others come from outside. Accreditation, public scrutiny and media coverage are some of the ways that prison operations are monitored.

Figure 3. Modern Prison Organizational Structure

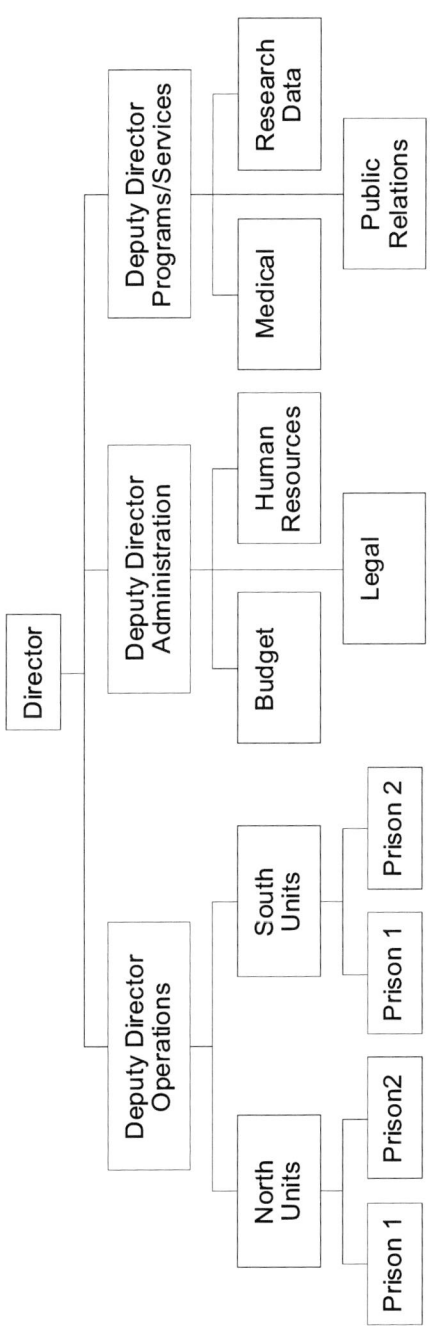

THE ACCREDITATION PROCESS

Up until the implementation of official standards, prison officials had little assistance in gauging the quality of their facility and staff performance. In the late eighteenth century, the Philadelphia Prison Society constructed guidelines for the treatment of prisoners that included such things as the separation of men and women, children and adults, a primary classification system, and the basics for prison industry (Bergsmann, 1981). More recommendations and reforms followed. In 1870, the National Prison Association (now the American Correctional Association) published its guidelines as the Declaration of Principles. Since that time, numerous commissions and councils have addressed the requirements of modern penal institutions and have developed model legislation, programs, and guidelines (Bergsmann, 1981).

In 1974, the American Correctional Association began its process of accreditation with its manual of 452 standards. The standards represent a consensus of professional currently working in the field. Of these, 40 (or 8.8 percent) are mandatory and must be met to achieve accreditation. Mandatory standards generally refer to conditions that insure the health and physical safety of staff and inmates (Sechrest, 1996). As Rauch (1988, 180) concludes, many mandatory standards simply direct compliance with local law such as building, fire, and sanitation codes. Many of the other standards reflect implications or directives from court rulings on constitutional practices in areas such as rules and discipline, visitation and mail procedures.

Today, accreditation through peer review is voluntary, but in many cases, federal monies can be tied to compliance. Reports from accreditation review committees are published indicating satisfactory compliance and areas that need work. It is not uncommon to see agency websites boast about how long their facilities have maintained accreditation. Obviously, the existence of professional standards would make it harder for administrators to claim ignorance in a lawsuit alleging negligence. That is, it would be difficult to claim that you didn't know something should have been done, or something was a danger, when your own professional guidelines make that clear. Legal tests of accountability often use the concept of what you "knew or should have known," and the presence of professional guidelines meet that standard. To Sechrest (1996), this is important because correctional officials may be liable for damages resulting from injurious conduct.

Courts could require accreditation as a way of resolving disputes over conditions of confinement as was the case in Oklahoma, South Carolina, and Kansas. A majority of professionals surveyed believed that accreditation would be an advantage for the state in defending themselves against law suits (Farkas & Fosen, 1983). However, according to Miller (1992) the courts have not adopted ACA standards as the primary tool for measuring corrections performance; in fact, in some instances they establish different standards.

Administrators argue that adhering strictly to standards could result in less creative problem solving and could work against facilities that have established conditions that are better than those required by accreditation. Others criticize the accreditation process as lengthy, exclusive of other expert opinions, and involving costly fees. Despite the drawbacks, over one thousand agencies in the U.S. and Canada are pursuing accreditation with the ACA (Sechrest, 1996).

PUBLIC RELATIONS

One of the effects of being an "open system" is that corrections must interact with the public and the media on a constant basis. Many correctional experts agree that the media often serve to reinforce negative images and stereotypes about corrections (Marsh, 1986). In trying to create more understanding and support from the public, corrections officials have actively sought better relationships with the press by scheduling press conferences, inviting press to meetings, and staffing their own public relations offices. The public relations office may have the responsibility for putting out press releases, scheduling media visits or public tours, publishing a newsletter, and responding to inquiries from other agencies as well as the general public.

Although most people see public relations as simply a source of factual information, the real goal is to develop good rapport and trust for the department in the community. Prison administrators must be aware of the public's concerns about any risks to the community that the prison might present, the safety and well-being of the employees, the spending of money generated by the prison in the community and the reputation of the management overall.

The way people interpret prison problems and needs in general is quite different from the way they react to prisons in their community. Traditional literature indicates that communities facing the prospect of a new prison have fears of escapes and concerns about increased crime rates and potential adverse economic conditions due to the negative image of a "prison town" (Carlson, 1988). In a survey of residents located near a new prison site in Clallam Bay, Washington, Carlson (1988) found that the most anticipated negative consequences were more demands on local law enforcement, more demands on schools and social services and increased crime particularly drugs.

On the other hand tax breaks and economic incentives have made it difficult for some communities facing downturns in other industries to reject a new prison. Small towns throughout the U.S. have been competing for prison site selection not only for the jobs, but for the salary revenues that will be spent in their areas.

The Media

With an open prison system, management of the media is very important for good community relations. In addition, the *Freedom of Information Act* has been used effectively by the media to access all types of previously inaccessible prison information. However, there are significant differences in approaches to the media from state to state and between state institutions. While each state will have certain set media policies, wardens and other facility administrators may vary in their relationships with the area's media. For that reason, most states like to control media through their centralized public information officer at their administrative headquarters.

It was not until a series of Supreme Court cases were decided between 1974 and 1978 that the First Amendment issues surrounding the visitation and interview rights of the media were clarified. In *Pell v. Procunier*, a suit was filed on behalf of four inmates and three journalists who claimed that the California prison policy that prohibited the press from obtaining face to face interviews with specific inmates violated their First Amendment rights. The court upheld the administration's policy citing the fact that prisoners have a range of expression opportunities that include the press, namely writing to them, corresponding with them through other visitors such as relatives and friends, or by having the journalist as a regular visitor. The courts have basically said that the media does not have special access to inmates for conducting face to face interviews and access to specific inmates may be denied (*Houchins v. KQED*). While prison authorities claim that managing an orderly institution requires that it not be forced to produce certain inmates at certain times at the media's beck and call, others claim that such media access is critical to monitoring potential abuses and unconstitutional practices.

In California, a controversial and confrontational relationship has developed between the department of corrections and the media as a ban on face-to-face interviews was imposed. The Department also began opening mail between inmates and media representatives. Under the restrictions, journalists are only allowed to interview randomly selected inmates during regular visitation hours and without reporters bringing in pens, paper and tape recorders. Also, talks with specific inmates have to take place over the phone which is closely monitored by prison staff (Yaffe, 1996). Although the media has brought suit on this issue and are attempting to cultivate the support of taxpayers on "opening" media access, the state has prevailed so far.

Attempts to control inmate contributions to media through books, journals, newsletters and websites have also been controversial. In 2007, University of Denver law students took up the case of a federal prisoner who has been restricted and even disciplined for writing accounts of his prison experiences (Finley, 2007). Although officials claim that notoriety could disrupt the balance of inmate life and thus, security, First Amendment freedoms are at stake as is the public's right to be informed about conditions behind bars. Without balanced coverage from multiple sources, much of the information we receive on prisons and prisoners is officially processed, government data.

PRISON DATA: PROFILE OF INMATES AND STAFF

Numbers and Rates

In 2005 there were approximately 7 million people on probation, parole, in prison or in jail. Of those, 2.3 million persons are incarcerated in the U.S. in either prisons or jails. This means that roughly one out of every 32 persons is in some type of correctional supervision in this country. Two-thirds of all those incarcerated are being held in state and federal prisons. There are roughly 491 prison inmates per 100,000 people in the U.S. population. The demographics of the prisoners are not even distributed however. One out of every 108 men and only one out of every 538 women make up this group. There are 3,145 Black male prisoners per 100,000 Black males in the general population, 1,244 Hispanic male prisoners for every 100,000 Hispanic males in the general population and 471 White males incarcerated in prisons for every 100,000 white males in the U.S. The number of prison inmates has continually increased over time, with 3.3% percent increases in each of the last two years (Harrison & Beck, 2006). Roughly 5.6 million people or 2.7 percent of the population has some type of prison experience (Beck, 2005). In Maryland, more people are in prison than in state colleges (Ruddell, 2004).

The federal prison system now has about 190,000 inmates in 114 institutions across the country (BOP, 2007) while the states combine for the rest of the incarcerated offenders. In state prisons, violent offenders represent more than half of those in custody (52%) while property (21%) and drug offenders (20%) make up the other significant segments. Those with public order offenses make up the remaining 7 percent.

One of the trends that alarms many sociologists is that prisons continue to be built in the most rural areas. In scenarios that resemble government subsidy programs, economically deprived areas or in places impacted by losses in mining, forestry, industry and farming are being awarded prison operations as a way to stimulate a suffering economy and stabilize declining employment rates (Huling, 1999). As we will see in the chapters ahead however, the moving of thousands of inner city and urban offenders away from their communities, families and potential resources for release has many possible negative effects.

Characteristics of the Inmate Population

There is no doubt that the Drug War of the last two decades has shaped the prison population we have today. In fact, the U.S. has more people in prison on drug related charges than most other first world nations have in their entire prisons systems (Ruddell, 2004). It is reported that two-thirds of those entering prison have histories of substance abuse (Leukefeld & Tims, 1992).

Thirty-eight states and the federal government had capital punishment statutes as of 2006. Approximately 300 inmates have been added to death row populations each year for the last ten years across the country while approximately 53 people were executed in 2006 (32 White and 21 Black inmates). In 2005, there were over 3200 persons on death row in the U.S. including 52 women (Snell, 2006). On the average, approximately 70 people are executed each year, with Texas executing more offenders than any other state. In addition, 22 death row prisoners died of natural causes nationwide, and 107 had their sentences commuted, or overturned in 2004 (Bridges, 2005).

The incarcerated population is approximately 44 percent African American, 36 percent White, 19 percent Hispanic, and 2 percent other races. The system is said to be over represented by minorities in that African Americans make up only 12 percent of the general population and Hispanics only 10 percent (DiMascio, 1995). The fact that roughly one in ten African American men is incarcerated has serious social ramifications. Prisoners are separated from families and neighborhoods and because in most states, are barred from voting, one in seven African-American men will have lost the right to vote (Palmer, 1999). Critics refer to this as the **"disenfranchisement"** of entire segments of society.

Overall, the median age of prisoners in the U.S. is 30. The percentage of the prisoners that are elderly varies with the age used to classify the population. A national definition of older offender was developed in 1993 using 50 as the tracking age (Anderson, 1999, 219). In 2006 California had 20,000 inmates, 4 percent of their total population, over the age of 50 including 717 over the age of 70 (Turley, 2006). Given their lifestyles and lack of health care resources over the years, many inmates begin having physical problems at this age which are consistent with those of a much older group on the outside.

It has been estimated that as many as 75 percent of inmates are functionally illiterate, and only 30 percent have completed high school. In a group of non-prisoner men of the same age, it is likely that 85 percent would have graduated from high school (DiMascio, 1995).

Women in Prison

In a 1955 report the Colorado Department of Corrections lamented the lack of constructive work opportunities for women offenders. At that time, the state was also holding women from Utah and South Dakota and there was some discussion of asking for federal funds to develop a multi-state collaborative female facility for the less populated western states. The roster lists the occupations of the 26 female offenders as housewife (8), waitress (5), steno (2), as well as a cook, bookkeeper, seamstress, nurse, housekeeper and cashier. The women were mostly under the age of 25 and White. Their offenses were predominantly larceny, false pretenses, confidence games, and second degree murder (Chapman, 1992).

Today, women represent about 8 percent of those incarcerated although the number of women in prison is growing faster than the number of men. The profile of adult female offenders has also changed over the years. In 1975 women were primarily incarcerated for larceny, forgery, embezzlement and prostitution. By 1995, offenses were more likely to be drug related as well as larceny. Over 60 percent of women prisoners have one or more children under the age of 18 (NCJRS, 1998). A large percentage had custody of their children prior to their incarceration. Six in ten females were raised in a single parent household and half had a family member with an incarceration history. A significant number of women had been physically or sexually abused or had come from a background of poverty and neglect (Lombardo & Smith, 1996). A comprehensive study of women in prison in 1991 found that African American women were more likely to have been raised by single mothers and were more likely to have lived with their children prior to incarceration (U.S. Dept of Justice, 1994).

The percentage of women incarcerated for a drug offense rose dramatically in the period from 1986 (12 percent) to 1991 (33 percent) (U.S. Dept of Justice, 1994) most likely as a consequence of the 1980s "war on drugs." In fact, many criminologists refer to the war on drugs as a war on women.

Mentally-Ill Offenders

There are many different types of mental illnesses and degrees of impairment, so this is a difficult group to make generalizations about and to design classification and treatment plans for. According to a number of studies, prisoners are more likely to have any of a number of mental illnesses, than the general population. Estimates are that anywhere from 1 to 40 percent of the inmate population has some type of psychiatric impairment and that 10 percent have significant or severe psychiatric impairments (McShane, Williams, Pelz & Quarles, 2005). A study of Ohio prisoners determined that while 22 percent had suffered some type of psychiatric disorder in their lives, 12 percent had a serious current episode. While prevalence rates appear to be high, institutional treatment rates appear to be very low. Monahan (1992) reports that the prevalence of violence is more than five times higher among people who have serious psychiatric impairments, such as schizophrenia, major depression, or bipolar disorder. The prevalence of schizophrenia is approximately three times higher in the jail and prison samples than in the general population samples; the prevalence of major depression is 3–4 times higher, and the prevalence of mania or bipolar disorder is 7–14 times higher. Females with schizophrenia were found to be ten times more likely to be homicide offenders than the general population.

Many officials will admit they do not have an accurate count of the number of mentally-ill within their corrections system. Still, mentally-disturbed prisoners have been cited as the number one health problem behind bars. Generally, mentally-ill offenders are older, more likely to never have been married and to have a lower education than offenders without symptoms of mental illness. Compared with other individuals, mentally-ill offenders received longer sentences for their crimes and served out significantly larger portions of their terms, as they were less likely to be paroled. Mentally-ill offenders were also likely to have been employed at the time of their arrest (Feder, 1991, 1995).

Because the mentally ill often have histories that overlap with substance abuse problems it is difficult to determine which factors may be related to recidivism risk (McShane, Williams, Pelz & Quarles, 2005). In some states, such as Kansas, Arizona, California, Minnesota, Washington and Wisconsin mentally-disordered sex offenders may now be held indefinitely in "civil confinement" once their prison terms have expired (Mauro, 1997).

Federal Bureau of Prisons

There are significant differences between the states' prison population and the federal. Eighty-five percent of federal inmates are housed by the Bureau itself (down from 91% in 1997) while the remainder are confined via a private contractor. The average age of federal prisoners is 37 and the racial composition of those incarcerated in 56 percent

White, 40 percent Black, 1.6 percent Asian and 1.6 percent Native American. In examining ethnicity, the BOP reports that 31 percent of the inmates are identified as Hispanic. Seventy-four percent of the federal inmates are U.S. citizens, 16 percent are Mexican, 3 percent are Colombian and 2 percent are Cuban. The others are citizens of a number of different countries.

In terms of security level, 18 percent of the inmates are in minimum custody, 39 percent in low level, 28 percent in medium and 11 percent in a maximum security setting. Only 3 percent of the inmate population is made up of lifers, while 50 percent are serving 5–15 years. Fifteen percent are serving shorter sentences of up to 3 years. The percentage of inmates serving time for drugs has steadily increased. In 1970 only 16 percent of the federal population had drug offenses but by 1970 that number was 25 percent and by 1994, at the height of the drug war, it was 61 percent. While today the percentage of drug offenders is still very high (59 percent) the other offenses are small percentages of those convicted of bribery, robbery, firearms and explosives violations, arson, extortion, immigration offenses and property crime. Only 3 percent of federal offenders have violent crime convictions (www.fbop.gov, 2007).

The Costs of Incarceration

From 1977 to 2001 this country's spending on state and local corrections increased 1101 percent (Ruddell, 2004). The true costs of incarceration include not only the building and operating of facilities, the employment of staff and allowances for their long term pensions and benefits but also the indirect costs of mass imprisonment on society and the lost opportunity costs of not spending in other areas of public need.

Across the country, states use many different formulas to calculate the cost per inmate per day. One state administrator admitted that he simply divides his total budget by the number of prisoners to arrive at the cost per inmate per day. Ironically, using this formula, the cost per inmate per day would actually go down as the population increases, a phenomenon we know is not true. The average cost per inmate per day in 1993 was approximately $52.38 or almost $20,000 per inmate per year (Camp & Camp, 1994). The way this figure is calculated by most systems, it is more like the cost of the average inmate, rather than the average cost. There are many different categories of special needs inmates from the mentally ill and elderly to AIDS-infected prisoners and those in protective custody and administrative segregation. The cost of all of these inmates is much higher than the average and for some medical treatments; special staffing and equipment drive the costs up to $300 per day.

In 2001 total spending on state and federal prisons was about 57 billion; and much of that was spent on capital improvements, which means that it is not part of the daily operations or services. Twenty years ago, spending was only 9.6 billion which illustrates the dramatic growth in this area of public spending. Realistically, it can be said that the states have used one out of every fourteen general fund dollars on prisons (Schiraldi & Greene, 2002) Overall, criminal justice represents about 7 percent of all state and local government expenditures, and amount equal to what is spent on health and hospitals (Butterfield, 2004).

A prison budget is mostly spent on personnel. Salaries and benefits make up the greatest portion in each state with operations expenses such as equipment, and utilities making up another significant portion. Most inmate recreational services and activities are paid for out of an account that is funded by profits from goods and services sold to inmates in prison stores.

And finally, another indication of the prison funding crisis that has resulted from the punitive trends of the past thirty years is that federal prisoners must now pay a real portion of their incarceration costs. Public Law 102-395 Sect 111 and 18 U.S.C. 4001 set out a Cost of Incarceration Fee system which is usually equal to the average cost of one year of confinement (U.S. DOJ/BOP PS 5380.03).

SUMMARY

Management of a contemporary correctional institution means that administrators must stay abreast of changes in the law as well as trends in public administration techniques. While being sensitive to public opinion, media inquiry and legislative directives, the manager must run a constitutionally viable facility within budget constraints.

There is some consensus that the style of management that administrators use with inmates is not the same style that will be effective with staff. It is believed that styles of management will vary with the level of security in a certain institution or the types of inmates held there. Most managers employ strategies such as walking around the facility, speaking with inmates and staff directly about their concerns and taking a "hands on" approach to many details of daily operations.

The organizational structure of prisons has become more complex with many specialized functions including legal counsel, legislative analysts and management information systems specialists. Borrowing from the private sector, administrators have also become more consumer oriented, periodically surveying staff as well as inmates to ensure meaningful feedback that may identify problem areas early and avoid confrontations later. Management training has also become a component in state as well as national initiatives. Several corrections management journals have been developed to disseminate research. All of these factors may contribute to reduced liability and fewer potential lawsuits (McShane and Williams, 1996).

Cases

Pell v. Procunier 417 U.S. 817, 94 S.Ct. 2800 (1974)
Houchins v. KQED 438 U.S. 1, 98 S.Ct. 2588 (1978)

References

American Correctional Association.(1999). *Directory of juvenile and adult correctional departments, institutions, and paroling authorities.* Lanham, MD: ACA.
Anderson, C. (2003, August 18). Prison experience shared by 1 in 37 American adults. *Houston Chronicle* from Associated Press, 3A.
Anderson, J. (1999). Special needs offenders. In P. Carlson & J. S. Garrett (Eds.). *Prison and jail administration: Practice and theory*, pp. 219–225. Gaithersburg, MD: Aspen Publishers, Inc.
Bergsmann, I. (1981). Correctional standards development in the United States. *Federal Probation, 45*, 3, 49–56.

Butterfield, F. (2004, May 3). With longer sentences, cost of fighting crime is higher. *New York Times*, A15.

Camp, C. G., & Camp, G. (1994). *The corrections yearbook.* South Salem, NY: Criminal Justice Institute.

Carlson, K. (1988). Community opposition to prisons. *Corrections Today, 50*, 2, 84–90.

Chapman, J. (1992). *This is the prison: Colorado Penitentiary Canon City* (3rd ed.). Canon City, CO: Colorado Territorial Prison Museum.

Di Mascio, W. (1995). *Seeking justice: Crime and punishment in America.* New York: The Edna McConnell Clark Foundation.

Farkas, G., & Fosen, R. (1983, December). Responding to accreditation. *Corrections Today, 45*, 40–42.

Feder, L. (1991). A profile of mentally-ill offenders and their adjustment in the community. *Journal of Psychiatry and Law, 19*, 1–2, 79–98.

Feder, L. (1995). Psychiatric history, due procedural safeguards, and the use of discretion in the criminal justice process. *Justice Quarterly, 12*, 2, 279–305.

Federal Bureau of Prisons (n.d.). Retrieved June 1, 2007 from www.bop.gov

Harrison, P. M., & Beck, A. (2006, November). *Prisoners in 2006.* NCJ 215092. Washington, DC: Bureau of Justice Statistics, U.S. Department of Justice.

Huling, T. L. (1999, April). Prisons as a growth industry in rural America. Paper presented to the United States Commission on Civil Rights. Retrieved June 6, 2007 from www. prisonpolicy.org/scans/prisons_as_rural_growth_shtml

Jacobs, J. (1977). *Stateville: The penitentiary in mass society.* Chicago: University of Chicago Press.

Lombardo, V. S., & Smith, R. (1996, October). A model program for female offenders. *Corrections Today,* 92–95.

Leukefeld, C. G., & Tims, F. (Eds.). (1992). *Drug abuse treatment in prisons and jails.* Rockville, MD.: National Institute on Drug Abuse.

Marsh, H. (1986). The media and correctional administrators: The time for mutual cooperation and understanding has come. *Criminal Justice Research Bulletin, 2*, 4, 1–4.

Mauro, T. (1997, June 24). Court: Sexual predators can stay confined. *U.S.A. Today,* 3A.

McShane, M., & Williams III, F. P. (1996). Administration. In M. McShane and F. P. Williams III (Eds.), *Encyclopedia of American prisons,* pp. 4–8. New York: Garland.

McShane, M., Williams III, F. P., Pelz, B., & Quarles, T. (2005). The Role of mental disorder in parolee success. *Southwest Journal of Criminal Justice, 2,* 1, 3–22.

National Criminal Justice Reference Service. (1998). *Women in criminal justice: A twenty year update.* Rockville, MD: National Criminal Justice Reference Service.

Palmer, L. (1999, March 21). More blacks serving time in U.S. prisons. *Arizona Republic,* A19.

Rauch, W. H. (1988). Achieving accreditation. *Corrections Today,* 50, 5, 180.

Ruddell, R. (2004). *America behind bars: Trends in imprisonment, 1950 to 2000.* New York: LFB Scholarly Publishing.

Schiraldi, V., & Greene, J. (2002). Reducing correctional costs in an era of tightening budgets and shifting public opinion. *Federal Sentencing Reporter, 14,* 6, 332–336.

Sechrest, D. (1996). Accreditation. In M. McShane & F. P. Williams III, (Eds.). *Encyclopedia of American Prisons,* pp. 1–4. New York: Garland.

Snell, T. (2006, December). *Capital punishment, 2005.* Washington, DC: Bureau of Justice Statistics, U.S. Department of Justice.

Turley, J. (October 7, 2006). Release elderly inmates. *Los Angeles Times.*

U. S. Department of Justice. (1994). *Women in prison: Survey of state prison inmates, 1991.* Washington, DC: Bureau of Justice Statistics.

Yaffe, D. (1996, April 17). Locking down the media. *The Recorder,* pages 1, 8, 9.

Online Exercise

Comparing Veterans and Non-veterans in Prison: Go to the National Criminal Justice Reference Service website (www.ncjrs.org) and look for a Bureau of Justice Statistics report from May, 2007 titled: *Veterans in State and Federal Prison, 2004* by M. E. Noonan and C. Mumola. Summarize what they found to be the difference between veteran and non-veteran prisoners.

Questions for Thought and Discussion

1. What are the most common features of the prison population today and what implications do these features have for management and treatment?

2. What do we know about the cost of incarceration compared to what many people in the community might think about it?

3. How would you describe the ideal relationship between prison officials and the media? What would you consider to be the features of adequate access to inmates for media representatives?

4. Explain the forces that influenced the shift in modern correctional institutions from closed to open systems.

Books You May Want to Read

Jacobs, James. (1977) *Stateville: The penitentiary in mass society.* Chicago: University of Chicago Press.
Harris, Jean. (1988) *They always call us ladies.* New York: Zebra Books.

Movies You May Want To See

American Me
Shawshank Redemption

CHAPTER 5
Prison Management and the Role of the Correctional Officer

Now the official in the lowest ranks of the custodial bureaucracy—the guard in the cellblock, the industrial shop, or the recreation yard—is the pivotal figure on which the custodial bureaucracy turns.
Gresham. Sykes (*The Society of Captives*, 1958, p. 58)

Experts will agree that the inmate's most important daily interactions, from both custody and treatment perspectives, are with correctional officers. Because the prison is a rapidly changing environment, an officer must learn not only the basic survival skills, but also how to adapt to a variety of new situations as well. Even more than the ability to adapt, the officer must be innovative and creative in his or her response to complex and emergency situations. The irony is however, that although innovation and creativity in responding to emergencies is a necessary survival skill, institutions, weary of lawsuits and challenges to authority through the courts, have relied more on standardized written policies and uniform procedures as the most effective response.

The balance between "doing what you are told" and "doing what works" has created dilemmas for correctional managers since the opening of the first prison. Administrators have long argued about the qualities needed in prison employees, those charged with the safe and humane operation of prisons. Often the debate centers on whether prison environments are truly different from other work places or whether a good employee in any business would also be an effective employee in the prison system.

A scroll through most departments of corrections' websites as well as the Federal Bureau of Prisons will indicate that most are always hiring. During the Drug War and the subsequent prison building, and thus staffing, boom of the 1980s, thousands of employees were hired that are now reaching retirement. Up to one third of the workforce in some areas is eligible for retirement now and the field is looking for new and innovative ways to attract employees.

THE CORRECTIONAL OFFICER

Qualifications

Across the country, applicants for entry-level correctional positions face two types of procedures: qualifying and screening. To qualify, each applicant must meet certain basic requirements to continue in the hiring process. Screening denotes the search for negative information or traits that may disqualify a person from being acceptable as a candidate, thus he or she is eliminated.

In corrections, unlike many other occupations, applicants may be required to take a series of qualifying tests. These may be educational and vocational tests, aptitude, or skills tests. Applicant scores are ranked and the selection process may focus on the top percentage of applicants. There are also screening tests such as medical exams and personality assessments.

The legal and practical necessity of conducting some type of personality screening is often related to the "peace officer" status of the security positions within corrections. Some of the most common personality tests include the Minnesota Multiphasic Personality Inventory (MMPI), the California Personality Inventory and the Inwald Personality Inventory. While the MMPI was originally designed to screen out potential mental health risk applicants for the military, the Inwald was specifically developed for correctional officer selection. The scales in this test measure stress reactions and deviant behavior patterns including absence, lateness, alcohol and drug use, anxious or rigid tendencies, and interpersonal difficulties.

In addition to testing, most departments also include personal interviews with a board of screeners to select candidates who have scored highest on initial tests. Interviews must conform to federal and state guidelines on fair hiring practices and other legislation that protects an individual's rights and privacy such as the *Americans with Disabilities Act.*

Training

Prison reformers of the nineteenth century sought to enhance the rehabilitation process by improving conditions within the penitentiary. Proper supervision of inmates was one area of interest. As Dorothy Dix (1845, p. 21) cautioned, "I would never suffer any exhibition of ill temper, or an arbitrary exercise of authority. The officers should be equally subject to rules and discipline as the prisoners." Ironically, the first training academy for correctional officers was not opened until almost one hundred years later.

Though training schools for correctional officers have been used in other countries since the late 1830s, the first in this country opened in 1930 in New York City. The philosophy of the school was to control prisoners by "intelligence and leadership rather than by force" (Schade, 1986). Courses in the academy included the history of crime and punishment, the study of the present crime situation, types of penal institutions and their functions, the prisoner and his background, prison discipline, and classification/segregation (Schade, 1986).

Correctional officer training today is more specific and technical than early academies and less likely to include theoretical material on crime and punishment. Training periods are usually much shorter than the three months residential preparation of the first academy. Today an average training period would be two-to-four weeks including a period of hands-on supervision. A curriculum often covers self-defense, firearms familiarization, riot and disturbance procedures, and the legal aspects of the treatment of inmates. The American Correctional Association (ACA) recommends that correctional officers have 40 hours of orientation and training before being placed on the job, 120 hours of additional training during the first year, and 40 hours of continuing service training each year thereafter. The ACA Commission on Accreditation specifies not only the topics for training but the minimum standards for officers' performance as they begin the job. The ACA also offers correspondence courses and online courses for correctional officer training, and many bookstores carry test preparation manuals for taking advance placement or civil service tests for these jobs.

Prison Staff in the United States

There are over 403,500 employees in juvenile and adult state corrections in this country. The race and gender breakdowns are still different from that of the inmate population although it is significantly more diverse than twenty to thirty years ago. Black males make up 11 percent of the workforce, Black females almost ten. White females make up 20 percent and White males, 46. Hispanic males constitute another 5 percent of the state personnel and Hispanic females, 2. The remaining 7 percent are men and women of other racial groups. Approximately 32,400 persons are employed in the Federal Bureau of Prisons (ACA, 2001). In all jurisdictions, 63 percent of those working with the adult population are correctional officers although the ratios of officers to inmates vary quite a bit. Other employees may be clerical and treatment staff, equipment and industry specialists and administrators.

Data from 2000 indicate that about 34 percent of correctional officers are minority and about 22 percent are female. African-Americans constitute 24 percent of officers and Hispanics approximately 8 percent (Camp & Camp, 2001). Information on salaries reveals that although pay for entry level positions vary across the country, the averages range between $16,000 and $30,000. What this does not include however, is overtime which often supplements an officers pay by as much as 30 percent.

Of the roughly 254,000 direct custody officers employed in state correctional institutions today, less than 56,000 are women and only 14 percent of them are in supervisory positions. This is similar to the number of women who are in supervisory positions within the Federal Bureau of Prisons (ACA, 1999) and only 10 of 97 warden positions are filled by women. In 1992, Kathleen Hawk was named as the first female head of the Federal Bureau of Prisons (see the box on the next page). Currently, nationwide, women hold 20 percent of the Warden and Superintendent positions in adult corrections and 34 percent of those in juvenile facilities. These figures are proportional to the total number of women employed in each custody career field (ACA, 1999).

Kathleen Hawk Sawyer, Director Federal Bureau of Prisons

Kathleen Hawk Sawyer was Director of the Federal Bureau of Prisons from 1992 until 2003. She was a career public administrator in the Federal Bureau of Prisons and the sixth Director of the Bureau that was established in 1930. Dr. Sawyer received a Bachelor of Arts degree in psychology from Wheeling Jesuit College, Wheeling, West Virginia, in 1972, and a M.A. degree and Ed.D. in Counseling and Rehabilitation from West Virginia University. Prior to her tenure with the federal prison system, she designed and implemented a psychological counseling program at the Sargus Juvenile Facility in St. Clairsville, Ohio.

Dr. Hawk Sawyer began her career with the Bureau of Prisons as a Psychologist at the Federal Correctional Institution in Morganstown, West Virginia in 1976 and was named Chief of Psychology Services for the institution in 1983. Soon after, she was selected as a Senior Instructor for the Bureau of Prisons' Staff Training Academy, Glynco, Georgia.

Dr. Hawk Sawyer was appointed Associate Warden for Programs at the Federal Correctional Institution at Fort Worth, Texas in 1985, a co-correctional facility housing up to 1,000 inmates. In 1986, she became the Bureau's Chief of Staff Training. She was responsible for all training at the Bureau's 3 training centers (Glynco, Georgia; Aurora, Colorado; and Fort Worth, Texas) as well as local training provided at each Bureau facility.

In 1987, Dr. Hawk Sawyer was named Warden of the Federal Correctional Institution at Butner, North Carolina, an all male population of 800 inmates. She was then selected as the Assistant Director for the Program Review Division in the Central Office of the Bureau. She was responsible for developing and implementing a system of internal controls and monitoring for all operations throughout the Bureau which was recognized by the Department of Justice as being the best in the agency. This led to Dr. Hawk Sawyer receiving the Attorney General's Award for Excellence in Management in 1992.

Dr. Hawk Sawyer was also an ex-officio member of the Federal Prison Industries Board of Directors; an ex-officio member of the National Institution of Corrections Advisory Board; a member of the American Correctional Association (ACA), a past member of the ACA Correctional Standards Committee, and a member of the Association of State Correctional Administrators. In 1993, she received the National Association of Blacks in Criminal Justice's William H. Hastie Award for outstanding leadership in the criminal justice field; and the League of United Latin American Citizens' National Presidential Citation Award. In 1994, she received the Presidential Meritorious Rank Award. In 1997, she received the Surgeon General's Medallion for "significant and noteworthy contributions to the Office of Surgeon General, the Public Health Service, and the health of the Nation."

THE ROLE OF THE CORRECTIONAL OFFICER

The role of the correctional officer is made difficult by the varying and seemingly conflicting goals that exist within the prison today. Writers cite the problems of the employee trying to balance between:
- Punishment versus the Rehabilitation of the offender
- Custody v. Treatment duties within the institution

Prevention of Crime Versus Eventual Reintegration into Society

As a result of the different philosophies operating within a prison, officers may experience role confusion. Besides often feeling that inmates have more power and rights than they do, officers also see themselves at odds with treatment professionals within the facility.

Occupational stress among officers has taken the form of emotional disorders, heart problems, and alcohol abuse and accounts for a majority of the disability claims filed by officers. Studies also show higher rates of hypertension, ulcers, heart disease and diabetes and most often a negative correlation between job satisfaction and job stress (Long et al. 1986; Lambert et al, 2004; Dowden & Tellier, 2004; Griffin, 2006; Brough & Williams, 2007). Some of the potential stress factors for officers are in the areas of:
- **Staff relationships**: poor communication with senior officers and supervisors; paramilitary management styles, perceived lack of support
- **Nature of the job itself**: such as irregular hours, lack of clear guidelines, low wages, inadequate resources to do job
- **Relationships with inmates**: being responsible for inmates, conflict between trying to control and also help, problem-behavior inmates, possibility of violence
- **Advancement opportunities**: poor external rewards, difficulty getting promoted, lack of promotional opportunities, lack of participation in decision making
- **Physical surroundings:** noise, lack of heating, cooling, lighting, exposure to weather, older buildings in disrepair
- **Impact on family life:** living in remote prison areas, impact of shift work on marriage. taking work home, rescheduling family activities

Both men and women seem to be affected by job stress, particularly work-family conflict. Elaborating on some of the problems officers perceive in their jobs, Kauffman (1988) points out that many resent the fact that assignments are often awarded based on seniority and not according to skills and capabilities. This means that the most dangerous inmate contact jobs are given to the newer, inexperienced officers. Those with seniority will opt for staff positions that involve little risk and less inmate contact. Shift assignments also seem to go with seniority as the preferred day shift is regularly used as a reward, leaving the newer employees to the later shifts. Also, poor communication between the shifts means that important information on the day's activities is not passed on to the later workers.

Although the public often expresses very punitive sentiments about how inmates should be treated and the conditions under which they should live, they overlook the effects that poor conditions have on staff. Today, a number of facilities are so old and deteriorated that working there may be cruel and unusual for staff. Twenty-five facilities were built before 1875, 79 were constructed between 1875 and 1924 and almost 150 were built between 1925 and 1949 (Senna & Siegel, 1996). Some of the earliest prisons such as Elmira, Auburn, Sing Sing and San Quentin are still in use.

Officers often feel a gap exists between themselves and the administration. Staff may feel that they are not supported and appreciated, especially when policies are implemented that appear to "favor" the inmates. Many times officers do not understand the changes that are made and often administrators do not take the time and effort to clarify why certain decisions will improve existing conditions. Not able to identify with either the inmates or the administration, officers tend to isolate themselves and, as a result, criminologists note that an officer "subculture" or code of behavior develops.

The Correctional Officer Subculture

According to Kauffman (1988), the officer code is a series of mutually understood guidelines for behavior to which the majority of officers would ascribe. It includes the following:
- the most important duty is to aid an officer in distress; this is the norm on which solidarity and officer culture are based, and grounds for evaluating new officers
- don't bring in drugs or other contraband for inmates

- don't rat on a fellow officer to an inmate or to an investigation about an officer's conduct towards and inmate
- never make a fellow officer look bad in front of an inmate, and always support an officer in a dispute with an inmate
- don't be too sympathetic with inmates, doing favors for them is beyond the call of duty

The demise of rehabilitation goals has given those who want to help inmates little motivation to work in corrections. The custodial nature of the job, with the emphasis on security, has been a disappointment for many extremely capable employees. High turnover and low pay add to morale problems. In maximum security units, officers have been shown to have a more custodial view of their job, and they have displayed more negative stereotyping of inmates than those in medium/minimum treatment-oriented facilities (Williams & Soutar, 1984). After a particularly dangerous encounter with a violent inmate, an officer at Walpole State Prison remarked (Kauffman, 1988, p. 258),

> I said right then and there, I'm getting another job…. There's got to be an easier way. I figured why should I subject myself to this kind of environment because I know that it does have some kind of profound effect….

USE OF FORCE

There are three basic types of force used by correctional officers in attempts to gain an inmate's compliance with an order or to deal with emergency situations. Force is usually described in degrees of seriousness categorized as minor use of force, major use of force, and use of deadly force. According to Sapp & Lopez (1985), minor use of force is any physical contact with an inmate in a confrontational situation. Such force is applied to control behavior or to enforce an order. For example an officer might place his hands on the shoulders of an inmate and turn him toward the direction he wants him to move. Minor force would become major when:

1. Restraints are applied to restore or preserve order. (This would not include routine uses of restraints such as on psychiatric patients or

any inmate being transported outside or any inmate whose status or classification requires restraints for movement outside the cell).
2. Chemical agents such as pepper spray, water, batons, or other "instruments of force" are used.
3. Any offensive or defensive physical contact is used including blows, pushes, or come-along holds.
4. Any injury has been sustained.

Major use of force automatically would become deadly force whenever firearms are used.

One of the most difficult things for an officer to learn is the proper level of force necessary in a variety of emergency situations. Many inmate behaviors must be interpreted and even the most experienced employees often have difficulty reading the signs and using the proper discretion. Normally, minor force may be required when immediate compliance is needed to maintain order and safety, when verbal persuasion is impractical or fails or when the usual disciplinary sanctions are inadequate. The use of major force, on the other hand, implies that there is some imminent and immediate danger of physical injury. The force then must be applied to maintain or regain control particularly in the event of a riot or disturbance. Major force might also be used to prevent an escape or serious property damage.

In most systems, a written report must be made whenever major force is used. These reports are usually reviewed for appropriateness of conduct and employees may be disciplined if it is determined that unnecessary force was used. Reports may also indicate patterns of difficulty from which officials can develop policy changes or special training programs.

A reasonable prelude to the use of major force would be an initial attempt to handle a disturbance with minor force. This would indicate that the officer had already listened to and attempted to calm the inmate, secured the area, requested additional staff assistance, tried to restrain the inmate, and in some cases, called for the use of a video camera. Deadly force may be indicated in order to prevent serious life-threatening injury, to stop an escape, or to quell a riot when there has been loss of life and serious injury to others.

According to a study from use of force reports in the Texas Department of Criminal Justice, most incidents occur in the main hallways of the prison or in segregation/solitary areas. Most often force is used to enforce an order that the inmate has refused. Also, most incidents take place during the first and second shifts when movement is at its peak (Sapp & Lopez, 1985).

During training, most officers are familiarized with use-of-force equipment. This includes restraint equipment such as handcuff, straight jackets, and belly chains; protective equipment such as riot helmets, gas masks, and batons; and control equipment such as chemical agents or gas. As stated in several court cases, chemical agents may only be used to control the most serious emergencies and may never be used as a punitive measure. However, as Krantz (1988, p. 197) points out, there have even been occasions where the "use of force or chemicals, such as tear gas, to quell a disturbance has been held to constitute cruel and unusual punishment" (See *Spain v. Procunier*, 1979).

Legal Interpretations of Use of Force

The concern administrators have for use of force is reflected in their investments in training correctional officers on the proper use of force and the development of written policies that explain procedures for reporting use of force incidents. Prison officials realize that the courts are likely to view the unnecessary use of force or injuries resulting from such force as cruel and unusual punishment in violation of the Eighth Amendment. This was the case in *Inmates of Attica Correctional Facility v. Rockefeller* when the actions of correctional officers following the resolution of a riot were interpreted as retaliatory brutality.

> Injured prisoners, some on stretchers, were struck, prodded or beaten with sticks, belts, bats, or other weapons. Others were forced to strip and run naked through gauntlets of guards armed with clubs which they used to strike the bodies of the inmates as they passed. Some were dragged on the ground, some marked with an "X" on their backs, some spat upon or burned with matches, and others poked in the genitals or arms with sticks. According to the testimony of the inmates, bloody or wounded inmates were apparently not spared this orgy of brutality.

The standards for determining when use of force violates an inmate's constitutional rights were first expressed in 1973 in *Johnson v. Glick*. In this case the court considered:
1. The need for the application of force
2. The relationship between the need and the extent of force used
3. The seriousness of the resulting injury
4. Whether the motivation for the force was a good faith effort to maintain or restore discipline or a malicious desire to cause harm (Krantz, 1988).

In addition to these criteria, the court may also look at punishment standards such as those evaluated in *Gregg v. Georgia*. In that case, the Court held that punishment (force) was excessive if it involved the "unnecessary or wanton infliction of pain" or it was out of proportion to the severity of the crime itself. For example, in *Sampley v. Ruettgers*, the Tenth Circuit Court applied the "unnecessary and wanton infliction of pain" standard to a case of use of force by a prison guard. The plaintiff would have to show the judges in this case a "severe pain" or "lasting injury" before they would find that the force used violated the Eighth Amendment. However, this has not been the holding of the U.S. Supreme Court. As explained in *Hudson v. McMillian,* an injury does not have to be serious if the finding is that the officer "maliciously and sadistically caused harm." In this case officers held down and beat up an inmate causing facial bruising and swelling and cracking a dental plate. What was significant was that a supervisor witnessed the unnecessary brutality and only admonished the officers "not to have too much fun." This was the criteria the court used to establish "malicious and sadistic" constituting liability in this case.

The criteria used in *Johnson* and in *Gregg* have also been expanded to interpret the constitutionality of force used during a prison riot. In *Whitley v. Albers*, the Supreme Court added two additional considerations to the criteria established in *Johnson*. They weighed:
1. The extent of the riot or disturbance's threat to the safety of prison personnel and other inmates, and
2. The efforts made to lessen the severity of force used.

In this case, the Court placed a heavy burden on the inmate plaintiffs to show that the defensive action taken by the correctional officers was unconstitutional. The Court assumed that during a riot all action taken by the correctional officers would be defensive. The judges recognized that in a riot officers must react, and they do not have the benefit of hindsight as do later evaluators. Therefore, not every infliction of pain that in retrospect seems unnecessary will constitute a violation of civil rights. The majority in this 5-to-4 decision was supportive of the individual officer's judgment and discretionary action in a riot or disturbance. Ironically, the disturbance in this case was precipitated by the inmates' perceptions that correctional officers were using unnecessary force in escorting a couple of intoxicated prisoners.

LEGAL RESPONSIBILITIES AND LIABILITIES OF CORRECTIONAL WORK

Today there are many sources of regulation for the duties of the correctional officer. As Rolando Del Carmen (1983) explains, the obligations of the officer in performing his or her duties come from:
- The U.S. Constitution (particularly the Bill of Rights and the Fourteenth Amendment that makes those rights applicable to the states)
- The state constitution that governs the state prison system
- The laws passed by Congress
- The laws passed by individual legislatures
- Case law (judicial decisions) in precedent cases
- Rules and regulations of the department of corrections
- Union agreements made between officers and the department

There are also a number of areas of liability should an officer fail to perform in the required manner. An officer's performance, like other rule/law enforcement occupations within the criminal justice system, is subject to personal and agency liability should there be a violation of duty. Violations may include not only actions taken by officers, but those they may fail to take as well. First, an officer may be charged with a violation of criminal law either according to state or federal statutes. Thus actions such as theft of government property or an assault on an inmate or other staff member may be prosecuted through the courts in criminal charges against the employee.

A recent incident in a Florida federal prison reinforced the importance of handling charges against staff as carefully as one would charges against an inmate. One of six officers at the Tallahassee Detention Center who was being arrested for sexual misconduct with female inmates fired on and killed a special agent as agents then shot and killed him in his assignment area. Officials are now considering whether officers should go through weapons screening before entering facilities just as visitors and inmates do (Johnson, 2006).

An employee may also face a civil suit for damages should he or she willfully cause harm or damage to the person or property of another. These cases would be filed and heard in a civil court. A third potential area for liability is in civil rights suits where an inmate or other employee may allege that an officer, acting on behalf of the state, willfully deprived them of their civil rights as protected by Section 1983 of the *Civil Rights Act*. Most of these cases are filed as federal suits but, if a state has a civil rights act of its own, the employee may be in violation of that law, and cases may be litigated under its jurisdictions. Overall, inmates have felt that the federal courts are more sympathetic to civil rights cases and tend to file there, rather than in state courts.

According to Rolando Del Carmen (1983), those who are responsible for the hiring, training and supervising of correctional officers face additional liabilities should they be found guilty of the following:

- *Negligent hiring*: employing someone who the department knew or should have known was not qualified or had some type of problem that kept him/her from performing his/her job in an appropriate manner. Failing to confirm that the person had the needed education level or license or not checking the person's references, police record, or mental health history would be examples of negligent hiring.
- *Negligent training*: failing to give any, or the proper degree of, training to an employee and having them responsible for tasks beyond his or her abilities experience or training. An example is lack of training in proper procedures, as in the use of force or on equipment such as firearms, chemical agents, or riot batons.
- *Negligent retention*: keeping someone in employment after discovering that they were not qualified for the job in the first place or that they are unable to perform tasks in an appropriate manner even after training. This includes not meeting performance standards required for the position held. An example would be finding out an officer had a serious drug or alcohol problem and keeping them in a supervisory position without treatment.
- *Negligent supervision*: the failure to properly supervise an employee, the absence of direct supervision when it is necessary,

the failure to check firsthand on the employees within one's area of responsibility.

The most obvious cost of liability is the direct payment of damages, court costs, and attorney fees. As Collins (1988, p. 17) explains, however, there are also indirect costs such as "the negative effects on morale from losing litigation and unwanted court intervention in correctional programs, the loss of staff from their assigned jobs to defending lawsuits and the loss of respect and credibility to the agency that comes from being labeled as being unable to meet the requirements of the Constitution." He adds that losing lawsuits "can create a feeling of vulnerability on the part of employees, causing a retreat into an attitude of defensiveness and stifling innovation."

TURNOVER

Turnover is when employees leave, either voluntarily or involuntarily. Terminations may be either desirable, as when unsuitable employees move on, or undesirable as when a new employee obtains a "better" position in another agency. Turnover is often viewed as negative when there is significant cost to the department in terms of the money spent on hiring and training and the expense of manpower when the employee is dropped from the schedule and his or her work done by an existing employee on overtime or at the expense of another set of tasks. Turnover is most expensive when employees quit within the first 24 months of work. In most cases there is lag time between one person leaving and another being selected, hired and trained. The funds to hire the replacement are frequently not available until after the exiting employee has officially left so that an overlapping transition is not possible. This process can cost anywhere from $10,000 to $20,000 per new officer (McShane et al., 1991).

Turnover rates vary in prisons across the country, from the lowest annual rates in states like Massachusetts (3.9%), New York (3.2%) and California (4.7%) to the highest rates in states like Alabama (68%) and Arkansas (49%). The average of all states is 22 percent and Texas hovers about the mean at 23.2% (ACA, 2001). Reasons for turnover in corrections are low pay, lack of advancement opportunities and "better" job prospects in other fields, and even other criminal justice agencies. Others cite boredom, the disruption of shift work and the physical danger and verbal abuse that go with the job. Still other explanations include the lack of prestige in prison and jail work and dissatisfaction with the nature of the officer's job. Some of the reasons employees leave jobs in corrections have to do with administrative policies and relationships. Inequities among shifts, assignments based on seniority and the lack of meaningful interaction between officer and administration are frequently cited as reasons for low morale. Some prison managers believe that there is nothing wrong with the job itself, but that there was something wrong with the employee or the employee's choice of career. Another group admitted to the problems of the job and the job's potential to discourage employees. This group cited poor working conditions, offenders' aggressiveness, long hours and the stress of crowding as reasons for employee turnover. Remote geographical locations also appeared to be a problem. Many have criticized the decision to built facilities in sparsely populated areas, however, this building trend continues because of the availability of land, its affordability and the willingness of the surrounding communities to accept correctional institutions (McShane et al., 1991).

UNIONS

A 1987 prison survey found that 53 percent had officers represented by a union through a collective bargaining agreement (Benton & Nesbitt et al., 1987). Though most officer unions are prohibited by law from striking (Hawkins & Alpert, 1989), "sick outs" and "work stoppages" have occurred from time to time. Though security officers and treatment staff may belong to separate unions, both have the potential to influence policies addressing their needs and interests. As noted by Wynne (1985), unions in the past have fought against such reforms as rehabilitative programs for inmates and affirmative action hiring. In Delaware, the employees union and management agreed that anyone working in the population would be notified if any inmate had or was medically suspected of having a communicable disease. Other topics of interest to union members are the administering of drug tests to employees and the loss of state jobs to private corrections facilities.

Unions may also use their bargaining power to increase the fringe benefits employees receive such as medical plans, vacation time and compensatory time, overtime pay and hazardous duty pay, as well as provisions such as uniforms, meals and tuition reimbursement. Fringe benefits may account for as much as 30 percent of a corrections officer's salary. Fringe benefits may also be easier to negotiate than salary increases because they can be "hidden" in various parts of the budget and are less susceptible to public and bureaucratic protest (Smith & Sapp, 1985).

In California, the correctional officers union had over 31,000 members in 2007 (Peirce, 2007) and a $3 million dollar headquarters building in the state capital. The union takes credit for doubling officer salaries over the last ten years and boasts 2,000 members who earn over $100,000 per year. Dues brings in over $9.5 million per year and the organization has contributed millions to favored political candidates in the past (Hurst, 1994). The union has also been criticized for stopping an investigation into officer brutality at the Pelican Bay facility. Objecting to the probe of officers, union officials brought pressure on wardens, administrators and then governor Wilson to stop the department's internal affairs office from pursuing brutality complaints. Testifying before the legislature, the head of the CCPOA (California Correctional Peace Officers Association) admitted that in the hiring process "we go through 40,000 applicants over a 24-month period. I can guarantee you, 10 or 15 out of 40,000 are psychos, and they slip through the system" (Lounibos, 2004). The union also funded the political campaign of the opponent of the district attorney who was bringing charges against officers suspected of brutality (Arax & Gladstone, 1998). More recently, "Govenator" Arnold Swarzenegger vowed that if elected, he would act independent of the powerful bloc and would not accept their campaign funds. However, not long into his term, he began secret meetings with the union which caused the state corrections director to quit in protest.

SUCCESSFUL PRISON MANAGEMENT

One of the most successful prison managers in recent times has been cited in a text on excellent management practices by expert Tom Peters. Warden Dennis Luther created a positive atmosphere for inmates and staff with encouragement, incentives and lots of creative programming.

Although his facility was critically overcrowded and housed many of the more secure inmate classifications, there were no disturbances and no incidents of violence either against inmates or staff during his tenure. Federal Prison System Environmental Climate ratings for his institution were in the highest percentiles possible and were unduplicated within the FBOP. His principles for management, some of which are listed below, focus on building trust and rapport.

1. Inmates were sent to prison *as* punishment not *for* punishment.
2. Correctional workers have a *responsibility* to ensure that inmates are returned to the community no more angry or hostile than when there were committed.
3. Inmates are *entitled* to a safe and humane environment while in prison.
4. You must believe in man's *capacity* to change his behavior.
5. Normalize the environment to the extent possible by providing programs, amenities, and services. The denial of such must be related to maintaining order and security rather than punishment.
6. Most inmates will respond favorably to a clean and aesthetically pleasing physical environment and will not vandalize or destroy it.
7. We do not treat all inmates alike any more than we treat all people in the "free world" alike. We must be sensitive to personality differences, cultural backgrounds, lifestyles and educational levels, and treat inmates as individuals.
8. Bringing racial bias into the institution that results in discriminatory actions can be every bit as dangerous to fellow staff members as the introduction of contraband.
9. Whenever possible *provide explanations* for changes in policies and procedures that the inmate perceives as detracting from the quality of his life.
10. *Be responsive* to inmate requests for action or information. Respond in a timely manner and respond the first time and inmate makes a request.
11. Be dependable when dealing with inmates. If you say you are going to do something, do it.
12. It is important for staff to *model* the kind of behavior they expect to see duplicated by inmates.
13. The indiscriminate use of foul language by staff can only detract from the professional image staff must try to maintain.
14. There is *inherent value* in self-improvement programs such as education, whether or not these programs are related to recidivism.

15. Inmates need *legitimate opportunities* to enhance their self-esteem.
16. Inmates are to be treated *respectfully and with basic dignity*. Staff can treat inmates respectfully without compromising the essential element of professional distance.
17. Be courteous, polite and professional in all dealings with inmates, *regardless* of their behavior.
18. Punish behavior that threatens order and security—swiftly and harshly.
19. Inmate discipline must be consistent and fair.
20. Send clear messages regarding the kind of behavior that cannot be tolerated in an institution.

SUMMARY

The correctional officer must be able to control and manage the day-to-day activities of prison inmates. While the rules and regulations of the institution govern the routine procedures that each officer follows, the officer must also rely on his/her own personal skills and experiences in order to successfully conduct his or her mission. The support of quality managers who can adapt to the legal, economic, political and social demands of the future are essential for this task.

Marilyn McShane and Frank Williams (1993) offer the following suggestions for management practices in the years to come:

1. Top administrators for corrections should be drawn from a variety of professional backgrounds but with direct experience in human services management.
2. Managers should adopt a management style that is consistent with their personality and beliefs.
3. There should be more dialogue between the personnel office of any agency and managers such as wardens and superintendents on the criteria for selection and hiring, promotion, regular work assignments, and job descriptions.
4. Correctional officer assignment policies, for both location and shift work, should be critically reviewed.
5. New arrangements and management strategies such as unit management and "podular direct-supervision" should be studied for feasibility.

6. Changes in supervision style or policy should be well planned with input from all levels of operation.
7. Opportunities for higher education, job enrichment or enlargement for all correctional employees should be aggressively pursued.
8. Correctional managers at all levels must become more involved with and more responsive to, influences outside the traditional correctional system such as the community, the media and governmental representatives.
9. Management training should incorporate, and emphasize, needs identified from management research.
10. Institutions should be reorganized and operated along a small city or hospital model with less emphasis on all activities being centered on the first shift. There should be more 24-hour utilization of facilities and activities.

Well-managed prisons appear to be favorably different in that they have lower rates of violence, less disciplinary, lower rates of employee turnover and more efficient operations. While Warden Luther was in charge of the McKean federal prison which housed a normal federal prisoner population, the average cost per inmate per day at that facility was $15,370 while the federal average was $21,350 (Sandler, Hudson, Weiss, & de Guzman, 1998).

Cases

Gregg v. Georgia, 428 U. S. 153 (1976)
Hudson v. McMillan, 503 U. S. 1 (1992)
Inmates of Attica Correctional Facility v. Rockefeller, 453 F. 2d 12 (2nd Cir. 1971)
Johnson v. Glick, 481 F. 2d 1028 (2nd Cir. 1973)
Whitley v. Albers, 475 U. S. 312 (1986)

References

American Correctional Association. (2001). *Directory of juvenile and adult correctional departments, institutions, and paroling authorities.* Lanham, MD: ACA.

Anderson, J. (1999). Special needs offenders. In P. Carlson and J. S. Garrett, (Eds.) *Prison and jail administration: Practice and theory*, pp. 219–225. Gaithersburg, MD: Aspen Publishers, Inc.

Arax, M. & Gladstone, M. (1998, December 16). Keeping justice at bay. *Los Angeles Times,* A1, A46.

Benton F., & Nesbitt, C., et al. (1987). *Questions and answers about correctional personnel Management: Prison personnel management and staff development Volume II—Summary of the National Survey.* College Park, MD: American Correctional Association.

Brough, P. & Williams, L. (2007). Managing occupational stress in a high-risk industry. *Criminal Justice and Behavior, 34*, 555–567.

Collins, W. (1988). Law and regulation. In *Prison personnel management and staff development.* American Correctional Association (Ed.). College Park, MD: ACA.

Del Carmen, R. (1983). *Legal responsibilities of correctional personnel.* Washington, DC: National Institute of Justice.

Di Mascio, W. (1995). *Seeking justice: Crime and punishment in America.* New York: The Edna McConnell Clark Foundation

Dix, D. (1845). *Remarks on prisons and prison discipline in the United States.* Montclair, N.J.: Patterson Smith, Reprinted 1967.

Dowden, C., & Tellier, C. (2004). Predicting work-related stress in correctional officers: A meta-analysis. *Journal of Criminal Justice, 32*, 31–47.

Feder, L. (1991). A profile of mentally ill offenders and their adjustment in the community. *Journal of Psychiatry and Law, 19*, 1–2, 79–98.

Feder, L. (1995). Psychiatric history, due procedural safeguards, and the use of discretion in the criminal justice process. *Justice Quarterly, 12*, 279–305.

Federal Bureau of Prisons. (1999). www.bop.gov.

Gilliard, D., & Beck, A. J. (1998). *Prison and jail inmates at midyear 1997.* Washington, DC: Bureau of Justice Statistics, U.S. Department of Justice.

Griffin, M. L. (2006). Gender and stress: A comparative assessment of sources of stress among correctional officers. *Journal of Contemporary Criminal Justice, 22*, 4–25.

Hawkins, R., & Alpert, G. (1989). *American prison systems.* Englewood Cliffs, NJ: Prentice Hall.

Hurst, J. (1994, February 6). The big house that Don Novey built. *Los Angeles Times Magazine*, 16–20, 38.

Johnson, K. (2006). In wake of Fla. Shootout, prison workers may be screened. *USA Today,* A7.

Kauffman, K. (1988). *Prison officers and their world.* Cambridge, MA: Harvard University Press.

Lambert, E., Hogan, N. & Barton, S. (2004). The nature of work-family conflict among correctional staff: An exploratory examination. *Criminal Justice Review, 29,* 145–172.

Lombardo, V. S., & Smith, R. (1996, October). A model program for female offenders. *Corrections Today,* 92–95.

Long, N., Shouksmith, G., Voges, K., & Roache, S. (1986). Stress in prison staff: An occupational study. *Criminology, 24,* 331–345.

Mauro, T. (1997, June 24). Court: Sexual predators can stay confined. *U.S.A. Today,* 3A.

McShane, M., Williams III, F. P., Shichor, D., & McClain, K. (1991). Examining employee turnover. *Corrections Today, 53,* 5, 220–225.

National Criminal Justice Reference Service. (1998). *Women in criminal justice: A twenty year update.* Rockville, MD: NCJRS.

Palmer, L. (1999, March 21). More Blacks serving time in U.S. prisons. *Arizona Republic,* A19.

Peirce, N. R. (2007, February 18). California versus New York: Grappling with the prison dilemma. Washington Post Writers Group. Retrieved June 2, 2007 from the National Academy of Public Administration, www.napawash.org

Peters, T. (1992). *Liberation management.* New York: Knopf.

Sandler, M., Hudson, D., Weiss, C., & deGuzman, N. (1998). *Beyond the bottom line: How to do more with less in non profit and public organizations.* New York: Oxford University Press.

Schade, T. (1986). Prison officer training in the United States: The legacy of Jessie O. Stutsman. *Federal Probation, 50,* 4, 40-46.

Senna, J. and Siegel, L. (1996). *Introduction to criminal justice.* St. Paul, MN: West.

Smith, B., & Sapp, A. (1985). Fringe benefits: The hidden costs of unionization and collective bargaining in corrections. *Journal of Police and Criminal Psychology, 1,* 2, 33.

U. S. Department of Justice. (1994). *Women in prison: Survey of state prison inmates, 1991.* Washington, DC: Bureau of Justice Statistics.

Williams, T. A., & Soutar, G. (1984). Levels of custody and attitude differences among prison officers: A comparative study. *Australian and New Zealand Journal of Criminology, 17*, 87–94.

Wynne, J. (1985). Prison employee unionism. In R. Carter, D. Glaser & L. Wilkins (Eds.), *Correctional institutions,* (3rd ed.), pp. 399-402. New York: Harper and Row.

Online Exercise

Go to the Federal Bureau of Prisons website (www.fbop.gov) and click on the "about" section that will take you to the organizational chart of the FBOP. Explain the main features of the organizational structure. Does it appear to be an effective management operation based on that structure? What would you change and why? Who is the current Director?

Questions for Thought and Discussion

1. What factors seem to be related to correctional officer stress and what do you think can be done to reduce stress?

2. What suggestions did Warden Dennis Luther make about the treatment of inmates in correctional facilities and how to you evaluate his "credo."

3. Describe some of the issues related to employee turnover. What suggestions would you have for addressing it?

4. Explain the legal aspects of correctional officer use of force and some of the practical solutions you might use to reduce the incidence of use of force.

Books You May Want to Read

Earley, Peter. (1992). *Hot house: Life inside Leavenworth Prison.* NY: Bantam
Washington, Jerome. (1994). *Iron House: Stories from the yard.* NY: Vintage Books

Movies You May Want to See

Dead Man Walking
McVicar

CHAPTER 6
Classification and Programming

The history of corrections is a graveyard of abandoned fads.
Robert Martinson (1976)

INTRODUCTION

Initially, diagnostic officials evaluate inmates as they are received into the system and classification committees make a series of decisions about the inmate. Decisions include where the inmate will live and work, the custody or security level, and whether the inmate is a gang member or an escape risk. Many treatment issues are also explored at this time including educational vocational skills and training potential and any physical and mental health problems that need to be addressed.

According to Clements (1986) the interests served by proper classification are threefold. Proper assessment and assignments will: (1) meet practical needs, meaning that appropriate classification will make it easier to manage the inmate and others around them; (2) serve ethical concerns, meaning that humane treatment and assignment will provide for the welfare of the inmate; and (3) serve the legal obligations that the courts find in the relationship between those incarcerated and the state.

Unfortunately, many inmates are misclassified either because of faulty or negligent screening, or the unavailability of beds at the proper level of supervision. Poor planning, population projecting or the inability to build or lease facilities that meet current classification needs are also to blame for inappropriate classification. This is a grave concern to any system because improper classification not only costs money but may lead to unnecessary violence, injury, and even death. A recent escape by two inmates with violent criminal histories in Texas demonstrates a worst case scenario. Although both were serving at least

50 year sentences, and one had a previous misconduct requiring unit transfer, they were assigned to a work crew outside the prison unit fences. After attacking officers and grabbing their weapons, they stole a nearby city truck and escaped. Although they were soon recaptured, it was not before one officer died from a fall from horseback, the horse was fatally wounded, an area resident was carjacked and in the vehicle when it was disabled by law enforcement fire (Lee & Babineck, 2007).

CONTEMPORARY CLASSIFICATION ISSUES

The classification process in any prison provides two functions. One is the initial housing and job assignment of the inmate, and the second is the periodic review that is done throughout the inmate's stay in prison. Updates on an inmate's status are usually done every six-to-nine months to insure that the prisoner remains properly classified.

The decisions about classification and future treatment are usually made upon reviewing the inmate's records and criminal and family histories and by interviews, written tests, and physical examinations. Inmates are usually kept in a central in-processing unit or reception station until their records have been compiled and all classification decisions have been made. Of course, missing data is problematic.

Although diagnosis and classification proceeds on the premise that offenders are not all alike, the decision-making process used in institutions involves the employment of official stereotypes about prisoners, their histories, and the probabilities of certain behaviors. According to Doran (1977), stereotypes allow administrators to make quick decisions. Such a process also keeps significant distinctions between staff and inmates and makes official action more predictable. Because of the presumed ability to predict such things as future behavior and risk, experts have developed models to assist in making classification decisions.

Classification Models

According to Amy Craddock (1996) there are three basic models for classification. The first is the ***consensus model*** which may be used where departments have unique populations that require non-traditional assessments or where departments do not have the resources to gather data on which criteria is most effective in making classification decisions. Under this model, staff usually agree on the most important factors to consider in the process. The Federal Bureau of Prisons used this model, surveying staff to come up with six items to use on their classification instrument: severity of current offense, expected length of incarceration, prior prison commitments, history of escapes, history of violence and the type of outstanding warrants or charges pending on an inmate.

The second model is the *equity based system* which focuses on the most legally defensible characteristics of past and present criminal behavior. In this case, subjective or potentially irrelevant variables are eliminated from the process and are less likely to be raised in complaints of unfair treatment.

The third format is a *predictive model* that uses a number of legal, social, psychological and medical factors to develop a comprehensive picture of the inmate and to predict behavior. Instruments are administered to predict risk, such as risk for suicide, or violent behavior, others look for potential adjustment problems, and still others indicate personality type. The *Level of Supervision Inventory (LSI)* claims to provide not only an assessment of risk, but also an identification of treatment needs. Tests may be used to determine an inmate's education level, vocational interests or tendency toward addiction. In some systems, psychiatric assessments such as the *Minnesota Multiphasic Personality Inventory (MMPI)* are used to develop classification categories of inmates. For examples, Megargee grouped types of MMPI results into ten distinct personality profiles that might be used to predict behavior and interaction as well as treatment needs.

Some systems use an equity model for determining housing and work status and a more predictive approach for assignment to treatment programs. With limited resources and size limitations on most programs, officials try to gear assignments to those who have demonstrated the most success in the past or those closest to being discharged. In the reclassification process many departments look for disciplinary violations, overall institutional adjustment and time until release to decide whether to promote, demote or retain inmates at their current classification (Craddock, 1996).

Critics, particularly feminists, have argued that little attention has been paid to the development of a separate, and perhaps more accurate classification system for women. Male population-based models tend to place women in a more secure status than is really needed. Most practitioners agree that female prisoners need less security and control within an institution and more treatment. Therefore, custody-based models will have more difficulty meeting the extensive treatment needs of women (Burke & Adams, 1991; Fowler, 1993).

High Profile Inmates

In any correctional setting there are a number of different types of high profile inmates. These are either notorious because of their offenses such as the Unibomber or Timothy McVey or because of who they were before they committed their offense such as former police officers, lawyers, Watergate politicians and Enron executives. These special cases provide a number of logistical challenges for corrections officials that range from media demands and safety issues to preferential treatment and souvenir seekers. It is not surprising then that while the judge and prosecutor were eager to make a "get tough" example of Paris Hilton by sentencing her to jail, officials at that facility were just as eager to discharge her at the first sign of some physical or emotional health problem that may have signaled an impending liability.

Often correctional administrators resort to costly and resource intensive administrative segregation to isolate high profile cases from potential reprisals from inmate violence. The murder of serial killer and "cannibal" Jeffrey Dahmer shortly after his incarceration was not unexpected, nor was the recent stabbing attack on Robert Bardo, who was serving a life sentence in the murder of actress Rebecca Schaeffer. Inmates who are serving life sentences, those without any chance of parole may see such acts of violence, particularly against a well-known inmate as a way of achieving status or fame.

Legal Aspects of Classification

The federal courts have consistently said that they are reluctant to interfere with classification and transfer matters because they prefer to defer to administrative expertise in the operation of daily functions. However, as Krantz (1988) points out, because the way inmates are

Classification and Programming

classified or reclassified can seriously jeopardize their parole eligibility or access to programming and jobs, these decisions cannot be irrational, discriminatory, or arbitrary.

In *Ramos v. Lamm,* the court held that the procedures used in Colorado were based on "unfounded assumptions regarding inmate behavior and that the criteria were not applied uniformly to all inmates." The court also asserted that "any system of classification, placement and assignment must be clearly understandable, consistently applied and conceptually complete. Methods of validation must be implemented and means of redress for irregularity must be provided." In addition, the courts have called for classification systems that would insure that all new inmates receive appropriate assignments and treatment. The courts do not want prisoners kept in a more secure condition or status than was absolutely necessary as dictated by some quantifiable risk.

Over the last few years a number of lawsuits by inmates have challenged classification procedures, particularly those that placed restrictions on prisoners. The courts have basically found in these cases that when policies stipulate that certain criteria and guidelines apply, then the inmates have a right to expect those to be followed and that systems must abide by them. Otherwise, classification decisions are not unconstitutional just because they create restrictions,(*Stephany v. Wagner, Lanier v. Fair, Wallace v. Robinson*) (Craddock, 1996).

Another important purpose of classification is that by properly identifying those inmates with violent tendencies, other inmates will not be inappropriately housed with them or fall prey to attacks and abuse. In some cases, records will indicate that a prisoner has a history of homosexual assault. Tattoos may identify rival gang affiliation and, when answering direct questions, an inmate may admit that he could not get along with members of other races. Assessing these types of risks may prevent future incidences of violence between inmates. Prison officials must also prepare for the possibility of housing and managing "terrorists" or inmates with AIDS which pose a number of new administrative dilemmas.

Integration and assignments

Prisons may not segregate inmates by race in either housing or job assignments or in recreational activities. Racial segregation may only be used in emergencies of security and discipline (*Mickens v. Winston).*

A vague fear that desegregation would result in violence is not sufficient to justify segregation (*U.S. v. Wyandotte County, Kansas*). It has also been held that even temporary segregation must meet the level of clear and present danger before being considered justified (*Wilson v. Kelley*).

Despite legal prohibitions, William Wilbanks (1987) asserts that racial segregation, although less blatant, still exists in prisons today. Potentially racist separation strategies include "gang affiliation," "dangerousness assessments," and "protective custody." Protective custody is included because it is often utilized by whites who find themselves in units where they constitute only 5–15 percent of the population.

While the problems of racially unbalanced prisons are clear, administrators argue that disparity occurs when prisoners want to be assigned close to families, and outside geographical areas are not well integrated. They also contend that inmates prefer to be celled with members of the same race. Fearing liability from violence that may occur if integration is forced, some administrators have racially-mixed wings and cell blocks but not necessarily individual cells. However, forced cell integration had been considered by other administrations as a way to combat the violence of gangs deeply embedded within their systems. The practice has only been attempted on a limited and experimental basis. According to Krantz (1988), inmate suits seeking to stop forced integration and allowing "freedom of choice" in assignments have been rejected by the courts.

HIV-infected inmates have legally challenged policies that segregate them from the general prison population in housing, work and recreational activities. While the court would not specifically say that health-risk inmates could not be segregated, it would require that such inmates not be subject to deprivations and lower levels of service because of their status. Because it would be very expensive and difficult to provide equal resources outside of the general population in an alternative setting, the administrators' first preference is usually to integrate special populations, where feasible, into the mainstream.

The Assessment Process

In addition to being constitutional, and meeting the needs of the inmates as well as operational security, a classification process must also consider the cost associated with particular assignments. Because it is much more expensive to keep inmates in higher levels of security, classification systems must be continually revised so that they accurately reflect the amount of management and control necessary.

Aspects of assessment may include:
- *Health*: examination for physical health problems, screening for infectious diseases, dental workup, disabilities detection, fitness for work determination
- *Psychological*: mental health screening, determine risk of suicide, test for personality disturbances, violence potential
- *Alcohol/Drug Abuse*: History of substance use or abuse, extent, nature, patterns, relationship to crime, family involvement
- *Intelligence*: IQ tests, or others
- *Academic/Vocational*: tests for levels of functioning, proficiencies, skills, interests and aptitudes
- *Work/Training History*: experiences, skills, marketability, appropriate prison work assignment
- *Personal/Social Skills*: hygiene, racial compatibility, self-discipline, gang affiliation, ability to work and live with others—temperament
- *Family and Friends*: locations of possible visitors, family in correctional system for determining assignment
- *Victimization Potential*: risk, any known enemies

Corrections officials will argue that safety is the primary concern in making inmate assignments for work, housing and treatment programming. In this process, three different types of prediction methods may be used. The first, clinical assessment, relies on expert diagnoses and evaluation such as psychological analysis or the interpretation of personality tests. These are often time consuming and expensive and rely on professionals who may be otherwise occupied. Thus, they such methods are most commonly used when inmates are suicidal or in crisis. There is also concern that many psychological instruments used today are not normed for or validated within the prison population. The second type of assessment is the use of statistical or actuarial information such as profiles or comparisons to inmates with similar behavior patterns or experiences. Thirdly, the most often relied upon approach is anamnestic prediction which relies simply on the past behavior of that person. Thus, records that reflect a history of escape or violence toward inmates or staff will most likely trigger restrictive treatment within the prison system.

The assessment process is also likely to uncover many deficiencies in the background and current functioning of new inmates. According to a Department of Justice study, at least 42 percent of inmates have a learning disability that causes them to function below the fifth grade level (Bell, 1983). Another survey shows that approximately 10 percent of adult offenders have some type of serious disability, while in juvenile populations that rate is 28 percent. One government report estimated, however, that only 1.4 percent of state and federal prisoners receive some type of social security disability benefit (Baum, 1984).

State institutions vary in the exact IQ score used to determine who is and who is not mentally challenged. For programming purposes, and often by court order, some cut-off point is established and applied for classification purposes. Most systems use a score between 68 and 72 and below on the Wechsler Adult Intelligence Scale. Bernard McCarthy (1985) estimates the average percentage of developmentally disabled in prison populations is 2.5 percent.

CUSTODY

The basic custody levels used by most institutions are minimum, medium, and maximum security. With some variation, the elements of each are usually as follows:

- *Minimum* — 36% of all male inmates and 48% of females.
  Security is not a main concern; inmates are unlikely to escape, have proven themselves trustworthy in prison, and are not considered dangerous. Headcounts are infrequent. The facility has a more normal life-style and more active programming. Inmates have some privacy, possible family visits and may work unsupervised. Housing is often large open bays. An inmate may be designated as a "Trusty." The focus is on reintegrating the inmates with society; pre-release centers are in minimum custody.

- **Medium** — 36% of all male inmates and 33% of all females. Security has features such as electric fences and razor wire, regular head counts and continuous surveillance but the inmates may go to work, eat and recreation unescorted. There is more inmate to inmate contact than in maximum custody. Visitation may be open style seating and housing may be a dorm-like arrangement. Inmates may be allowed more variety in personal possessions than in maximum. These inmates have probably committed serious crimes but have proven trustworthy while incarcerated.

- **Maximum** — 22% of all male inmates and 13% of females.
  Most dangerous and disruptive inmates are here. High-tech security in multiple, and overlapping layers. Armed guards are often on the perimeters with continuous electronic surveillance. Emphasis is on security and control. Limited movement by prisoners who are often videotaped and cuffed as they are escorted, visitors separated by partitions, inmates may shower and eat alone with no group activities. Solitary confinement is common with frequent strip searches and personal possessions are restricted to basic necessities. Protective custody inmates are in this category as well.

Over the years, this traditional custody classification system has become increasingly sophisticated to allow for a greater variety of inmates and institutional needs. As a result perhaps, the number of inmates in maximum security appears to have declined. The first edition of this textbook reported that 52 percent of inmates were in maximum custody which is a dramatic departure from the figures reported today. One system, developed by Herbert Quay, separated inmates as passive, aggressive, and situation normal. In another example, Texas employs at least six custody levels, which indicate housing and security assignments but not necessarily how inmates are classified for good time earning purposes, work or treatment. The 2006 Statistical Report for the state outlines the breakdown of inmates by level as follows.

Those ***minimum*** inmates who are considered "trustees" are allowed to roam the institutional grounds with little or no supervision. Other minimum custody inmates are also provided little or no supervision but are required to remain within the fenced compound. Three quarters of state prisoners are classified as minimum. Those designated as ***medium*** custody must remain within the institution unless closely supervised. Another seven percent of Texas prison inmates are in this group. About 2800 inmates (or 2 percent) are designated for **Safe-Keeping**, as they have been identified as likely targets for harm or unable to defend themselves from others. Most must volunteer for this status, and they may not be mixed with other custody inmates. Fifth are the **Close custody** inmates who require close supervision both inside and outside the institution and are severely restricted in movement. This is another two percent of the total state prison population. The last category includes two types of **Administrative segregation** inmates. The A status inmates are considered predatory and assaultive. They are placed one to a cell The other group is B status and may be double-celled but are still restricted from access to the rest of the prison population. Currently about 7 percent of the inmate population is in administrative segregation status. The remainder of the inmate population is in transition or in other custody status arrangements.

In making custody or housing assignments the classification specialist or committee will look at the inmate's offense, incarceration, and escape histories, immigration status, potential for violence, membership in gangs, as well as other indicators of hygiene, racial compatibility, self-discipline and ability to live with and work with others. Committees are often made up of staff from security, work sites, health services and administration so that all points of view are considered in the process. In some cases, inmates appear at a classification review hearing in order to make statements or answer questions. While attempts are made to keep known enemies apart, only the most volatile and vulnerable inmates can be kept in solitary confinement or in protective custody.

Protective Custody

Protective custody is one way prison administrators attempt to isolate and protect inmates who are likely to be victimized. Protective custody (PC) is a small restricted housing area that usually is made up of maximum security single cells located in a wing of a larger institution. PC is often referred to as a "prison within a prison." In almost all instances, inmates must request PC and cases are reviewed by prison officials. In one survey, 37 states acknowledged that they usually grant

Classification and Programming

requests even though it is difficult to substantiate all fears as legitimate (Pierson, 1988). Usually the inmate must provide some concrete evidence that his or her life is in danger or the specific name of the potential threat. Most requests for PC come from inmates with known enemies, sex targets, informants or those with gambling debts, poor social skills or low intelligence. Drug trafficking and gang activity usually spawns requests for PC (Fields, 1996).

The use of PC is creates problems for administrators. While they may be held liable for injuries to inmates who are denied protection, the courts have also made it clear that PC units cannot be punitive in nature so that basic amenities, programs and privileges must also be available. This makes PC very expensive to furnish and operate. Inmates leaving PC to return to the general population are often targeted for retaliation as a result of that status or are regarded with suspicion. Some states agree to coordinate exchanges of at-risk inmates who can be held safely in the general population of another jurisdiction rather than use PC. In *Walker v. Lockhart,* an inmate was ordered into federal custody as it seemed his safety could not be guaranteed in the state system (Fields, 1996).

Administrative Segregation

Unlike protective custody, administrative segregation (ad seg) is a punitive status and the courts have a lowered expectation of the conditions there. However, the ad seg environment must meet constitutionally acceptable standards (as not cruel and unusual) and the time spent there must be limited, although the courts have not specified a certain amount of time as critical.

According to Barbara Belbot (1996) assigning someone to administrative segregation for as long as two years has been held constitutional, while 30 days has been found to violate the constitution. The determining factors in these decisions have been living conditions and reasons for confinement (*Graham v. Willingham, Knuckles v. Prasse,* and *Hutto v. Finney*). In general, the courts expect states to develop and follow their own specific operational policies for the use and management of a constitutionally viable administrative segregation area.

In most cases, prison facilities have an area or wing designated as administrative segregation. Inmates are usually sent there following a disciplinary hearing for a specified amount of time. At the end of that time period, the inmate's case may be reviewed for further punitive detention or for return to the general population. If a facility only has temporary ad seg quarters, the inmate may be transferred to a more secure, maximum-security unit and reclassified. Offenses resulting in ad seg time are typically assault, drug smuggling, continued failure to work, weapons possession, threatening a staff member or certain types of gang related activity.

The cells in administrative segregation usually contain the basics (bed, toilet, and sink) with no personal possessions. Inmates are confined to the cell almost 23 hours per day with minimal recreation and shower time. Security and surveillance is heavy during all activities and prisoners are usually escorted from place to place in handcuffs and chains, if moved at all.

PROGRAMMING AND TREATMENT

There are a variety of treatment programs in prisons although there is much less emphasis on programming today than in the late 1960s and early 1970s. Programs can be divided into categories such as education, skills training and therapy or counseling.

National studies indicated that roughly 27 million people, or 10 percent of the population, are functionally illiterate. Research also shows that more than 75 percent of prison inmates are functionally illiterate and that the average inmate functions only on a sixth grade level. According to Schwartz & Lewis (1987) 42 percent of the incarcerated population has some type of learning deficiency, meaning that they are functioning below a fifth grade level. Of this group, 82 percent have a specific learning disability. There has been some recent controversy over the estimates of the percent of the inmate population that is illiterate. Depending on definitions and criteria used, the types of tests and assessments given and the separation of categories for nonnative English speakers, the true numbers of illiterate, functionally illiterate and reading impaired may vary.

Education programs are the backbone of treatment and most facilities have a GED program for those without a high school education. While it is unclear whether participation in GED programs can be mandated, some states have enacted legislation to this effect.

Currently, laws also require that most juveniles be enrolled in education programs. Moreover, under both the *Education of All Handicapped Children Act of 1975* and the *Individuals with Disabilities Education Act of 1990*, prisons must provide access to special education programming as well as transition planning for release for those inmates who are qualified for these services.

Drug and Alcohol Treatment

Many reports cite a disproportionate amount of drug and alcohol abuse among prisoners. According to research by Belenko (2002) 83% of those in prison or jail are seriously involved with alcohol or drugs. A report by the Bureau of Justice Statistics (2006) indicates that 60 percent of female and 53 percent of male state prisoners in 2004 were abusing or dependant on drugs prior to incarceration. Roughly one-third of state and one-fourth of federal inmates admitted that they had committed their offense while under the influence of drugs. Two-thirds of state prisoners also admit that that they had used drugs regularly at some time in their life. Drug abusers were much more likely to be recidivists and one in seven was homeless prior to prison admission. These figures appear to have been consistent for at least the past decade.

While a significant portion of the inmate population is in need of substance abuse treatment, only about 40 percent of those designated as drug dependant/abusing actually receive such services. Still, more recent figures indicate an increase in treatment services over previous years (BJS, 2006). It is estimated that most state departments spend only five percent of their budgets on treatment—the federal system spends less than one percent. However, one study estimates that while treatment may cost $6,500 per inmate over the regular cost of incarceration, the cost savings from each successful release would be $68,000 per inmate in the first year (National Center on Addiction and Substance Abuse, 1998).

A 2006 study by the Urban Institute that focused on the Texas state jails that house predominantly repeat drug offenders found that inmates there were less likely to receive drug treatment than inmates in regular prison settings. They were also less likely to receive education, job training and other self-improvement programs even though they were more likely to be serving shorter sentences and had an immediate need of employment skills. The data collected also indicated that while about half of prison inmates had a history of frequent drug use, compared to 68% of those in state jails, those in state jails had a much harder time obtaining a job within a year of release than did prisoners from the state prison system (O'Hare, 2007). Overall, this indicates that a drug or alcohol abuse history may be a more significant barrier to successful community integration than a felony conviction and prison sentence.

The most common substance abuse programs available, perhaps because they are so inexpensive, are Alcoholics Anonymous (AA) and Narcotics Anonymous (NA). AA has been in prisons since 1935, while drug treatment is much more recent. Although one of the basic tenets of AA is that the meetings are voluntary, many inmates believe that participation in this self-help group based treatment will reflect positively on their record and enhance chances for early release. Other inmates enjoy the social aspects of the treatment meeting at which refreshments are often served. While there are few evaluations available to measure the success of this particular twelve-step process, it is likely to be continued because it is a popular approach. According to Gary Green (1996), about three-fifths of drinking inmates have been involved in at least one alcohol intervention program in their life and 20 percent of these inmates join an alcohol treatment program while incarcerated. At the present time, there are over 1800 AA groups in prisons across the country.

The 1966 *Narcotic Addict Rehabilitation Act* required treatment for federal offenders who had violated U.S. narcotic laws. Although by 1978 there were over 33 drug treatment units in the federal system, only a small proportion of offenders are able to participate in these programs (11 percent). A 1991 survey of state institutions found that about 30 percent of all inmates participate in some type of drug treatment intervention (Krause, 1996).

Some intensive treatment programs are located in separate facilities adjacent to the prison or in nearby secured treatment centers. Officials sometimes voice concern that inmates may volunteer for such programs only because they offer a diversion from the normal prison routine; however, most all inmates could benefit from the skills practiced in these sessions.

Treatment programs vary in philosophy, approach to recovery, and length of time spent in treatment, which may vary from one to six months. They also vary in the intensity of services (live-in versus one-visit-per-week for hourly sessions). Some programs are self-help, some use group therapy, cognitive therapies, educational videos, relaxation techniques, or medicines to combat addiction (Krause, 1996).

One of the concerns about drug treatment in prison is that it represents a very protected environment, apart from the influences of the street. Some say it is difficult to gauge the success of an intervention until the participant had proven resistant outside, amid the stresses of daily life. Others argue that there are many real "street influences" inside prison, including many types of drugs, and that prison treatment programs are a valuable resource for providing the every day skills needed by persons facing even long term incarceration.

Other Treatment Initiatives

Other treatment offerings include a variety of self-help programs which appear to be cost effective as well as meaningful to inmates. Recognizing that effective counseling or treatment must be voluntary and not forced, some therapists simply act as facilitators for the groups inmates select to work with. Often, those who have recovered from or shared in the same traumatic event or problem have a credibility and legitimacy in the eyes of the offender that the "professionals" do not.

In one system, a support group was formed of women who had committed crimes resulting in the deaths of their children. All of the inmates represented in this group suffered from stigma and ostracism within the prison, guilt and low self-esteem, as well as the inability to interact with others relative to their grief. Many of the women had family problems, drug habits, and emotional problems to resolve as well. Over a four-year period, fourteen different offenders have found the program helpful in reducing their feelings of isolation, gaining understanding of their crime, and planning for their future. Explained one inmate, "maybe because of what we've been through, we see things more clearly; perhaps we can be preventive medicine to others like ourselves. Women don't realize you can love your children, and this can still happen. By exposing ourselves, maybe we can help others" (Kaplan, 1988, p. 9).

In addition to the programs mentioned above, a wide variety of specialized offense treatments are being developed for inmates such as treatment for combat stress (disorders suffered by veterans), anger management for spouse abusers and sex offender treatments. In many jurisdictions, participation in a sex offender treatment program is required by the courts. Other programs, not therapeutically-oriented but also generated for special-needs inmates, include assistance to illegal aliens with immigration problems, daily life-skills training for the developmentally disabled and coordination with social security administrators to resolve work or health related issues. These functions can be performed by counselors, social workers or community volunteers. Resolving routine issues that trouble the inmate when separated from families or outside agencies may help reduce stress and facilitate positive adjustment to institutional life.

SUMMARY

Classification systems usually emphasize characteristics of the offender rather than the offense. Inmates' labels such as recidivist, gang member, addict, mentally disturbed, and sexually predatory are often employed in making choices about separating groups of offenders. In order to be effective, a classification tool must be able to predict reasonably well, must reflect reality, and it cannot remain fixed over time in a dynamic setting (Rans, 1984).

While a more conservative public seems to favor tougher, more austere prison conditions there is some indication from research that inmates housed in higher security levels are as likely, if not more likely to recidivate than those who lived in minimum security. This means that not only is the more secure confinement more expensive during incarceration, but that it also predicts future expenses in terms of the likelihood of return to prison (Chen & Shapiro, 2007).

Current prison overcrowding ensures that there are many more inmates who need treatment than can be realistically served. The numbers of inmates needing basic educational and work skills, and the growing number of offenders with substance abuse problems have put a strain on existing program structures and resources. As a result, administrators have three options: (1) reduce the percentage of inmates receiving treatment in order to insure quality services; (2) reduce the number of different services offered to insure all inmates get some treatment, or; (3) modify the programs to somehow expose more inmates to some aspect of treatment. For example, South Carolina reports that the number of prisoners with sex-related offenses has doubled over the last five years, leading them to resort to group rather than individual therapy treatments. Besides being less expensive, administrators find that the group method appears to be as effective as traditional individual approaches (Szymanowski & McGee, 1988).

Cases

Graham v. Willingham 384 F.2d 162 (7 Cir., 1988)
Hutto v. Finney 437 U.S. 678 (1978)
Knuckles v. Prasse 435 F.2d 1255 (3 Cir., 1971)
Lanier v. Fair, 876 F. 2d 243 (1st Cir., 1989)
Mickens v. Winston 462 F. Supp 910 (1978)
Ramos v. Lamm 458 F. Supp 128 (1979)
Stephany v. Wagner, 835 F. 2d 497 (3^{r}Cir., 1986)
U.S. v. Wyandotte County Kansas 343 F. Supp. 1189 (1972)
Walker v. Lockhart 713 F.2d 1378 (8 Cir., 1983)
Wallace v. Robinson, 940 F. 2d 243 (7 Cir. 1991)
Wilson v. Kelley 294 F. Supp. 1005 (1968)

References

Baum, E. (1984). Handicapped prisoners: An ignored minority? *Columbia Journal of Law and Social Problems, 18,* 3, 349–379.
Belbot, B. (1996). Administrative segregation. In M. McShane & F. P. Williams III, (Eds.), *Encyclopedia of American prisons*, pp. 8–11. New York: Garland.
Bell, R. (1983). *Learning deficiencies of adult inmates.* Washington, DC: National Institute of Justice, U.S. Department of Justice.
Bureau of Justice Statistics (October, 2006). *Drug use and dependence, state and federal prisoners, 2004.* Washington, DC: Office of Justice Programs, U.S. Department of Justice.
Burke, P., & Adams, L. (1991). *Classification of women offenders in state correctional facilities: A handbook for practitioners.* Washington, DC: National Institute of Corrections.
Chen, M. K., & Shapiro, J. M. (2007). Do harsher prison conditions reduce recidivism? A discontinuity-based approach. *American Law and Economics Review, 9,* 1–29.

Clements, C. (1986). *Offender needs assessment.* College Park, Maryland: American Correctional Association.
Clements, C. (1987). Assessing offender needs—Developments and prospects. *Corrections Today, 49*, 7, 112.
Craddock, A. (1996). Classification system. In M. McShane & F. P. Williams III, (Eds.), *Encyclopedia of American prisons*, pp. 87–96). New York: Garland.
Doran, R. (1977). Organizational stereotyping: The case of the adjustment center classification committee. In D. Greenberg (Ed.), *Corrections and punishment.* Beverly Hills, CA: Sage.
Fields, C. B. (1996). Protective custody. In M. McShane & F. P. Williams III (Eds.), *Encyclopedia of American prisons*, pp. 373–374. New York: Garland.
Fowler, L.T. (1993). *Classification of women offenders.* Columbia, SC: South Carolina Department of Corrections.
Green, G. (1996). Alcohol treatment programs in prison. In M. McShane & F. P. Williams III (Eds.), *Encyclopedia of American prisons,* pp. 24–26. New York: Garland.
Kaplan, M. F. (1988). A peer support group for women in prison for the death of a child. *Journal of Offenders Counseling Services, and Rehabilitation,* 13, 1, 5–13.
Krantz, S. (1988). *Corrections and prisoners' rights.* St. Paul, MN: West.
Krause, W. (1996). Drug treatment. In M. McShane & F. P. Williams III (Eds.), *Encyclopedia of American prisons,* pp. 171–174. New York: Garland.
Lee, R. C., & Babineck, M. (2007, September 25). Prison guard killed in escape. *Houston Chronicle,* A1.
Martinson, R. (1976). California research at the crossroads. *Crime and Delinquency, 22*, 2, 180–191.
McCarthy, B. (1985). Mentally ill and mentally retarded offenders in corrections: A report of a national survey. *Sourcebook on the mentally disordered prisoner,* Washington, DC: U.S. Department of Justice.
National Center on Addiction and Substance Abuse at Columbia University. (2002, August). *Trends in substance abuse and treatment needs among inmates--Final Report.* Washington, DC: U. S. Department of Justice.

National Center on Addiction and Substance Abuse at Columbia University. (1998). *Behind bars: Substance abuse and America's prison population.* New York: Columbia University.

O'Hare, P. (2007, June 1). Many inmates miss out on drug rehab. *Houston Chronicle.* Retrieved June 1, 2007 from www.chron.com.

Rans, L. (1984). The validity of models to predict violence in community and prison settings. *Corrections Today, 46*, 3, 50.

Schwartz, G., & Lewis, K. (1987). Effective special education for juveniles. *Corrections Today, 49*, 3, 26–30.

Szymanowski, D., & McGee, G. (1988). Computer profiles guide sex-offender therapy. *Corrections Today, 50*, 7, 150.

Texas Department of Criminal Justice Executive Services. (2006). *Fiscal Year 2006 Statistical report.* Huntsville, TX: Texas Department of Criminal Justice.

Wilbanks, W. (1987). *The myth of a racist criminal justice system.* Monterey, CA: Brooks Cole.

Online Exercise

Go to the website for the Texas Department of Criminal Justice. Look up the Offender Orientation Handbook which is given to all new inmates upon arrival in the system.

1. What is the department policy on the collection of DNA blood samples?

2. Explain how the amount of good time credit that an inmate can potentially earn is determined.

3. What is the classification system used for categorizing inmates for work, good time credit, privileges and housing and how easy is it to understand?

Questions for Thought and Discussion

1. What is the purpose of classification and what do you think the most important priorities should be?

2. Discuss some of the legislation that has been used to help bring treatment to prison.

3. Describe the assessment process. What types of information do you feel is most helpful for making decisions about security and treatment?

4. What types of policies might you have for dealing with high profile inmates?

Books You May Want to Read

Santos, Michael. (2003). *Profiles from Prison*. Westport, CT: Praeger.
Martin, Danny, & Sussman, Peter. (1995). *Committing Journalism*. New York: W.W. Norton.

Movies You May Want to See

Bird Man of Alcatraz
Doing Time: Life Inside the Big House

CHAPTER 7
Prisonization, Rules and Discipline

Prison is a place where all sorts of things are not there.

Bruce Jackson

INTRODUCTION

To sociologists in the mid-1900s, prison represented the perfect controlled environment in which to study human behavior and reactions. An astute observer could watch the formation of individual strangers into groups—some friendly, some violent. Students of the prison environment sought answers to technical questions about how lawbreakers could be led or coerced into conforming behaviors, how they interacted, and whether or not they changed. The more philosophical questions included how societies formed, how power or leadership roles emerged, and how man treated man in a captive world.

According to Garfinkel (1961), the entire criminal justice process from arrest to prison represents a **status degradation ceremony** where the subject is transformed into a lower social type. Separated from the rest of society, the convicted is denounced as he/she takes on the identity of the crime and becomes know as a burglar, robber or murderer. In prison, the person's identity is revised into this lower status; a haircut, uniform, and the assignment of a number all indicate that the new inmate is no longer what he/she was but is now like other offenders.

The process of "becoming" a prisoner also involves the recognition of a **stigma**, according to Erving Goffman (1961). Those with a stigma, such as being a prisoner, learn that they are excluded from the normal perspective and must associate with others of the same stigma; they search for leaders or representatives from among themselves. They also learn the rules for their behavior now and the consequences of being what they are. Many professionals argue that the adoption of stigma-related attitudes by offenders makes rehabilitation through self-esteem difficult. Often discouragement from other inmates regarding the futility of trying to get out from under the stigma of being a "convict" works against treatment.

To Goffman (1961), prison is a total institution where inmates under similar circumstances live and work, cut off from the rest of society in an enclosed, formally administered life. There are specific rules, a few clearly defined rewards, and a variety of possible punishments. Though inmates bring cultural identities with them, they are stripped away at the door in a process of **mortification** and **role dispossession.** Men are no longer fathers or husbands; women are no longer mothers or wives. Indoctrination into the institution involves a series of debasements, degradations, and humiliations. A person is stripped of possessions, searched and often shaved. Goffman explains the admissions process as an obedience test and a contest for breaking the will of the defiant inmate.

What is more striking about prison to the new inmate, who according to Goffman (1961) is now the lowest of this group of low status, is the lack of privacy. Your body and your necessary articles are subject to continuous scrutiny. Your records or life history are common knowledge among the institutional staff where little confidentiality is maintained. In order to survive, Goffman postulates that the resident adopts one of four modes of adaptation: (1) withdrawing from the situation; (2) challenging authority; (3) colonizing with others to make the best of the circumstances; and (4) converting to the administrative perspective, trying to be a perfect inmate.

In the process of becoming a prisoner, or **prisonization,** Goffman (1961) found that many devise secondary adjustments—deals, gimmicks that while not particularly legitimate, are not necessarily a challenge to staff either. Inmates construe games, or interactions that result from their bitterness and the commonality of their "unjust" condition. In a sense, this creates a fraternity, a **prison subculture.**

PRISONIZATION

One of the first studies on inmate subculture was conducted by Clemmer at Menard Prison in Illinois. For Clemmer (1940), prisonization was "the taking on, in greater or lesser degree of the folkways, mores and customs, and general culture of the penitentiary." How strongly one identifies with other prisoners and prison ways, according to Clemmer, depends on the housing area he/she is assigned to, the strength of relationships or ties one has on the outside, and the vulnerability of his/her own personality—whether they join groups, accept the codes of others, and change to suit peers. Clemmer assumed that most inmates did not join groups.

Clemmer's theory about prisonization was tested by Stanton Wheeler at the Washington State Reformatory. Wheeler (1961) found that the degree to which an inmate becomes prisonized depended upon which phase of their incarceration they were in. Prisoners in the middle of their sentence were more likely to be involved with other inmates in subcultural identification. Inmates in the early and pre-release phases of their stay were more likely to relate to administrative definitions of order and outside values. Wheeler plotted the degree of prisonization over time; the result has been labeled **Wheeler's U-shaped Curve.** In the diagram below, the early (thicker line at the left) stage is when the inmate would be attempting to obey rules, earn privileges and impress authorities with a good attitude. Friends and family still seem close, as do ties to one's outside life. The thin line dipping down over time, represents the loss of contact with the outside, feelings of hopelessness, vulnerability to other inmates, getting into trouble and joining gangs and cliques that may lead to disciplinary problems. Over time, as the inmate nears release, they once again engage in contacts with the outside, good behavior and attempts to dissociate one's self with negative relationships inside (the second thick line at the right).

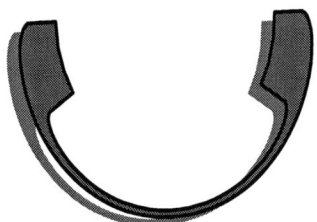

The importance of the middle phase of a prisoner's sentence was also explained by Miller (1973). Attention focuses on establishing relationships with other inmates and trying to secure some form of power base. Miller's concept of the middle phase is described by Love et al. (1987, p. 4).

> The future is ignored as an impossible perspective with unreal qualities. Coping with the passage of time is one of the most important activities. Boredom is fought by getting into programs, hobbies, reading or ritualistic activities (e.g. making chains with cigarette packs). Many seek stimulation through rule violations, gambling, and encouraging violence among others. Guilt and shame... frequently addressed with grandiosity and compensatory fantasies (including pursuit of professional careers, being a hero, etc.....

Love et al. also relate that depression, anger and anxiety are also common at this stage, and inmates resort to frequent sick call visits and attention getting mechanisms.

Another of the early works on prisonization was Sykes' 1958 book, *Society of Captives*. Sykes labels the psychological and sociological problems that the inmate goes through in adjusting to incarceration as the **pains of imprisonment.** Prisonization, for Sykes, was the process of adapting to the deprivations of prison life. The five deprivations include the:

1. Loss of liberty or restriction of movement
2. Loss of autonomy or self-direction
3. Lack of normal, heterosexual relationships
4. Deprivation of previously enjoyed goods and services
5. Lack of personal security and safety

Deprivation and Importation Models

Under the **Deprivation Model**, theorists view the structure of prison organizations and lifestyle as shaping the inmate subculture. The goal of security requires that inmates be stripped of possessions and privileges that are enjoyed on the outside. This creates a common bond among prisoners. The strength of that bond is described by Bartollas et al. (1976).

No formal structure, no matter how coercive, can deny or prevent a counterculture and structure from emerging. What the institution denies in the way of self-respect, freedom, privileges, normative standards, and benefits, the inmates create for themselves on a surreptitious but nevertheless very effective level.

From the beginning, the in-processing procedure creates uniformity among the inmates (giving them numbers, perhaps haircuts and uniforms), making it even easier for them to identify with each other. It is hardly surprising that inmates bind together in groups which many sociologists call a "negative consequence" or "latent dysfunction" of the nature of prisons.

The inmate's need to adapt to the deprivations of the prison environment often forces them into situations where they get special privileges from the staff by being cooperative and maintaining the status quo. Cloward called this process **structural accommodation**. By using the existing power structure, the inmate plays along to get whatever limited benefits exist in the otherwise bleak surroundings. While entering into mutually beneficial relationships with the staff works for some inmates, others become alienated from this same organizational structure. As Thomas and Petersen (1977, p. 50) write, high levels of alienation are "strongly associated with the degree of assimilation or 'prisonization' into an inmate society that is in direct opposition to the goals of the prison and its official representatives." These writers also conclude that there is support (Clemmer, 1940 and 1950; Wheeler, 1961; Garabedian, 1963) for the idea that "as the duration of exposure to the deprivations of imprisonment increases, so does the degree of integration into the oppositional inmate subculture."

Contrasting the deprivation model is the notion that subcultures form because of the habits and traits inmates bring into the prison from outside. Values and styles of interaction are learned on the street and "imported" with the offender. The development of the importation model was in response to the inabilities of the deprivation model to explain or predict the type of responses inmates would have to the prison setting. Particularly now, it is clear that parts of street gangs and drug cultures are carried over into the prison and, though somewhat revised, operate within. The relationships between gang members inside and outside the prison are the theme of the 1992 movie *American Me*, based loosely on events in the California Prison System which was an excellent example of the importation model although there are aspects of the deprivation model as well. Another, *Cool Hand Luke*, better exemplifies the deprivation model as does the *Shawshank Redemption* and *Sleepers*. Typically, films that document older prison times seem to portray them as isolated worlds where the harsh conditions change the "vulnerable" offender, most often for the worse. Films based on more contemporary incarceration experiences tend to emphasize the notion that rough and dangerous people enter together as in the importation model which can be seen in *Bad Boys* starring Sean Penn.

Some argue that the absence of violence and gangs in prisons in other countries tends to support the importation model. Without underlying cultural differences being brought into the prison by inmates, wouldn't all prisons with equal deprivations result in similar behavior? Also, research on women's prisons seems to imply that adjustment patterns cannot be understood outside the context of women's roles in society (Gibbons, 1979).

A number of studies on women's' prisons have emphasized the importance of the roles inmates award each other in kinship or family structures (Heffernan, 1972; Giallombardo, 1966; Propper, 1981). Two inmates, often involved in a homosexual relationship will begin the family—one taking on the masculine role and one assuming the "wife" role; they will add children, brothers, aunts, etc., as the relationships develop. As Giallombardo (1966) notes, family units may be interracial, may include up to 100 members, and may involve switching from one family group to another. As Propper (1981, p. 155) notes, not all kinship groups center on sexual relations. "Participation in make-believe families seems to be less motivated by a desire for sexual gratification than by a need for security, companionship, affection, attention, status, prestige, and acceptance."

Researchers today suggest an integration of the deprivation and importation models. Together pre-prison experiences as well as adaptations to deprivations within the prison explain much of inmate behavior. Prison homosexuality is often discussed as a result of the deprivations of prison life. However, the very different character of relations in male and female institutions suggests the influence of imported values. Estimates are that only 10 percent of the males (Clemmer, 1940) and 5 percent of the females (Burkhart, 1976) had had homosexual experiences prior to prison, but that 30 percent of the males and females were involved in homosexual activities while in prison (Van Wormer, 1984). While the literature suggests that widespread fears of homosexuality still dominate the inmate culture, there are distinct differences between the purposes of sex in male and female institutions. As the research of Ward and Kassebaum is explained by Van Wormer (1984, p. 24):

> While men in prison are more concerned with the mere physical dimension and inclined to make use of material goods as a medium of exchange, women are more concerned with the emotional commitment of sexual relationships.

Though there is much variety in patterns of adaptation, some theorists have designed typologies or categories of inmate subcultures. A few are listed below.

Clemmer (1940)	**Heffernan*** (1972)	**Schrag** (1961)	**Irwin & Cressey** (1962)
clique men	*square*	*Square John*	*convict*
group men	*life*	*Right guy*	*thief*
semi-solitary men	*cool*	*con-politician*	*straight*
completely solitary men		*Outlaw*	

*women's prison

Regardless of the typology used, there are a few aspects of the inmate subculture that seem to be shared by all. One is the inmate code or unwritten set of values that seem to be agreed upon by inmates as the best way to do time. As Sykes and Messinger (1960) note, the norms of this code include:
1. Don't interfere in other inmates' business.
2. Don't lose your head, stay cool, do your own time.

3. Don't use or exploit other inmates.
4. Don't weaken, whine, or be a sucker.

Interestingly enough, research by Ward and Kassebaum (1961) seemed to indicate that the inmate code is not as strongly upheld by women prisoners and that the taboos against snitching are not as absolute.

Most Hollywood dramatizations of prison life include one character as the snitch or rat (i.e., *The Big House* with James Cagney). This is probably because of the role they play in bringing inside information to official authorities and because of the tension they create within the inmate subculture. During riots like Attica (1971) and New Mexico (1980), the snitches were sought out and killed. Sykes (1958, p. 88) explains:

> Most of the ratting that occurs in the prison is done for the sake of personal gain, but we can distinguish two different forms. First, there are those rats who reveal their own identity to the officials, who hope to win preferential treatment from their rulers in exchange…. Second, there are those rats who prefer to remain anonymous, not because their betrayal is an unselfish act committed for the good of the custodians, but because they wish to get rid of a competitor or to settle a grudge. Thus, the officials may find themselves being manipulated by their prisoners into a position where they are serving unintentionally as a weapon in the battles taking place among the inmates.

As Kessler and Roebuck (1996) explain, theoretically, the administration's successful use of snitches would depend upon a weaker inmate code and the absence of other inmate avenues of control and intelligence. And, although the courts have appeared to validate the use of snitches as the practice of not revealing the identity of informants in prison disciplinary hearings was upheld in *Wolff v. McDonnell,* justices would nonetheless be wary of any systematic violence that results from the use and abuse of informants.

Prisoner Argot

> Prison is an oral place. There's not much to look at in a cell, so inmates do a lot of talking. They talk to their neighbor, or the guy locked five cells away, two above, or one below. Even in the yard, it's an oral place. Jiving. Joking. Shouting. Laughing. Crying. Often just plain lying. Inmates will rap about anything to anyone, to keep the tension off of them. And when no one else will give us any rap, we talk to ourselves.
>
> Jerome Washington (*Iron House*, 1994)

Another aspect of prison life unique to the inmate culture is a special language or argot that develops among the prisoners. Though the terms vary from state to state and even between units, prison slang is invented for everything from an illegally transmitted message (kite) to a best friend (road dog) to taking a bus (pulling chain). It is not unusual to hear the officers using many of the commonly understood terms as well.

According to Jones (1996) argot is more distinctive than slang in that it is purposively meant to be significant only to the members of the subculture themselves and it is used to convey shared values and sentiments such as making fun of the system or differentiating between types of prisoners. Although the specific phrases in the language are constantly changing, the implication is that shared terminology, like shared values, is necessary for survival.

Age, Race, Sex and Subculture

In a study of prisoners in a Midwestern penitentiary, Gillsepie and Galliher (1972) found that a majority of prisoners in their twenties believed the prison had matured them, while most of those who were middle age reported that prison had preserved them, and the older prisoners felt that incarceration had aged them. This is not surprising since most of the young people are maturing anyway and use their confrontation with the law as an opportunity to publicly announce, and believe, they will change their ways. The middle-aged prisoner, on the other hand, has been locked up through a period where his peers on the streets are falling to the effects of drugs, alcohol, and younger, tougher competition. They view their current incarceration as saving them from the fate of their friends. Faced with their mortality, the older prisoner has the most to loose. They see time passing them by and regret that what little time they have left will be wasted behind bars.

Contemporary literature on the subculture of prisoners is dominated by the issues of race and gangs. While blacks represent 12 percent of the U.S. population, they are roughly 46 percent of those incarcerated. While the research on disciplinary actions in institutions appears mixed, more of the more recent studies find that African Americans were more likely than whites to be written up for misconduct (Free, 1996). Previous research has also indicated that white officers find African American inmates to be more threatening and dangerous than other inmates, which may mean closer scrutiny and a greater tendency to "write up" offenders which may contribute to the disproportionate infraction rates. Studies of inmate adjustment and race have also concluded that African American inmates had higher self-esteem than other inmates, were more likely to feel safe in prison and less likely to consider suicide. Other researchers have found that an economically disadvantaged background, regardless of race, often meant a smoother adjustment to incarceration (Free, 1996).

Many theorists of prison culture view the prisoner rights movements and the general civil rights movements of the 60s and 70s as disrupting the "traditional" prison culture where the older convict had status and authority. In this period of social unrest and policy reform, a new internal social structure emerged aligned on the variable of race and human rights. A 1978 study by Slosar reported that race was the most important element in the prisoner's selection of friends and leaders.

Research on Adjustment

Many officials consider prison adjustment a prerequisite for parole. Parole boards look at disciplinary records and participation in educational, vocational, drug and alcohol treatment, and other self-improvement programs as an indication that the person has adjusted to the expectations of society. Research has examined the link between disciplinary problems and overall adjustment as well as time spent in solitary and on restriction. Other indicators of adjustment include contact with outsiders (MacKenzie et al., 1987), the absence of mental health problems (Toch et al., 1987), and the ability to maintain a prison job (Coe, 1961; Wolfgang, 1961) or a housing assignment (Coe, 1961) over a significant period of time.

Measurements of adjustment, like other research done in the prison, must recognize that characteristics of the inmate population may change over time. Thus models used to predict behavior must be flexible enough to accommodate these changes.

In a study of young inmates who had committed their crimes prior to age 17, McShane and Williams (1989, p. 266) found that the 55 younger prisoners:

> ...were approximately twice as likely to be problem inmates than the group of young adult inmates most often associated with disciplinary incidents. Fully one-third of the juveniles were in some form of administrative segregation and barely half were given work assignments.... These findings suggest that the youngest offenders will be in prison longer than mot other inmates with comparable sentences. Further, their disciplinary histories implied that they will, as a group, remain problem inmates for a longer period of time.... As a group they tend to be assaultive, place inordinate demands on expensive segregation facilities, and require extra security measures.

Age is consistently found to be one of the best predictors of disciplinary misconduct (Jensen, 1977; Flanagan, 1983; Gentry, 1987). Other inmate characteristics have been examined such as race, work history, marital status and education but have had mixed results or have interacted with age in some way to make interpretations difficult (McShane & Williams, 1989).

In a study of Texas prisoners, Gentry (1987) found that a relatively small number of inmates serving shorter sentences were responsible for a large percentage of the disciplinary problems within a facility. He called these inmates **chronic violators** and divided them further into two groups. Most were non serious violators that committed frequent, but less serious offenses which took up a greater percentage of time and resources. The second, the serious violator was a continuous threat to the safety of others and the security of the institution,

Prison Rules

Prison rules, like bars, are used to control behavior and promote the smooth operation of the institution. Some rules prohibit the same behaviors that are proscribed in general society such as assault, theft, and possession of drugs. Other offenses are particular to prisons as in refusal to work, lying to an officer, or use of vulgar language. In all cases, it is critical that rules be clear, specific, and widely disseminated in writing to each inmate. As an extreme example in the 1950s, Stateville Prison in Illinois had an inmate rule book with over 200 rules and regulations (Fox, 1983). Today, most state prison systems average 30–50 rules as well as additional regulations particular to each individual unit or building. One of the most fundamental rules in prisons everywhere is the prohibition of contraband.

Contraband

In most prisons, contraband is the broad, generic term associated with the prisoner's possession of prohibited items. These items may be in any of the following categories.
1. Goods no inmate is allowed to have such as pocket knives, alcohol, lighter fluid, or currency.
2. Goods certain inmates may be allowed to have but not the inmate found in possession of them, for example, mirrors, or immersion heaters. Distinctions in types of items one may be allowed to keep.
3. Items for which you do not have a property slip or receipt that verifies that the object was obtained legitimately. This would include the possession of any item the administration does not have on your property inventory. The purpose of this type of contraband category is to cut down on theft and extortion or buying, selling and trading between inmates particularly in actions of gambling and drug trafficking.
4. Possessions that are permissible in their original form but have been altered in some way to now constitute a security risk (radio wires stripped, pens or bombs sharpened into weapons, bandanas tied or sewn together).
5. Goods that are permissible in limited quantities, but the accumulation of an excess amount constitutes contraband (i.e.

more than one pound of coffee, ink that could be used in tattooing, etc.). Such a "stash" would be punished as contraband when the more serious suspected illegal activities of gambling and extortion could not clearly be established.

Most forms of contraband have an economic value for unauthorized buying, selling, and trading within the prison. Contraband usually enters the prison in one of four general ways. First, it may be smuggled in by visitors during contact visits. Secondly, it may be brought in by staff engaged in corrupt activities. Contraband may also enter the prison with inmates returning from furloughs, outside work details or court appearances. Finally, contraband may also come into the prison via commercial deliveries, especially where inmates are involved with unloading and receiving process. Once inside the prison, the flow of contraband is facilitated by the freedom of movement that inmates have between activities like dining, recreation, educational classes, medical appointment, and even church.

Experts believe that although contraband cannot be eliminated altogether, it can be significantly reduced by administrative procedures such as random strip searches of inmates who have contact visits and drug testing in cases where they establish probable cause. Metal detectors are often used for inmates returning from work especially where tools are used. Policies may also include random searches of employees of all ranks or possibly polygraph exams. In addition, cell searches, often using drug sniffing dogs may be conducted periodically to seek out contraband. When there has been a violent attack on a staff member or inmate without a weapon recovered, searches are conducted and often many varied weapons are seized.

Advances in technology have also made more sophisticated tests for contraband possible. In an experiment conducted by Sandia Labs on mail coming into the Pima County Jail in Arizona, tests indicated that about 10 percent of incoming mail had traces of meth, LSD, cocaine and marijuana. The hand held portable, or benchtop scanners provide trace drug detection analysis in 4–10 seconds and can also detect PCP, heroin, and THC at subnanogram levels. Although no one can be prosecuted from the interception of these materials through the mail, stopping the material from dissemination within the institution is considered critical (Falcon, 2005).

Sociologists writing about inmate culture often stress the important role played by contraband. The acquisition of prohibited goods often relieves some of the material and psychological deprivations of prison life. According to Kalinich (1996) many inmates who are active in contraband are otherwise careful and try to avoid causing problems. They keep busy and try to encourage order in their "market place" because disruptions would only bring institutional scrutiny.

The existence of an economic system of contraband also creates leaders in the inmate subculture. This type of leadership is not always popular, and rivalry and fighting often result. As Kalinich (1980, p. 76) writes, "The perception of many residents is that the 'rich get richer while the poor get poorer.' this leads to some bitterness on the part of the 'have-nots' toward the relatively well-off inmates. Residents who cannot afford to purchase contraband often turn to theft and extortion for income."

Not everyone, however, is privy to the network of contraband goods. As Williams and Fish (1974, p. 218) write:

> Certain types of inmates are not allowed by the inmate community to participate in the illicit economy regardless of their financial condition. These are the low status inmates— snitchers, inmate cops, and occasional squares. By reason of the fact that these inmates disobey the code, they are pushed away when it is time to share the scarce illegal goods that circulate in the prison. To carry on a flourishing illegal business requires a certain amount of secrecy and the social types of inmate cop, snitchers, and squares cannot be trusted.

According to Gleason (1978) the probability of getting caught dealing in contraband or "hustling" depends on four things. They are (1) the frequency of the hustle (obviously the more often an offense takes place, the greater the chances of being observed); (2) the larger the quantity of merchandise, the more likely it will be observed; (3) the vigilance of the officers; and (4) the experience the person has in performing the "hustle" which is often equated with time spent in prison and the development of good "techniques" to avoid discovery. Often the prices associated with the goods and services reflect the risk or potential punishment involved if detected.

Discipline

Discipline has long been considered the essence of control in operating penal institutions. In its 1931 report, the Wickersham Commission asserted that "discipline... determines the influence of the institution upon inmates. It determines the relationship between the prisoners and prison officials. It sets the mood and temper of all other activities within the prison."

Discipline in the early 1800s was part of a penal philosophy aimed at individual reform through silence, solitude, and repentance. Work, separation from amoral influences, and strict rules were aids to instill character in the inmates' "lost souls" (Barnes & Teeters, 1943). As prisons grew in size and administrative complexity, humanitarian reformists were replaced by state bureaucrats, and individual rehabilitation was replaced by economic efficiency as an institutional goal.

Insisting that most reformers had abandoned the notion of rehabilitation, many officials in the mid 1800s defended the use of corporal punishment as a way of forcing inmates to behave. One assistant warden at Sing Sing argued that convicts "must be made to know that here they must submit to every regulation and obey every command of their keepers" (Rothman, 1971, p. 101). In 1883, the Texas Legislature had the Penitentiary Board draw up specific rules and regulations for employees and inmates outlining the only punishments allowed. According to Copeland (1980), these included:
1. Confinement in a dark cell (not exceeding 7 days at a time).
2. Confinement in a dark cell or other cell in irons.
3. Ball and chain, shackles, or spike on ankle.
4. Deprivation of privileges in whole or in part.
5. Forfeiture of communication in whole or in part.
6. Whipping (only a special order in writing of superintendent, assistant superintendent, or inspector).

Although corporal punishment has virtually been eliminated by major reforms that have taken place in the last century, the philosophy of controlling behavior through strict discipline remained critical to the management of penal institutions. In 1967, the President's Commission on Law Enforcement and Administration of Justice stated, "...no institution can be operated safely and efficiently unless its occupants conform to some minimal standards of orderly behavior." The expectations for inmate behavior often meant unfettered discretion for prison officials. As Jones and Rhine (1985, p. 53) report, "in many instances severe sanctions were imposed not because of disciplinary infractions per se but because of militant racial and political beliefs expressed by prisoners themselves. In such cases, the inmates were summarily removed from the general population and placed in long-term segregation units for as long as a decade." Cases of extreme abuse of the disciplinary process reached the courts at the same time as judges began requiring officials to follow constitutional standards in most other areas of prison operations.

The Role of the Courts in Prison Discipline

Involvement by state and federal courts in inmate discipline represented a departure from a tradition of noninterference in matters which were once considered the discretion of administration. In *Jackson v. Bishop,* the Supreme Court found that the use of the "strap" or corporal punishment was unconstitutional. In the lower courts, other forms of punishment were also prohibited such as "beating, slapping, kicking or otherwise physically abusing juvenile inmates, in the absence of exigent circumstances" and the performance of "repetitive, nonfunctional, degrading, and unnecessary tasks for many hours" (*Morales v. Thurman*). By this, the court meant "pulling up grass without bending the knees in an area not intended to be cultivated; to buff a door for long periods; to move dirt by shovel to one area and then back again" (Reid, 1981, p. 435).

The courts looked at the length of time spent in segregation and the conditions of segregation and instituted procedural safeguards to protect the rights of the incarcerated. For example in *Hutto v. Finney,* the Court found that 30 days should be the most time allowed in solitary given the conditions of solitary confinement there. In addition, solitary cells must be sanitary, and have heat, light, and ventilation. However in more than one case, federal prison officials have complied with their own form of punishment, leaving the glaring fluorescent lights directly on the inmates 24 hours a day, seven days a week.

While in segregation, inmates must be given clothes, regular exercise (but not necessarily exercise outdoors) legal mail and medical treatment. Anticipating that the court would rule against the bread and water diet in solitary, Director Beto suspended the practice in Texas prior to a hearing on appeal. Noting judicial trends in the 1970s many other states revised their operations and initiated their own "due process" formulas for the disciplinary system.

We know from court rulings that punishment for disciplinary rules violations cannot be cruel or unusual or out of proportion to the particular offense committed. After that, there is much variation in the way that institutions punish inmate misbehavior. The range of punishments usually include minor restrictions such as verbal reprimand, loss of visitation, loss of recreation or entertainment privileges, loss of commissary or craft shop use, a restriction to one's cell or living quarters, or extra work duty. More serious punishments include loss of accumulated good-time credit and terms of solitary confinement. Some of the collateral consequences of receiving discipline are the negative effects punishments have on the opportunities for better job assignments, promotions to higher status levels, and future parole decisions.

Because the results of disciplinary action can alter the length or conditions of confinement, it became necessary to formalize the due process concern associated with the disciplinary process. This was accomplished in 1974 when the Supreme Court decided *Wolff v. McDonnell*.

In *Wolff*, the Court determined that certain procedural steps are required before an inmate can be deprived of statutorily granted "good-time" credit. Most courts have subsequently extended *Wolff* to hearings that could result in solitary confinement and cell restriction since these too, are considered deprivations of liberty. The safeguards outlined by *Wolff* include:

- written notification of the charges at least 24 hours before the hearing, describing specific conduct upon which charges are based.
- the right to call witnesses and present documentary evidence
- an impartial tribunal for hearing
- a finding of guilt must contain a summary of the evidence relied upon, a specific statement of the reason for the finding of guilt.

Wolff does not entitle inmates to confront or cross-examine witnesses, nor does it require that witnesses requested by the inmate be presented under all circumstances. Often times, security concerns will prohibit the presence of some witnesses at the hearing. Other reasons for denying the presence of certain witnesses include that their testimony will only be cumulative to that already presented, their written statements are available, or that their testimony only addresses a side issue rather than the main point. Though *Wolff* did not require that assistance be afforded to inmates in the disciplinary process, it recognized a limited need in cases where an inmate is illiterate or the issues were complex.

During the time of the *Wolff* case, the American Bar Association conducted a survey of the states on the availability of the possible 21 general elements of due process. Each state had written rules specifying the offenses for which one could be charged. All of those questioned used impartial tribunals to conduct hearings and allowed the inmate to appear at the haring. In addition, all respondents allowed the inmate to be present during the taking of evidence and to make his own statement. Only 14 (or 37 percent) of the states responding allowed the inmate to be represented by counsel (most often at the inmate's own expense), while 39 (or 89 percent) allowed representation by a counsel-substitute (ABA, 1974). Many states followed the 1973 recommendation of the National Advisory Commission on Criminal Justice Standards and Goals that offenders be allowed to select someone, including legal counsel to assist them at the hearing. These counsel-substitutes range from other inmates to law students to a list of staff members to assist with the inmate's defense.

Disciplinary Issues since *Wolff*

Since the *Wolff* decision in 1974, a number of additional issues covering disciplinary actions have been addressed. In *Baxter v. Palmigiano,* the Supreme Court stated that although an inmate may remain silent in response to questioning at a disciplinary hearing, negative inferences may be properly drawn from that silence. The opinion stated:

Prison disciplinary hearings are not criminal proceedings; but if inmates are compelled in those proceedings to furnish testimonial evidence that might incriminate them in later criminal proceedings, they must be offered "whatever immunity is required to supplement the privilege and may not be required to waive such immunity… (but) permitting an adverse inference to be drawn from an inmate's silence at his disciplinary proceedings is not, on its face, an invalid practice (as appears in Krantz, 1988).

The Court also held that the inmates' refusal to testify may not be the sole grounds for a finding of guilt. This case also illustrates that it is not uncommon to see disciplinary actions followed up by later criminal charges prosecuted in the local courts. It does not constitute "double jeopardy" to be found guilty and punished by a disciplinary hearing and later prosecuted by local authorities because institutional actions are administrative and not criminal in legal nature.

Additional cases have found that an inmate may be transferred to another unit as a result of disciplinary action without jeopardizing liberty interests or raising due process concerns (*Meachum v. Fano*). However, transfers in status from the general population to maximum security would require proper due process safeguards such as in *Wolff (Wright v. Enomoto)*.

In *Cleavinger v. Saxner,* the Supreme Court acknowledged the potential for abuse of discretion by prison authorities dispensing discipline. The justices considered the members of a disciplinary committee to only have **qualified immunity** in actions challenging their performance. The justices also decided that members were subject to damages if they were found to have violated an inmate's constitutional rights. Again, the court pointed out the differences between a disciplinary hearing in prison and a criminal trial.

> The prisoner was to be afforded neither a lawyer nor an independent nonstaff representative. There was no right to compel the attendance of witnesses or to cross-examine. There was no right to discovery. There was no cognizable burden of proof. No verbatim transcript was afforded. Information presented often was hearsay or self-serving. The committee members were not truly independent. In sum, the members had no identification with the judicial process of the kind and depth that has occasioned absolute immunity.

In order to find committee members liable, it would have to be shown that they "knew or should have known" that they were violating the inmates' rights or that officials maliciously intended to violate their rights (Earl, 1987). Recognizing the potential scope of lawsuits resulting from cases on this issue, the federal government began a special training program for a new cadre of hand-picked disciplinary hearing officers.

SUMMARY

From the beginning of American corrections, emphasis has been placed on the role of discipline to not only control, but to reform the criminal. The reality that exists today, however, is that there are a number of prisoners that are not concerned or deterred by disciplinary action. Once inmates have lost all of their good-time credit, had all of their privileges revoked, and have been housed in a segregation area, there is no other punishment that can be imposed. Take for example, Tom. The Missouri prison system is home to Tom. At 16, he fatally shot a convenience store clerk, robbed an elderly man, stole his car and kidnapped and raped the elderly man's wife. The public now feels safer knowing that Tom received life with no parole. What the public doesn't realize is that Tom is a very expensive problem inmate. He has a long history of disciplinary actions including many assaults against staff and has twice stabbed other inmates. He has forfeited all the privileges other inmates look forward to and has twice been transferred to stricter units.

Administrators are frustrated by their inability to find a way to reach or change the behavior of problem inmates like Tom. Segregation or solitary confinement appears to be the only avenue; the prison within the prison. However, Barak-Glantz (1983, p. 29) reports that doing time in solitary confinement appears to have "little deterrent effect on subsequent experiences with punitive solitary confinement." Often inmates become adjusted to solitary and often even purposefully seek it in order to avoid some threat or conflict in the general population.

Cases

Hutto v. Finney 437 U.S. 678, 98 S.Ct. 2565, 57 L.Ed.2d 522 (1978)
Jackson v. Bishop 404 F.Supp 571 (1968)
Morales v. Thurman 364 F. Supp 166 (1973)
Wolff v. McDonnell 418 U.S.539, 94 S.Ct. 2963, 41 L.Ed. 2d 935 (1974)

References

Barak-Glantz, I. (1983, June). Who's in the hole? *Criminal Justice Review,* June, 29–36.

Barnes, H., & Teeters, N. (1943). *New horizons in criminology.* New York: Prentice Hall.

Bartollas, C., Miller, S., & Dinitz, S. (1976). *Juvenile victimization: The institutional paradox.* New York: Halsted Press.

Burkhart, K. (1976). *Women in prison.* New York: Popular Library Education.

Clemmer, D. (1940). *The prison community.* Boston: Christopher Publishing Company.

Coe, R. (1961). Who is the inmate? Characteristics of well-adjusted and poorly adjusted inmates. *Journal of Criminal Law, Criminology, and Police Science, 52,* 178–84.

Copeland, R. (1980). *The evolution of the Texas Department of Corrections.* Unpublished master's thesis. Huntsville, TX: Sam Houston State University.

Earl, D. (1987). *Cleavinger v. Saxner*: Determining immunity for prison officials who sit on disciplinary committees. *Utah Law Review,* 427–450.

Falcon, W. (2005, July). Special technologies for law enforcement and corrections. *NIJ Journal.* Washington, DC: U.S. Department of Justice.

Flanagan, T. (1983). Correlates of institutional misconduct among state prisoners. *Criminology, 21,* 29–39.

Fox, V. (1983). *Correctional institutions.* Englewood Cliffs, NJ: Prentice Hall.

Free, M. (1996). *African Americans and the criminal justice system.* New York: Garland.

Garabedian, P. (1963). Social roles and processes of socialization in the prison community. *Social Problems, 11,* 139–152.

Garfinkel, H. (1956). Conditions of successful degradation ceremonies. *American Journal of Sociology, 61,* 420-424.

Gentry, H. M. (1987). *A comparison of the chronic rule violator, the occasional rule violator and the non-violator in the Texas Department of Corrections.* Unpublished master's thesis. Huntsville, TX: Sam Houston State University.

Giallombardo, R. (1966). *Society of women.* New York: John Wiley.

Gibbons, D. (1979). *The criminological enterprise.* Englewood Cliffs, NJ: Prentice Hall.

Gleason, S. (1978). Hustling: The 'inside' economy of a prison. *Federal Probation, 42*, 32–40.

Goffman, E. (1961). *Asylums.* Garden City, NY: Doubleday.

Heffernan, E. (1972). *Making it in prison: The square, the cool, and the life.* New York: John Wiley.

Jensen, G. F. (1977). Age and rule-breaking in prison. *Criminology, 14*, 555–568.

Jones, R. S. (1996). Argot. In M. D. McShane & F. P. Williams III (Eds.), *Encyclopedia of American prisons*, pp. 39–41. New York: Garland.

Jones, C., & Rhine, E. (1985, Winter). Due process and prison disciplinary practices: From *Wolff* to *Hewitt. New England Journal on Crime and Civil Confinement, 11*, 44–122.

Kalinich, D. (1996). Contraband. In M. D. McShane & F. P. Williams III (Eds.), *Encyclopedia of American prisons*, pp. 111–114. New York: Garland.

Kalinich, D. 1980. *Power, stability, and contraband.* Prospect Heights, IL: Waveland.

Kessler, R., & Roebuck, J. (1996). Snitch. In M. D. McShane & F. P. Williams III (Eds.), *Encyclopedia of American prisons*, pp. 449–450. New York: Garland.

MacKenzie, D., Goodstein, L., & Blouin, D. (1987). Personal control and prison adjustment: An empirical test of a proposed model. *Journal of Research in Crime and Delinquency, 24*, 49–68.

McShane, M., & Williams III, F. P. (1989). The prison adjustment of juvenile offenders. *Crime and Delinquency, 35*, 2, 254–69.

Propper, A. (1981). *Prison homosexuality.* Lexington, MA: D.C. Heath.

Reid, S. (1981). *The correctional system.* New York: Holt, Rinehart & Winston.

Rothman, D. (1971). *The discovery of the asylum.* Boston: Little, Brown.

Slosar, J. A. (1978). *Prisonization, friendship and leadership.* Lexington, MA: D.C. Heath.

Sykes, G., & Messinger, S. (1960). Inmate social system. In R. Cloward et al. (Eds.), *Theoretical studies in social organization of the prison.* New York: Social Science Research Council.

Thomas, C., & Petersen, D. (1977). *Prison organization and inmate subcultures.* Indianapolis, IN: Bobbs-Merrill.

Toch, H., Adams, K., & Greene, R. (1987). Ethnicity, disruptiveness, and emotional disorder among prison inmates. *Criminal Justice and Behavior, 14*, 93–109.

Van Wormer, K. (1984). Becoming homosexual in prison: A socialization process. *Criminal Justice Review, 9*, 1, 22–27.

Ward, D., & Kassebaum, G. (1965). *Women's prison: Sex and social structure.* Chicago: Aldine.

Wheeler, S. (1961). Socialization in correctional communities. *American Sociological Review, 26*, 697–712.

Williams, V., & Fish, M. (1974). Convicts, codes and contraband: The prison life of men and women. In R. Carter, D. Glaser, & L. Wilkins (Eds.), *Correctional institutions,* (3rd ed.), pp. 215–227. New York: Harper and Row, reprinted 1985.

Wolfgang, M. (1961). Quantitative analysis of adjustment to the prison community. *Journal of Criminal Law, Criminology and Police Science, 51*, 608–618.

Online Exercise

Go to the website for the Florida Department of Corrections and at the site, search for Florida Administrative Codes; or, go directly to www.dc.state.fl.us/secretary/legal/index.html. Scroll down through the contents to Classification & Central Records (English). This is section 33–601. Then find the section for Inmate Discipline Investigation. This is Chapter 33–601.305.

1. What are the steps in the process of investigating an inmate disciplinary infraction?

2. Summarize the elements of the process.

3. Note what efforts have been taken to incorporate due process.

Questions for Thought and Discussion

1. Describe the two opposing models that are often used to explain prisonization and the formation of prison subcultures. Which do you think has the most merit and why?

2. What is contraband, what has been done about it and what other policies might you use to prevent its spread in prison?

3. Discuss the prison disciplinary process and the legal safeguards that guide it.

4. What does the research on prisoner adjustment to institutional life tell us? Are there implications for classification and treatment?

Books You May Want to Read

Bergner, Daniel. (1999). *God of the rodeo*. New York: Ballantine Books.

Conover, Ted. (2001). *New jack: Guarding Sing Sing.* New York: Vintage.

Movies you May Want to See

Escape from Alcatraz
Midnight Express

CHAPTER 8
Prison Violence

It is not even clear that there is more violence in prisons than there is in the communities where the inmates come from. Indeed, one wonders why there is not more violence in prisons; there seems to be so much to be violent about.

Albert K. Cohen (1976)

INTRODUCTION

Only a small portion of the inmates in prison are responsible for a majority of the disciplinary problems. Also, not all disciplinary problems are serious or involve violence. Many of the rules violated are those designed to help the offender develop self-discipline like getting to work on time, keeping one's cell neat, and observing proper grooming standards. These do not involve the safety and security of the staff and other inmates. However, major violations would be those actions that constitute risk to others such as assaults, fights, disturbances, and gang-related activities. Much training and supervision goes into preparing the staff to prevent or at least control the various types of violent incidents that may occur.

Currently, about 30 percent of those entering prison have been convicted of a violent crime and 47 percent of the overall population is serving violent crime sentences. This indicates that violent offenders are serving longer terms than other offenders who leave the system much quicker.

Though the prison is made up of both nonviolent (often property and drug) offenders and violent offenders, most are able to adapt to prison and avoid disciplinary trouble. Those involved in disciplinary actions will be both types of criminals, although violent criminals may be more likely than nonviolent criminals to commit violent offenses in prison. The relationship can be diagramed as in Figure 1.

Figure 1. Relationship between Violent Offenders and Disciplinary Problems.

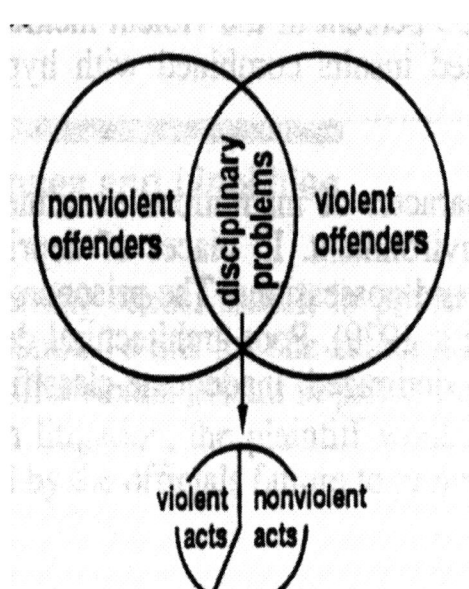

PRISON VIOLENCE

One measure of both the degree of order and the quality of prison life is the amount of violence. Courts often use the level of violence as an indicator that a prison is being maintained in a constitutional fashion and is part of the "totality" of conditions for judicial scrutiny. Violence may take the form of riots, disturbances, rapes, fights, assaults, and homicides. Often, analysts compare the safety of the streets to prison, but it is critical to realize that not everyone on the street is at the same risk. While young males have the highest victimization rates in society,

Prison Violence 151

they are also overrepresented in prisons, so it is not surprising that prisons are characteristically violent.

A report on the amount of violence in prisons in 1992 and 1993 found that 276 inmates had suffered violent deaths. Overall, the number of violent deaths has decreased over the last ten years despite increases in incarceration rates. Prison data also indicates that approximately 290,000 men and 135,000 women report being sexually assaulted in prison each year. Between 2000 and 2004 Federal officials in the Justice Department began investigations on 351 people accused of sexually abusing prisoners. Sexual misconduct particularly by male officers abusing female inmates has been indicated in all but one state in a recent survey by the government (Kallestad, 2006). One correctional officer, anticipating his arrest by arriving federal agents, opened fire killing one investigator and wounding another with a weapon he smuggled into the Tallahassee Federal Correctional Facility.

Overall, 13% of inmates report having been sexually assaulted (Roberston, 2004). Officials estimate that there are more than 60,000 unwanted sexual acts occurring each day (Prison Issues, 2004). Information relative to a lawsuit in the Texas prison system argued that 30 percent of new inmates would be sexually assaulted within their first 48 hours of incarceration (Ward, 2005).

Inmates are almost twice as likely to assault other inmates as they are to assault staff. The actual ratio is probably much higher, because many inmate assaults are unreported, while few staff assaults would be. Inmates often feel that it is useless to report victimizations or that there would be retaliation if they do. In addition, many correctional officers see violence as a normal part of prisoner life and believe that male inmates must defend themselves. Current estimates indicate that prison assault rates can run as high as 32 per 100 inmates (Finn, 2005). Interestingly, a study by Wolff et al. (2007) found that inmate on inmate physical assault rates were the same for females as for males although males were more likely to experience physical violence perpetrated by staff.

Although the number of inmate deaths resulting from inmate to inmate violence appears to have decreased over the past decade (from 82 to 51), assaults are more common. In a study by Wooldredge (1998) 50 percent of inmates report experiencing some type of crime ranging from property damage, theft and robbery to assault, only 10 percent reported a physical assault over the six month period preceding the survey.

Explanations of Prison Violence

There are many explanations for the violence in prison. Some reasons focus on the character of inmates; others examine the nature of institutions. In discussion of the former, some argue that the internal controls of inmates are weaker than the rest of society, and if the prison's (external) control is imperfect, violence will occur. Theories often link violence to values and behaviors that the inmate brings into the prison setting. These influences range from street fighting habits to gender role behaviors, particularly the "macho" or manliness of self-defense, to racism (which is often incorporated into gang violence). Theories of male aggression are supported by the fact that men are more likely to be incarcerated for a violent offense than women. Critics argue that this reasoning allows for "attribution error" or the tendency to attribute causes of behavior to the personality of the individual even in the face of contradictory evidence such as the presence of situational or environmental factors. This is important given that institutions across the country with similar inmate populations do not have similar rates of violence.

Other individual characteristics of the offender are also involved in explanations of prison violence. Age is a significant variable, with younger inmates more anxious to prove themselves with toughness and fighting. According to some experts, younger inmates have more opportunities to become aggressive and are more likely to be instigated into aggression by their peers and are more often rewarded with praise and respect. Because of their immaturity, young inmates are less likely to view the consequences they face as costly.

The violent inmate's background may include drugs, gangs, and mental health difficulties. They may also have spent time in other prisons or in juvenile facilities where survival skills include success in assaultive or predatory behaviors. It is not uncommon for attacks to occur when someone perceives that they have been "disrespected" or threatened.

More recently, patterns of inmate violence indicate that high risk or volatile situations are created when groups of inmates are moved, either between institutions as when new facilities are opened and all of the inmates are moved in from other facilities, or when a number of inmates are received and housed from out of state. There have also been incidents with ethnic violence between groups that have a history of violent confrontation on the outside such as Croatian and Serbian inmates or Shiite and Sunni inmates.

In June 2007, a melee broke out at a Maryland prison between Bloods gang members and Sunni Muslim prisoners that sent 18 prisoners to the hospital. Shanks made from Plexiglas and other broken pieces of metal were used in the disturbance that officials say was related to older Muslim inmates attempting to exert more control and send a message to the younger, more aggressive gang members. It appears that the earlier closing of an antiquated house of correction may have reorganized the distribution of power when inmates were transferred to other facilities (Garland, 2007).

Predicting Violence

Attempts to predict which inmates will be violent are not highly scientific or effective. Prisoners who are predatory and engage in sexual assaults on weaker inmates may be different from the inmate who carries out assassinations ordered by gang leaders. Initial classification systems use prediction devices such as personality tests or records screening to score inmates on their risk potential when they arrive. Prior violent behavior is the best predictor of future violent behavior that experts know of. Based on these scores, inmates may be assigned to more secure facilities and housing areas but they can also be promoted to a less restrictive area if their behavior warrants.

Because there has been at least one major prison riot every year in the U.S. since 1951, there has been great opportunity to study the conditions associated with riots. Of the more than 300 riots on record (Martin & Zimmerman, 1990), 56 percent have occurred in maximum security prisons. Larger capacity prisons have a higher incidence of riots as do older facilities and those where the structure resembles a warehouse. Another significant finding has been that as the amount of contact time between a warden and the inmates decreases, the incidence of riots increases (South Carolina Department of Corrections, 1973). A review of official reactions to prison riots prior to 1972 reveals that when a policy of force is adopted, inmate deaths are more likely to occur than when a policy of restraint is followed. The study also demonstrated that hostage deaths were not related to the adoption of either strategy (Garson, 1972).

Violence and the Prison Environment

Theories that focus on the character of institutions examine the nature of prisons and see inmates reacting to an unreal environment. In places of deprivation, prisoners are cast into a struggle for the limited power and possessions available. The prisoner's inability to control privacy and space increases stress. Poor architectural design, the availability of weapons, and limited staffing, create places and opportunities in which victimization can occur. Inadequate classification or overcrowding can lead to a mixing of weak and exploitive inmates. Undereducated and poorly trained correctional officers or inexperienced administrators lead to inadequate inmate supervision and control. It may even mean the corruption of officers or intimidation of staff by the more powerful inmates.

Research has been conducted that indicates that specific types of violence are more likely to occur at certain times of the day, certain places within the institution, and during certain types of activities. For example, Steinke (1991) found that violence toward staff was
more likely to occur in areas where inmates were engaged in a loosely structured activity such as dining, recreation, or showers, and that inmates were more likely to be alone when aggressive toward staff. Violence against other inmates was more likely to occur where inmates were allowed to congregate and less common in single-celled housing areas. While in some instances, the presence of others served to deter violence, it seemed to enhance tendencies toward violence in other cases. Some research has associated violence with levels of heat and the summer months, while other studies have found that older prisons with less surveillance, because of the architecture, are more violent. The degree of overcrowding has also been correlated with violence. Still other studies associate more experienced correctional officers with lower levels of violence in institutions.

Theories have also been developed that argue that violence is normal and even useful in the prison environment. Given the backgrounds of those incarcerated and the unnatural conflict orientation of the institution, it is not unexpected that there is violence. In fact, many wonder why there is not more. It can be argued that power struggles, the resulting awards of status, and position in the social hierarchy result in order, and even stability, in the prison subculture, which are essential to its structure and survival. During the settlement of the *Ruiz* lawsuit in Texas when traditional inmate-building tenders, acting as "guards" were replaced by newly hired correctional officers in established inmate/officers ratios, there was a great deal of violence attributed to the adjustment period. This is also often the case when a new prison unit opens. Inmates transferred from around the state compete for power and authority in the new facility. From these struggles, placements in the subculture are determined.

Some argue that violent incidents allow inmates to blow off steam or experience releases in the otherwise constant tension of incarcerated life. In a pattern of activity engineered so that inmates have no control over or effect on events, striking out against another or one's self is not only expression, but also a confirmation that they still have some degree of power. As one lifer explains (Rideau, 1992),

> Prison deprives those locked within of the normal avenues of pursuing gratification… and leaves them no instruments but sex, violence, and conquest to validate their sense of manhood and individual worth. And they do, channeling all of their frustrated drives into the pursuit of power, finding gratification in the conquest and defeat, the domination and subjugation of each other.

Many administrators believe that it is more practical to talk in terms of controlling and regulating violence than eliminating it altogether.

Responses to Prison Violence

Historically, prison officials rarely recorded incidences of violence or their response. From unofficial stories and reports, however, we know that retaliation and brutal punishments were common. Today, accurate logs are kept on all incidents, including witness statements, photographs and videotapes. Official reports are monitored by administrators, evaluated and used in training.

One aspect of training involves sensitizing officers to the telltale signs of trouble "brewing" within institutions. In general populations, requests for transfers, or protective custody, increases in mental health problems, increases in the number of grievances and disciplinary charges filed, accumulations of contraband, hoarding of commissary items, and rumors of retaliation may all indicate impending violence.

Decreases in attendance at programs or activities are also important barometers of violence.

Physical controls such as the use of force and restraints may be employed by officers in contact with inmates. Many prison systems have special teams that are highly trained in the technical and legal aspects of successful emergency response. Other systems have tried and abandoned such teams because of the need to train all officers in these skills because of the unpredictable nature of such emergencies. The existence of the elite teams of tactical response may undermine the confidence and morale of regular officers, who are first on the scene of most prison disruptions.

Legally, prison administrators have an obligation to protect inmates and staff from violence. Liability may be incurred when officials knew or should have known of a potentially violent situation and no corrective action was taken. This may include failure to protect informants from retaliation or vulnerable inmates from sexual assaults, understaffing high risk areas, failing to secure tools that could be used as weapons, and lack of training for officers in how to respond to a disturbance.

Gang Violence

There seems to be some academic debate over whether prison gangs developed as an extension of street gangs on the outside (importation model), or whether they had an independent origin based on the unique nature of the prison environment (deprivation model). Regardless of their origin, contemporary prison gangs do have operating memberships on the outside and carry out many activities in ways that transcend the prison walls. The reason for this is that prison gangs on the inside, like the outside, have lifetime membership and the only way to leave the gang is through death. Thus, as prisoners leave the institutions or come into them, they bring their affiliations with them.

The structure of prison gangs is highly sophisticated and rules are strict. Gang activity within institutions has involved drug trafficking, extortion rings, and sophisticated assassinations. According to Gillespie (2003) gang involvement prior to incarceration seems to enhance prisonization, which supports the importation model of adjustment, rather than the affiliation with gangs inside of prison (the deprivation model). As gang activity and the presence of gangs increases, so do disciplinary problems at most institutions. Theorists seem to agree that violence, prison riots and disturbances often reflect problems in adjustment, particularly when small groups compete for limited resources and power within an institution.

In a 1988 case from the Pontiac Correctional Center in Michigan, white inmates argued that from 75–99.5% of the inmate population was either a gang member or gang affiliate. They alleged that those who weren't gang members (primarily whites, who made up only 12 percent of the total institutional population) were coerced to aid and assist gangs in return for protection. The price for protection was the performance of deeds like carrying weapons or making "hits." As a result, many whites (40 percent of all whites) had resorted to protective custody where, they complained, they led a much more restricted routine. In Michigan's protective custody housing, as in other states, inmates are confined more hours per day and have fewer opportunities for work activity. Privileges are offered at irregular times or not at all. The suit, *David K. v. Lane*, asked for an injunction against an administrative policy that permitted nonviolent displays of gang membership. Plaintiffs argued that the policy signaled an acceptance of gangs, and consequently, the gangs flourished. The gang activity forced the white inmates, they alleged, to seek protective custody where they were subject to a loss of freedoms.

The court, however, found that it was not the intent of the policy to discriminate or to cause such an effect. In other words, in order to prevail, the inmates would have to prove that officials established this policy intentionally to disadvantage whites, which they could not. For the courts, proof of disparate impact was not enough to show a discriminatory intent in violation of the Equal Protection Clause. Though they did not grant the inmates relief, they did exhort prison officials to take firm action against the gangs and not let them control the prison.

According to Berryhill (1999) membership in prison gangs continues to rise. In Texas, authorities confirm that about 5,000 inmates are tagged as official gang members while another 10,000 are documented as "gang affiliated." The largest gang memberships are with the Mexican Mafia and Texas Syndicate, while about 900 belong to the Crips or Bloods and about 700 to the Aryan Brotherhood or Aryan Circle (Berryhill, 1999). Many other, lesser known gangs exist with an institution specific membership which the administration often calls "cliques" perhaps as a way of keeping their official gang totals lower.

Sexual Violence

Estimates of the number of inmates sexually assaulted in prison range anywhere from 1 to 30 percent of the total population. It is difficult to accurately assess the amount of sexual violence because there is no consensus on what acts constitute a sexual assault, many inmates are reluctant to admit being victimized, many are afraid of further reprisals if they do report being victimized and there are those who are not sure that the administration would be of any assistance anyway. A prisoner who was beaten and gang-raped by three men explained his feelings afterward (Hassine, 1996, p. 74):

> After I was raped, the only medical attention that I received was a physical examination of my rectum to confirm that I had been assaulted. I was placed back into protective custody by myself without anyone to talk to, alone and deserted like a dirty rag. I received no therapy from either a psychologist or psychiatrist. I was left to deal with it on my own. I didn't cry out then because no one seemed to care, and so I stripped myself of all and any emotions….

Chastising the Texas Department of Corrections for its indifference to the plight of inmates, federal judge, William Wayne Justice, noted recently that no systematic records of sexual assault or requests for protection were kept. Finding that only 6 sexual assaults were on file in a year with 140,000 inmates the court decided not to release the system from its 25 years of judicial oversight (Berryhill, 1999).

According to one study, sexual assault was one of the most common motives for single-assailant murders (Sylvester et al., 1977). As Nacci and Kane (1982) point out, of all the potential areas for conflict within a prison, sexual pressuring is the most dangerous. As Lockwood (1985, p. 91) explains, one predominant myth concerning such pressures is that the sexual aggressor is successful in converting the victim into a "punk" or consensual partner. Instead, he argues, that many "targets" cope with the confrontation by reacting violently or developing a protective lifestyle. And, as one inmate asserts, there may be long lasting effects from being sexually victimized (Hassine, 1996, p. 73):

> It has caused me to become attracted to other young men sexually, so as to continue the nightmare by further subjecting myself to punishment for my past crimes, and to also inflict my nightmare on others so they too can carry the terrible burden I've carried.

The common observation concerning sexual assault in prison is that a potential victim has limited options: fight, flee, or submit. To this list one author has added a fourth and relatively new option, sue. Inmates who suffer sexual assault in prison may bring civil (tort claim) suits against their custodians. In such litigation, the plaintiff would seek monetary compensation for the pain and suffering caused by the official's failure to protect.

A lack of adequate protection against sexual assault may also be grounds for a civil rights suit. In *Stokes v. Delcambre,* an inmate filed suit against a sheriff and deputy after he was beaten and sexually assaulted by other inmates in a Louisiana jail. In awarding $380,000 in compensatory and punitive damages, the court pointed out that the deputy was deliberately indifferent to the fighting that was taking place, and that he "should have known" that he had an "obligation" not to detain an inmate in a manner which made it likely he would be beaten or sexually assaulted.

In a Missouri case, the U.S. Supreme Court held that individual acts of violence rather than the usual patterns of violence would be all that would have to be established to win a claim (Levin, 1985). Though punitive damages are rare in inmate civil rights cases, the Court found it appropriate when "the defendants' conduct is shown to be motivated by evil motive or intent or when it involves reckless or callous indifference to the federally protected rights of others" (*Smith v. Wade*). In this case, Wade, an inmate in a first offenders' facility, was harassed, beaten, and sexually assaulted by two cellmates. In deciding that the guard, Smith, knew or should have known that Wade was at risk, the jury awarded the plaintiff $25,000 in compensatory and $5,000 in punitive damages. According to Levin (1985, p. 525), such a decision should have a "cautionary effect on corrections officials. Prison officials who view inmates as potential plaintiffs might be more inclined to prevent situations conducive to assault."

Fear of impending sexual assault has also been cited by defendants facing criminal charges for escape. Most courts hearing cases where the prisoner claims he/she fled because of duress will allow such a defense if the situation meets the criteria outlined in *People v. Lovercamp*. That is, a prisoner (Levin, 1985):

> (1) must face a specific threat of death, forcible sexual assault or substantial bodily injury in the immediate future, (2) must have no time to complain to authorities and no prior history of frivolous complaints, (3) must have no time or opportunity to resort to the courts, (4) must commit no violence against prison personnel during the escape, and (5) must report immediately to prison authorities upon escaping.

Interestingly enough, Lovercamp was a female inmate harassed by a number of lesbian inmates and one of a few defendants to use the rape/duress defense successfully.

PRISON RAPE ELIMINATION ACT

Concern not only about sexual violence in prison but a lack of accurate reporting about the problem led to the passage of the *Prison Rape Elimination Act* in 2003. The Act was the result of the work of the National Prison Rape Elimination Commission which is charged with studying policies and practices related to the prevention of sexual assault in prisons and jails nationwide. States are mandated to submit a comprehensive data set on all sexual violence incidents in prisons which is published in an annual report, *Sexual Violence Reported by Correctional Authorities*. This document is available on the web through the Bureau of Justice Statistics. The database will allow researchers more insight not only into the causes and nature of prison sexual violence but may suggest strategies and interventions for reducing the predatory violence. Critics argue however, that while states may be mandated to report incidents that come to their attention, inmates are still reluctant to file reports for fear of repercussions.

The 2006 report indicates that there were 2.9 allegations of sexual assault per 1,000 inmates and that most incidents involve the use of force or threats of force and occurs in the evening in the victim's cell. (www.Ojp.usdoj.gov/bjs/abstract/svrca06.htm). While this is an increase from the previous year, it is difficult to determine whether there are more incidents or simply more reporting taking place.

RIOTS AND DISTURBANCES

The first prison riot recorded in this country was in Connecticut in 1774 (Dillingham and Montgomery, 1985). Riots in early American prisons, however, appear to be independent and isolated occurrences unrelated to outside social forces. They were triggered primarily by the intolerable conditions, insufficient and contaminated food, lack of clothing and heat, sadistic brutality by guards and continuous backbreaking labor (Reid, 1981). Later riots, often termed "collective riots," mirrored social movements on the outside and borrowed the philosophies and ideas of the protests of the 1960s and 70s. In addition to demanding improved medical, recreational, and educational programs, organizers of riots questioned the legitimacy of incarceration, criticized the political nature of crime definitions, and called for a "humanizing" of the prison environment (Reid, 1981).

Prior research seems to classify the various models used to explain riots as focused on either environmental conditions, spontaneous events, conflict or the perception of power as official repression, collective behavior and social control which focuses on the stability of cooperative relationships between inmates and staff, a power vacuum and finally, rising yet unfulfilled expectations on the part of inmates particularly regarding privileges or deprivations (Martin & Zimmerman, 1990). According to Toch (1977, p. 71), there are different forms of violence associated with different phases of riots. Some occur before riots such as catalytic incidents which tend to be staff-inmate confrontations. During riots, many private violent acts are committed under the pretense or color of riots, such as vandalism, rapes and the executions of suspected informants. Violence is often used by authorities to quell a riot, as did the state police at Attica. Prison staff may also retaliate with violence against the inmates after a riot has ended.

By the time of the Attica riot in New York in 1971, ethnic and political groups of inmates had already organized and carried out a successful work strike. They had met with the corrections commissioner and had lobbied state officials for reforms. Administrative response to such activity was repressive and punitive and sparked confrontations that escalated into a riot on September 9th. Forty-three hostages were taken. One guard died from injuries suffered in a beating and fall, and three unpopular inmates had their throats slit. The riot was characterized by the solidarity of the inmates and a complex series of open negotiations with special observers, key press, and political figures. When negotiations broke down on the fourth day over the issue of amnesty, state police were sent in, and 29 inmates and 10 guard/hostages were gunned down in an attack of tear gas and shooting.

The New Mexico riot, nine years later, was unlike Attica and demonstrates the unique character of each uprising. Hindsight shows there were many warning signs of trouble at the Santa Fe facility. Personality tests conducted by an outside agency found that correctional officers and inmates had surprisingly similar potentials for violence. Brutality was tolerated by the "get-tough" administration, and psychiatric services facilitated the use of snitches (Saenz, 1986). Groups of maximum security inmates were housed in minimum dorms due to renovations, and 1,160 inmates occupied a building designed for 820. In the days preceding the riot, staff recognized several indicators listed in a riot control plan, an increase in requests for transfers from the unit; undue tension within the prison population; and a change in the contacts between inmates and guards" (Saenz, 1986).

Capitalizing on a serious breach of security, the inmates took complete control of the prison in 45 minutes. Death squads formed and went after the snitches who were tortured, mutilated, and burned with torches. New prisoners were tied up, raped, and beaten, and the weak in special protection areas were preyed upon. Administrative offices were destroyed, and the pharmacy looted. High on drugs and any chemicals available, the inmates carried on a crazed 36-hour orgy of violence with only a minimal attempt at serious reform negotiations.

The Santa Fe and Attica institutions were both overcrowded and inmates complained about dehumanizing conditions. Administrators lacked consistency in policies and goals, legislators ignored the troubles of the system, and the press focused only on the negative aspects of corrections. Though each had prior warnings of trouble, the guards were basically unprepared for a major riot (Mahan, 1985).

One of the significant differences between the two institutions was the almost ten year differential during which many administrators believe the inmate population had become more violent and dangerous. Administrators had taken lessons from Attica that altered their approach to the Santa Fe riot. Another difference was the contrasting racial compositions of the inmate populations, as indicated below.

	New Mexico	Attica
Black	10%	55%
Hispanic	58%	8.5%
White	30%	36%
Native American	2%	0.5%

The differences can also be contrasted in a description of key factors about the riots.

New Mexico (1980)	**Attica (1971)**
inmates were brutal, cruel & angry	inmates were well-organized, political, & articulate
no plan, spur of the moment demands	underlying plan, previously drawn up demands
no leadership or control, splinter groups, went on rampage	strong leadership, good control, cohesive action
no official negotiation process, corrections officials only	political observers, negotiators, press, clergy
wide spread destruction	withheld destruction
Governor stepped in	Governor would not participate
no guards killed	one guard died

New Mexico (1980)	Attica (1971)
hostages raped, brutalized, tortured	hostages were treated well
33 inmates died from torture/ killing by inmates	only 3 inmates killed by inmates, execution of snitches
no one killed by police	32 inmates, 11 civilians and trooper gunfire

Many theories have been offered to explain prison riots. They include (1) racial-political ideological tensions; (2) prisons as environments of deprivation; (3) the disruptiveness of administrative changes to delicate power balances; and (4) the conflicts inherent in mixing custody and treatment goals (Barak-Glantz, 1985). According to Fox (1983), riots are spontaneous events characteristic of the "time bomb" nature of prison. This theory might explain how a power blackout at the Lorton Correctional Complex in Washington, D.C. spawned a melee in which one inmate was fatally stabbed and part of the prison was damaged by fire (Allen, 1989). Fox also categorized the phases of a prison riot sequentially as (1) the explosion or initial uprising; (2) the organizational phase where leadership emerges; (3) the negotiation phase where discussion periods may include voicing demands and grievances; (4) the termination stage where force may be used to retake control and finally; (5) the explanation phase where usually an outside agency investigates and reports on the riot.

The various commissions appointed to study riots have always come to similar conclusions about the precipitating factors. They include (1) mismanagement and poorly trained staff as well as low pay and low morale of employees; (2) rural prison locations that create an unnatural environment; (3) inmate overcrowding and inadequate facilities; (4) lack of rehabilitation in the form of educational and vocational programs; (5) meaningless inmate employment without viable rewards; and (6) the antisocial nature of inmates.

The role of timing in explaining prison riots is also critical. A 1981 riot in Michigan appeared to have begun when guards initiated an unauthorized shakedown and threatened to lock down the institution for the long Memorial Day holiday. Faced with being locked in a small cell for three full days without a warden's consent, the prisoners felt provoked (Barak-Glantz, 1985).

According to some experts, conditions that enhance the probability of a riot include strain or tension, the growth or spread of generalized beliefs or rumors, and precipitating or instigating incidents. These ideas reflect the situation that occurred in two detention facilities for Cuban detainees, a protest erupted in November 1987 over what detainees feared were U.S.-Cuban negotiations to deport them. In the two weeks that followed, the cost of the destruction soared into the millions; over 120 hostages were taken. The government adopted a patient wait-it-out posture that resulted in peaceful resolutions in both facilities.

What we have learned about riots over the years appears to have been used wisely in this Cuban facilities incident, as one warden explained, "We have some extremely skilled, professionally-trained hostage negotiators at the scene, who throughout the crisis did an excellent job." Another warden commented, "the professionalism displayed by the hostages appears to have diffused much of the tension.... (T)hey had established a good relationship with the detainees prior to the crisis" (Millard, 1988). (This is opposed to other riots where officers with White Supremacist tattoos were singled out for torture.) One of the major differences between this riot and others, however, is that the detainees were not on a criminal par with most state prisoners and were in a sense, political detainees. As one warden remarked, "At no time did the detainees intend to harm any of our staff. They simply wanted to publicize their plight to the world." Obviously they realized that their potential bid for citizenship would have been greatly tarnished by the injury or death of any hostages.

One year after the immigration riots in Atlanta, Georgia and Oakdale, Louisiana, the Cuban detainees were still double-celled and confined to their cells 24 hours a day. The federal government contended that the riot had been instigated by two of the detainees who they took to trial. However, a jury found the defendants not guilty and theorized that the riot was "spontaneously triggered by the intolerable conditions of confinement" (Keller, 1988).

More Recent Riots

Despite advancements in technology and sophisticated training, disturbances and riots continue to claim lives and cause extensive damage. Riots have taken place in state correctional facilities, federal prisons and immigration detention centers. The Lucasville riot in 1993 was one of the longest ever as inmates controlled a wing of the Southern Ohio Correctional Facility for 11 days. One officer and nine inmates were killed. Inmate grievances included religious restrictions and forced cell integration. Almost two years later the leader of the riot was convicted of kidnapping and aggravated murder. Other issues that seemed to precipitate riots were mandatory haircuts (Columbia, South Carolina, 1995), racial conflict (Ft. Leavenworth, Kansas, 1992) and continued fear of deportation in Cuban detainees (Talladega, Alabama, 1991) (Reid, 2000).

Although gang activity is a major source of prison violence, gang issues are less likely to inspire riots, in fact, gangs often join forces and even mediate in riots. Fights, racial disturbances or brawls are more common and give the appearance of being gang-related although membership may or may not be a factor. A 2007 melee at a Baltimore facility, for example, was said to involve a dispute between the Bloods gang and older Sunni Muslim inmates (Garland, 2007).

Assaults on Correctional Officers or Staff

According to Light (1994, p. 219) many assaults on staff occur subsequent to an order or a command to do something that the inmate rejects. He explains that "Whether the order relates to a search, to a move to another area, or to general routine and discipline, prisoners constantly evaluate the legitimacy of the command in relation to powerful unofficial norms." Officers may also be assaulted when attempting to break up two inmates who are fighting, attempting to confiscate contraband or simply in the daily management of mentally ill offenders. Joliet State Prison in Illinois erupted in a gang war and three correctional officers were taken hostage in retaliation for the slaying of a gang member who was shot while stabbing a correctional officer (Reid, 2000).

In December 1999, prisoners at Angola in Louisiana beat a correctional officer to death and held two others hostage in an attempt to win release. The inmates had heard that Cuban detainees at an Immigration Center had been returned to Cuba after a disturbance there, and mistakenly assumed that they could negotiate some type of release. Administrators were quick to reinforce that policies nationwide never allow negotiations of release for hostages. The Cuban detainee deportation was a different set of circumstances involving long term federal planning and no hostages had been taken or harmed in the incident the Angola inmates referred to.

THE COST OF PRISON VIOLENCE

There are many direct and indirect costs associated with prison violence. Obviously, the most serious are loss of life and physical and psychological injury. Staff may be placed on worker's compensation or permanently disabled. Loss of property and damage from fires, riots, and disturbances create overwhelming expenses. Other costs following a violent incident include paperwork, clean-up, and overtime. There are also the expenses of disciplinary hearings, or even criminal trials, transfers to other units, and the placement of inmates in more costly, solitary housing.

After the police opened fire at Attica, 80 of those wounded required medical care. Lawsuits initiated by inmates' families resulted in awards ranging from $35,000 to $475,000. Eighteen years after the incident, seven settlements involving prisoners who "neither participated in the uprising nor resisted in the retaking of the prison" totaled $1.3 million (Associated Press, 1989). A few of the guards beaten and gang-raped in the New Mexico riot were so traumatized that they were never able to work again. Loss of property and repair at the New Mexico riot was $28.5 million and $17 million at Oakdale.

Fear of violence may keep some inmates, particularly older inmates, from participating in meaningful programs or recreation. They may prefer to isolate themselves in their cells rather than risk confrontations. Fear of victimization may lead to medical problems as well as psychiatric illness.

ATTEMPTS TO REDUCE PRISON VIOLENCE

Strategies for reducing the amount of prison violence range from segregating violence-prone inmates to improving building design to provide greater surveillance. Special management or housing units (SMUs or SHUs) or restricted housing units (RHUs) are the names commonly used for entire facilities or wings dedicated to the control of violent prisoners. These are all maximum super-security units that have many controls built in specifically to limit the prisoners' access to people and things that may result in additional harm. All cells are constantly monitored with audio and video surveillance. Inmates are released one at a time from cells by remote control to the shower or recreation areas or may be escorted in handcuffs and chains. Partly as punishment for serious offenses committed in prison, partly preventive, special housing is used when prisoners have demonstrated that they cannot adjust to the general inmate population. Because these units are resource intensive, the goal is to control the inmates' behavior and then move them progressively with reward privileges through various phases until they can be reintegrated into the general prison population. Officials in the Pennsylvania Department of Corrections claim that 85 percent of those reassigned from the RHU to the general population are successfully reintegrated (Beard, 1994).

Some prisons have developed special programs for teaching inmates conflict resolution and new techniques for stress and anger management. Cognitive theories suggest that poor judgment and reasoning cause inappropriate responses such as threats and violence. Education and counseling strategies attempt to alter inmates' attitudes and prevent future violence by teaching communication skills and more successful approaches to problem solving.

In general population units' contemporary architectural designs stress open living spaces with enhanced surveillance. The new style of direct supervision has officers within, instead of outside, the population, so that they can more carefully control activities. Their presence seems to deter acting out. Many experts recommend that the officers' role be expanded to emphasize the rehabilitative aspects of inmate-staff relations. Besides increasing job satisfaction, better supervision may reduce the opportunities for predatory behavior.

Some would argue that solutions should be developed at each individual prison given its unique population and environment. Data-collection systems should track information on each incident of violence and be analyzed for trends and solutions. Classification systems should seek to develop the most effective screening devices and assessment procedures for accurately predicting violence among inmates. Bowker (1982) also recommends the use of ombudsmen to resolve tension-producing problems between inmates and administration; a normalization of prison industry programs to include better wage incentives; facilitation of family visits, and initiation of conjugal visiting programs.

Cases

David K. v. Lane 839 F.2d 1265
People v. Lovercamp 43 Cal App 3d 823, 118 Cal. Rptr 110 (1974)
Ruiz v. Estelle 503 F. Supp 1265 (1980)
Smith v. Wade 416 U.S. 30, 103 S.Ct. 1625 (1983)
Stokes v. Delcambre 710 F.2d 1120 (1983)

References

Allen, C. (1989, February 13). The success of authority in prison management. *Insight*, 8–19.
Barak-Glantz, I. (1985). The anatomy of another prison riot. In M. Braswell, S. Dillingham, & R. Montgomery (Eds.), *Prison violence in America.*. Cincinnati, OH: Anderson.
Beard, J. A. (1994). Using special management units to control inmate violence. *Corrections Today, 56*, 5, 88–91.
Berryhill, M. (1999, December 27). Prisoner's dilemma. *The New Republic, 221,* 26, 18–23.
Bowker, L. H. (1982). Victimizers and victims in American correctional institutions. In R. Johnson & H. Toch, (Eds.), *The pains of imprisonment*. Prospect Heights, IL: Waveland.
Dillingham, S., & Montgomery, R. (1985). Prison riots: A corrections' nightmare since 1774. In M. Braswell, S. Dillingham, and R. Montgomery (Eds.), *Prison violence in America*. Cincinnati, OH: Anderson.

Finn, M. (2005). Violence. In M. Bosworth (Ed.), *Encyclopedia of prisons and correctional facilities*, pp. 995–999. Thousand Oaks, CA: Sage.

Fox, V. (1983). *Correctional institutions.* Englewood Cliffs, NJ: Prentice Hall.

Garland, G. (2007, June 5). Fight at prison said to involve gang members, Muslims. *Baltimore Sun.* Retrieved June 5, 2007 from www.baltimoresun.com.

Garson, G. (1972). Force versus restraint in prison riots. *Crime and Delinquency, 18*, 411–421.

Gillespie, W. (2003). *Prisonization: Individual and institutional factors affecting inmate conduct.* New York: LFB Scholarly Publishing.

Hassine, V. (1996). *Life without parole: Living in prison today.* Los Angeles: Roxbury.

Kallestad, B. (2007, June 22). Former inmates, experts say prison sexual abuse out of control. *USA Today.* Retrieved August 28, 2007 from www.USATODAY.com/news/nation/2006-06-22-prison-rape_x.htm.

Keller, O. J. (1988, Fall). Cuban detainees face further frustration, unfair treatment. *The Journal of the National Prison Project, 17*, 24.

Light, S. (1994). Assaults on prison officers: Interactional themes. In M. Braswell, L. Lombardo, & R. Montgomery (Eds.), *Prison violence in America* (2nd ed.), pp. 207–223. Cincinnati, OH: Anderson.

Levin, M. (1985). Fight, flee, submit, sue: Alternatives for sexually assaulted prisoners. *Columbia Journal of Law and Social Problems, 18*, 505–530.

Lockwood, D. (1985). Issues in prison sexual violence. In M. Braswell, S. Dillingham, and R. Montgomery (Eds.). *Prison violence in America.* Cincinnati: Anderson.

Mahan, S. (1985). An 'orgy of brutality' at Attica and the 'killing ground' at Santa Fe: A comparison of prison riots. In M. Braswell, S. Dillingham, & R. Montgomery (Eds.), *Prison violence In America* (2nd ed.). Cincinnati, OH: Anderson.

Martin, R., & Zimmerman, S. (1990). A typology of the causes of prison riots and an analytical extension to the 1986 West Virginia Riot. *Justice Quarterly, 7*, 4, 711–737.

Millard, P. (1988). Lessons learned after the riots. *Corrections Today, 50.* 3, 16.

Reid, S. T. (2000). *Crime and criminology* (9th ed.). Boston: McGraw Hill.

Rideau, W. (1992). The sexual jungle. In W. Rideau & R. Wikberg (Eds.), *Life sentences: Rage and survival behind bars.* New York: Times Books.

Robertson, J. E. (2004). Compassionate conservatism and prison rape: The Prison Rape Elimination Act of 2003. *New England Journal on Criminal and Civil Confinement, 30,* 1–18.

Saenz, A. (1986). *Politics of a prison riot.* Corrales, NM: Rhombus Publishing Co.

South Carolina Department of Corrections. (1973). *Collective violence in correctional institutions: A search for causes.* Columbia, SC: State Printing Co.

Steinke, P. (1991). Using situational factors to predict types of prison violence. *Journal of Offender Rehabilitation, 17,* 119–32.

Sylvester, S., Reed, J., & Nelson, D. (1977). *Prison homicide.* New York: Spectrum.

Toch, H. (1977). *Police, prisons and the problems of violence.* Washington, DC: Center for Studies of Crime and Delinquency, National Institute of Mental Health, U.S. Government Printing Office.

Wolff, N., Blitz, C., Shi, J., Siegel, J., & Bachman, R. (2007). Physical violence inside prisons. *Criminal Justice and Behavior, 34,* 5, 588–599.

Wooldredge, J. (1998). Inmate lifestyles and opportunities for victimization. *Journal of Research in Crime and Delinquency, 35,* 480–502.

Online Exercise

Go to the website for the National Criminal Justice Service (www.ncjrs.org) and look up a report by Allen Beck and Timothy Hughes dated July 2005, Sexual violence reported by correctional authorities—2004 (report # NCJ 210338). Look at Table 5 for the rates of substantiated inmate on inmate nonconsensual sex acts and compare it with staff sexual misconduct.

1. What does it show?

2. What might explain the differences, what dynamics operate to influence the reporting of one versus the other?

Questions for Thought and Discussion

1. What institutional and inmate factors appear to be related to prison violence?

2. Describe the major differences between riots like the one at Attica and that of Santa Fe.

3. What specific strategies have been indicated for preventing violence in prisons and what other solutions might be possible?

4. How are politics and management involved in the control of prison violence?

Books You Might Want To Read

Saenz, Adolph. (1986). *Politics of a prison riot.* Corrales, NM: Rhombus Publishing Co.

Wicker, Tom. (1975). *A time to die.* New York: Quadrangle

Movies You Might Want to See

Midnight Express
The Last Castle

CHAPTER 9

Issues in Medical Care: Disabled Inmates and the Elderly

The tendency to incarcerate special groups of offender who perhaps in the past, would have received alternative sentencing has created unique problems for prison administrators. In one state, a judge imprisoned a man who weighed over 500 pounds, in another a paraplegic received a life sentence, and a 78-year-old man who assisted his cancer-stricken wife in committing suicide was given ten years. Today, the "just desserts" philosophy and new mandatory prison statutes have put a number of people behind bars who may not have been incarcerated years ago. These prisoners have special treatment needs that must be met according to both medical standards and court orders. While this "equal opportunity" justice may appear to be more "fair," it also creates challenges to staff and administrators. Providing adequate care means designing creative solutions to the problems of these inmate subgroups.

MEDICAL CARE AND REHABILITATION

Corrections officials have long recognized that good health, the ability to work, and a positive self-image are critical aspects of any rehabilitation effort. It is quite common among incarcerated populations, however, to find that poor socio-economic backgrounds—and the related conditions of improper diet, drug and alcohol abuse, and lack of medical and dental attention—have created serious health problems. For some, involvement in crime and delinquency has also meant frequent injuries, disfiguring scars and exposure to communicable diseases.

The government's role in providing access to health care is a complex and hotly debated issue in our society particularly services for the unemployed, immigrants, and prisoners. While it is widely agreed that no one expects the quality of responsiveness that may be available through insured benefits programs, the courts have held that minimum constitutional standards must be maintained. Thus, there is concern over findings such as a California study that found one in six deaths within the system were likely preventable (Reiterman, 2007) or in *Women Prisoners v. The District of Columbia* that found reproductive health care so lacking, it appeared to represent cruel and unusual punishment.

Important elements of the prison's medical system are those services provided immediately upon a prisoner's arrival. Screening can take place for transmittable diseases such as AIDS, hepatitis, and tuberculosis. Treatment plans can be arranged for everything from ongoing conditions like asthma, epilepsy and diabetes to the completion of a sex change process begun on the outside. According to Allen and Simonsen (1989, p. 509), "In the most progressive prisons, cosmetic medicine—plastic surgery—is available on request of the treatment staff, to reshape the offender's self-image and thus increase his or her self-confidence. As a matter of fact, in a survey of over one hundred types of treatment, it was note that plastic surgery appeared to be one of the most effective rehabilitation treatments." In Texas, a young deaf mute with mental health problems was recommended for such treatment because his ears stuck out to the extent that he was continually ridiculed by other inmates. Their teasing often resulted in temper outbursts and fights that kept the young man in disciplinary status. After his ears were surgically "pinned back," the teasing stopped, and his treatment for emotional difficulties continued successfully.

Officials estimate that an effective health services program will require approximately 10 percent of the facility's total budget. While medical care is hardly the most expensive aspect of prison operations, certain medical programs may be relatively expensive to operate. AIDS patients, for example, may require care that may range from $40,000 to $60,000. Elderly prisoners also require a disproportionate amount of medical care costs particularly those bedridden or on a variety of medications.

Attracting qualified medical professionals, particularly nurses, to work in prisons has always been difficult. Some of the personnel

Issues in Medical Care

shortages have been offset by the use of private contracts for the provision of medical services. This has also been done where units are too small to require a full time dentist or physician or too remote to make sharing with other facilities practical. This is usually quite easy to arrange as most standards for operations have been outlined by the National Commission on Correctional Health Care (NCCHC).

AIDS IN PRISON

Current estimates place the number of federal and state inmates who are HIV positive at 23,046. The number known to have confirmed AIDS (acquired immunodeficiency syndrome) is approximately 6,027 (Maruschak, 2006). Although the number of new cases of HIV was down between 2003–2004 and the number of deaths attributed to AIDS appears to have decreased, this may be a product of how cases are categorized and whether testing is conducted. The rate of AIDS in prison is roughly three times that of the general population and female prisoners were much more likely than males to be HIV positive. Histories of intravenous drug use and sharing needles account for much of this high risk population. Many inmates have multiple risk factors. As one inmate explained in an interview (Hassine, 1996, p. 86):

> I've been an active IV drug user for 21 years, a homosexual all my life, and had a blood transfusion in 1985... a normal person's T-cell count is 2,000 or more. Mine is down to 88, and I am considered to have full-blown AIDS.... The prison administration didn't give me any support when I was first told. No physical or psychological help. I was only told to stop having sex and that, if I was caught having sex, they would put me in the Hole. They did nothing to help me in any way for the remainder of the 18 months I had left to do.

Current estimates place the HIV positive population at 1.9 percent of all state prisoners and 1.1 percent of federal prisoners (Maruschak, 2006). The Northeast has the highest rate (4.6%) and the West has the lowest (.7%). The racial breakdown of the AIDS population in prison is 44% Black, 42 % Hispanic and 14% White which coincides with profiles of the reported drug abusers in this country. The over representation of minorities in prison is also a factor with this data (Lachance-McCullough & Tesoriero, 1996).

The first AIDS prisoner was identified in New York in 1981. Since that time, states as well as the federal prison system have worked with the courts in developing safe, effective and constitutional practices for the care and management of the HIV/AIDS infected prisoner. While most states track AIDS and the HIV positive populations within their institutions, they vary in degrees of testing and avenues for the detection of infected prisoners. They also vary in treatment strategies and specific policies for housing and operations with this population.

The policy of segregating AIDS inmates was challenged in *Cordero v. Coughlin*. The inmates alleged that such segregation was a violation of the Eighth Amendment's prohibition against cruel and unusual punishment (deliberate indifference to serious medical needs) because the practice fostered depression and deterioration of their medical condition. The segregated inmates claimed that due process (the Fourteenth Amendment) had been violated as they were denied access to benefits and programs that others in the general population enjoyed. They also argued that they were living under conditions worse than inmates who had been disciplined, just because they had AIDS.

The court found that inmates have no constitutional right to freedom from segregation so long as it is instituted to advance a "reasonable correctional objective." Segregation was found proper if used to protect inmates with AIDS from abuse by others and other prison inmates from being infected. The court refused to find a violation of the Eighth Amendment because the inmates had not shown they were denied adequate food, shelter, or clothing. Finally, a denial of equal protection was not supported because there was no dissimilar treatment of similarly situated individuals. The judges determined that AIDS inmates and non-AIDS inmates were not similarly situated so this standard could not be applied.

As it appears that AIDS patients will have a difficult time contesting medical segregation policies, it is also likely that healthy prisoners will have as much difficulty trying to force segregation (see *LaRocca v. Dalsheim)*. Decisions handed down to date seem to indicate that mass screening and segregation of inmates with AIDS, AIDS related complex (ARC) or HIV will not be mandated by the court. In 2004, eighteen states were testing all inmates for HIV upon entering their prison systems. A few states, like Alabama test both upon arrival into and departure from the systems. Other states and the federal system test only inmates who appear to belong to high risk groups. Almost all states provide tests for inmates who request them (Maruschak, 2006).

THE MANAGEMENT OF INFECTIOUS DISEASES

A closed prison environment which is usually overcrowded and has a high rate of inmates with poor medical care histories and high rates of serious medical conditions is often the breeding ground for infectious diseases. Many prisoners have come from countries or backgrounds without immunizations and inoculations for diseases we mistakenly think of as unlikely risks. Prisons today have much higher rates of hepatitis, tuberculosis (TB) and influenza as well as AIDS and HIV infection than the general population (Glaser & Greifinger, 1993). Inmates may also contract chicken pox and measles with very serious consequences. The maintenance of accurate health histories on all inmates and a rapid response to potential outbreaks may be critical to the prevention of mass infection and death. In 1993, in New York 36 inmates and one correctional employee died after an outbreak of TB. The agency was widely criticized for its slow response to the potential threat and many states used this incident as a "wake-up" call to institute mandatory TB screening for all inmates (Texas Dept of Corrections, 1995).

Most states have instituted AIDS education and awareness programs for prisoners, additional training on AIDS and other infectious diseases for staff and policies for the protection of information on inmates who have AIDS or have tested positive for HIV. Some states have special medical care units or hospice services for terminally ill AIDS patients while others have designated facilities that provide specialized care for all terminally ill prisoners.

In the process of resolving *Ruiz v. Estelle* in Texas, the department spent millions of dollars updating standards for ventilation, humidity and temperature, critical factors in the control of airborne diseases (Texas Dept of Criminal Justice, 1995). Some prisons have installed isolation cells that utilize negative air pressure to halt the spread of disease and serve as quarantine stations.

CONSTITUTIONAL ISSUES

It is perhaps easiest to examine the issues of prison medical care by dividing the obligations into two categories. The first group involves the responsibilities the courts have attributed to the state as the caretaker of the inmate. Primary among these is the duty to establish medical service programs and to make them accessible to inmates.

The right to appropriate medical care has been clarified in the recent class action suit in California *Plata v. Schwarzenegger* where a receiver was installed to improve health conditions that had been found to violate the 8th Amendment. Cases cited included an inmate with chest pains who died waiting over eight hours to see a doctor, an asthmatic who died after going more than 48 hours without his medicine and a third who died after a two-year delay in diagnosing his testicular cancer. According to a report by the receiver (Sillen, 2007) that he terms "a wake up call" there were 426 deaths in 2006. Of those,

> ...66 of them—or 15 percent—were preventable (18) or possibly preventable (48). Among the non-preventable medical deaths (315), more than half, reflected lapses in care that may have contributed to earlier death or more suffering among terminal patients.

The problems cited in California's system are common everywhere namely (Sillen, 2007),

> delays in diagnosis and access to care and needed tests; misfiled, incomplete or illegible medical records; lack of space, sanitation and staffing; botched handoffs of medical information during inmate transfers; failures by clinicians to recognize and evaluate "red flag" symptoms, follow published guidelines, perform basic physical examinations, or respond to patient complaints; abdication of responsibility for patient care and lack of critical thinking or requests for help in difficult cases.

Courts also expect officials to hire a reasonable number of qualified medical personnel and establish procedures by which inmates can seek medical attention. This is usually accomplished through a system of appointments as well as "sick call" hours. The states' responsibilities would further include the provision of adequate screening devises for potential health problems and appropriate preventive responses to certain identified health risks. Another possible avenue of liability for the state would occur if security personnel deliberately interfered with or violated a course of treatment ordered by a physician. Conflicts between treatment and security are usually viewed as disrespect for territory and arise when decision making is not shared in areas of mutual responsibility. Good management and professional courtesy is important to resolve potential problems in the delivery of quality health care.

The second set of prison medical care issues, for which the state is responsible, is the actual quality of medical care provided in each individual circumstance. Questions concerning the adequacy of medical care have always been problematic for the courts because of the inherent difficulties in evaluating decisions and actions taken by trained physicians. Understandably, unless a doctor's treatment is grossly incompetent, it is difficult to get other physicians to testify, and their testimony is critical to winning a malpractice suit.

Ironically, the courts often defend not hearing medical complaint cases as civil rights violations because they feel that the inmate can address such grievances through tort action such as civil malpractice suits (Hawkins, 1989, p. 413). One of the few cases taken up by the U.S. Supreme Court on the issue of medical care was *Estelle v. Gamble* (1976). Over a three month period, Gamble sought medical treatment on over 17 separate occasions for a back injury and high blood pressure. He filed a civil rights suit (Section 1983) alleging violation of the Eighth and Fourteenth Amendments for failure to provide adequate diagnosis and medical treatment. The court held that although the state was responsible for providing medical services, not all complaints would rise to the distinction of cruel and unusual punishment. In order to constitute a violation of the Eighth Amendment, authorities must demonstrate **deliberate indifference to serious medical need** and such indifference must result in the unnecessary and wanton infliction of pain. These are the standards, the court decided, that should be used in determining when medical care presents a deprivation of constitutional rights. Obviously, an inmate faces an uphill battle to establish violations according to these standards, particularly because they require an interpretation of intent which is difficult to assess, as is what constitutes a serious medical need.

One court defined a serious medical need as "one that has been diagnosed by a physician as mandating treatment or one that is so obvious that even a lay person would easily recognize" (Gobert & Cohen, 1981, p. 338). An accident, simple negligence, or a disagreement as to the "best" treatment option would not meet this criteria. Cases that have been won have been extreme and thus would "shock the conscience" of the average person. As Hawkins and Alpert (1989, p. 413) explain,

> An inmate has an ear cut off in a prison fight. Prison doctors discard the ear rather than resuture it. One physician comments that the inmate does not need the ear, and discards it in the prisoner's presence. The court ruled deliberate indifference. Another case involved an inmate suffering from congenital scoliosis, who attempted to see a prison doctor over 100 times, but was seen only 5 times. A court found deliberate indifference. A prisoner suffering from circulatory problems was not allowed to wear prescription shoes, because the shoe height violated a prison rule. A court found the amputation that resulted could have been prevented by proper shoes and deliberate indifference was found. (See Carrabba, 1981, for these and other examples)

As explained by Krantz (1988, p. 216), "Neither lack of sufficient resources nor difficult administrative burdens can justify unconstitutional restrictions on needed medical care" (see *Hamm v. DeKalb County,* 1985). Thus regulations requiring pregnant inmates who seek to terminate pregnancy to obtain a court-ordered release to arrange personally for an abortion on a cost and administrative burden rationale was held to violate the deliberate indifference standard of *Estelle v. Gamble* (see *Monmouth County Correctional Institution Inmates v. Lanzaro,* 1987).

PREGNANT INMATES

Some 6–10 percent of women entering prison are thought to be pregnant (Bloom, 1995). Research indicates that these prisoners are at higher risk for miscarriage than nonprisoners. Miscarriages have been linked to: (a) the difficulty in identifying women with high risk pregnancies; (b) problems transporting women from inside to outside medical facilities for routine treatment; and (c) less capable medical staff in prisons and community hospitals (McCall et al., 1985). Other problems include the management of perinatal drug addiction and the use of shackles and restraints in transportation and delivery processes. Aside from a few programs like New York's that allow infants to remain with their mothers for up to one year, most systems separate the infant from the mother after a day or two. In some cases, this leads to depression and mental health problems for the mother (Bloom, 1995).

THE PHYSICALLY CHALLENGED

Physically challenged prisoners are usually distinguished from those with medical problems when their disability is in a "steady-state," meaning that although it causes them difficulties, it will not deteriorate from lack of treatment (Baum, 1984). Some disabled inmates have been disabled from birth or from accidents early in life, although not all disabilities are permanent. However, inmates who have incurred injuries in the course of committing crimes or while incarcerated often find themselves overwhelmed with trying to adjust to the institution as well as the new disability.

Protection of the interests of disabled prisoners comes from the recognition of the rights of the disabled in general. The ***Civil Rights of Institutionalized Persons Act*** guarantees procedural protections for disabled persons. This act empowers the Attorney General to seek relief in federal court if the state subjects institutionalized persons to egregious or flagrant deprivations of constitutional rights. This legislation does not require that specific programs or services be provided for the disabled, only that they may not be discriminated against in their exercise of constitutional freedoms.

The Rehabilitation Act of 1973 insures that the disabled are not excluded because of their disability, from participation in programs that receive federal money. Disabled prisoners under 21 years of age can also benefit from **Public Law 94–142** which mandates that they receive free and appropriate educational programs. This applies to young people who may have a wide range of health impairments including but not limited to those who are mentally retarded, hard of hearing, deaf, orthopedically impaired, speech impaired, visually handicapped, learning disabled, or suffering from serious emotional disturbance. The law requires states to identify, evaluate, and develop individualized educational plans for such disabled persons. However, according to Schwartz and Lewis (1987, p. 28), compliance has been difficult. "Limited official arrangements between corrections and education agencies, the relatively short period of incarceration for juvenile offenders, and the geographic isolation of many correctional facilities frequently stand in the way of implementation…."

THE MENTALLY ILL IN PRISON

Touring prisons in the early nineteenth century, reformer Dorothy Dix commented that great inconvenience was experienced by those who dealt with the insane inmates, an "unhappy class of prisoners in all prisons" (Dix, 1845, p. 42). Detailing the particularly vile and inhumane conditions suffered by the insane, she concluded that they could not receive the appropriate and peculiar care that their conditions demanded while in prison. Her impassioned pleas to the legislature of Pennsylvania were soon followed by a law establishing a separate institution for the insane who were then removed from the prison (Atherton, 1987, p. 21).

For the most part, criminals were then sent to prisons and the insane went to hospitals; even a few institutions were specifically established for the criminally insane. This separation continued until the early 1970s.

The return of the mentally ill to prison was spearheaded by massive releases of patients from state hospitals under the **Community Mental Health Act.** While this deinstitutionalization movement was seen as a reform, it did not provide the mentally ill with adequate alternative community services. As a result, many simply wandered the streets. Often, their irrational behavior drew police attention and brought them into the criminal justice system.

During this time of deinstitutionalization, there were also changes through legislation and court decisions creating mental health patients' Bill of Rights which led to stricter criteria for committing someone to a mental institution and limiting the time that a person may be held without a case review. As the mental institutions emptied out their chronic patients, they achieved great cost savings. Consequently, they could maintain lower operating costs by making it very difficult to get in (Cameron, 1988). Many original nineteenth-century facilities were in such poor condition that they had to be closed permanently. The lack of alternative facilities to confine those deemed dangerous or disturbed left judges with few sentencing choices except prison.

Over the last two decades, there appeared to be a public mandate for punishment that was less likely to view mental illness as mitigating the necessity of incarceration. Many feared that psychiatric hospitals would release violent criminals too soon, as a result, many offenders received prison terms instead. The designation of prison as a "dumping-ground" for the mentally ill (Toch & Adams, 1987) comes at a time when incarcerated populations are already at an all-time high. As Toch and Adams (1986) explain, correctional systems were unprepared for the influx of patient-prisoners and soon realized that they did not have the staff or resources to accommodate this special population.

In addition, recent concern that overcrowding in prisons will now release offenders too soon has led to legislation, particularly in California, where sex offenders deemed to be mentally ill can be confined indefinitely in state "treatment" custody after their sentences have expired. Public sentiment seems more concerned with which custody arrangement will keep offenders the longest rather than which is the most appropriate place for treatment.

Ironically, the mentally ill are often sent to prison because they have failed in other treatment and residential settings, and judges see no place else to send them. In light of what one report calls their "demonstrated incapacity to negotiate life," prison appears to be a humanitarian choice since they will get a bed, three meals, and hopefully some supervision (Toch & Adams, 1987). However, what may be overlooked is that prison is also a hostile and potentially dangerous environment where the weak are easily abused and exploited. It is a placed where a great deal of competence and savvy are necessary just to survive. Supervision is often insufficient to fully protect the mentally ill inmate and assist him or her in learning to cope and adjust. In a study of New York prisons, Toch (1977) found that inmates with a history of emotional disturbance were more often victimized while incarcerated than more emotionally stable inmates.

Another reason mentally ill offenders may be incarcerated is their potential for violence. though notably difficult to predict and unreliable in forecasting (Monahan, 1984), aggressive psychiatric patients have been profiled as more likely than other psychiatric patients to be the following: young, male, suffering from an organic mental syndrome or a substance abuse disorder, more likely to have shorter lengths of illness (might be related to the younger age), suffer depression, and more likely to have difficulty in delaying gratification (Kay et al., 1988). It is not surprising that this profile also fits the description of many other prison inmates.

Significant research has been done by Toch and Adams on the effect that mental illness has on inmate disciplinary problems. As one might predict, inmates with a history of hospitalization for mental illness prior to incarceration were more likely to engage in prison rule violations (Adams, 1981). Also, patterns of disruptiveness included violence more often among the emotionally disturbed than other inmates. In addition, the disciplinary violation rate for schizophrenics and antisocial personalities was higher than that of other disturbed inmates (Toch & Adams, 1986).

Inmate psychiatric patients appeared in another study to have higher rates of the types of rule infractions that could be associated with severe personality disturbances. These inmates had a higher number of charges of causing a disturbance, damaging state property, using vulgar language, refusing to obey an order and assaulting staff than did non-psychiatric inmates. Though the psychiatric inmates had more staff assault charges, they did not have a higher rate of inmate assaults (McShane, 1990). This finding may indicate that there is more actual conflict between staff and psychiatric patients or that there is a greater tendency for staff to interpret the inmate's behavior as threatening or assaultive. Either way, the problem appears to lie in the role relationship between officers and psychiatric inmates and is not characteristic of the psychiatric patients' interactions with other inmates. A typical staff assault by a psychiatric inmate might be reported as follows (Thirty-ninth Monitor's Report to the Special Master in Ruiz v. Estelle, November, 1986, p. 80):

Two officers responded to a disturbance and found the prisoner "going into very abnormal behavior." The disciplinary report states: "Inmate _____ just keep running on about someone coming to get him and kill him." The officers tried to escort him to pre-hearing detention. During the escort an altercation occurred in which one officer was hit in the nose and one officer was hit in the leg.

It is not surprising that correctional officers who are not well trained in the management of psychiatric patients will have a physically and emotionally difficult time dealing with these special needs inmates. In many departments, specifically selected officers attend extensive additional training before being assigned to a mental health unit. Many are still unprepared for the stress of working in the conflicting roles of security and treatment. Compounding the problem is the likelihood that the numbers of mental health staff are insufficient and that current treatment practices are inadequate (Johnson, 1987).

ELDERLY PRISONERS

Approximately 6 percent of the prison population consists of older offenders and most of those are incarcerated for a violent offense. Many victimized family members and were under the influence of alcohol at the time of the offense (Camp & Camp, 1993). The typical profile of an elderly inmate is a white male, who is unmarried at the time of incarceration, without a high school diploma, a recidivist, serving a sentence for a crime of interpersonal violence. According to Morton (1996) there are three distinct groups of older offenders; (1) those who commit their first serious offense after the age of 50; (2) those who are career offenders, going in and out of the prison system throughout their lifetime; and (3) those who enter prison at an earlier age with a life sentence and age through their extended stay.

Whether prison has more serious negative effects on the older inmate, as compared to other age groups, varies between research studies. Some have found that the physical and mental condition of older inmates deteriorates rapidly during prison terms. A 1990 study of Maryland inmates found that the older inmate averaged three chronic illnesses which meant medical costs that were three times that of younger inmates. The two most common illnesses, heart disease and hypertension, are expected to cost the Federal Bureau of Prisons alone, more than 93 million dollars to treat per year.

Research also indicates that as the length of imprisonment increases, marital ties, visits with family and friends, and contacts with outside groups tend to diminish, leaving the older inmate more dependent upon the institution. Age itself has traditionally been a variable closely associated with prison adjustment; research indicates that younger inmates experience greater adjustment problems. It has also been shown that the elderly inmate is much more likely to have serious mental health problems than their younger counterparts. Using the MMPI, a personality inventory, Panton (1976–77) found that the aged demonstrated greater anxiety, despondency, apprehension, and concern about physical functioning. They were also more demanding of attention and support, more neurotic though less psychotic than younger inmates, and finally, more eager to avoid responsibility. Panton (1974) explains that the number of mentally ill older inmates is more than twice that of younger inmates and that the average IQ of the older inmate is considerably lower.

While some research has found that older inmates have a higher degree of insecurity and more fear of correctional officers and of authority figures in general, Jensen (1977) relates that the older inmate is less prone to violate rules, and he/she does not try to escape but instead has a low activity level and fewer expectations for such things as furloughs and parole (Hormuth et al., 1977). This is somewhat ironic because studies also indicate that the older inmate is a better parole risk and that the likelihood of him/her violating parole is low (Goetting, 1984). Although older inmates, on the whole, are better behaved than younger prisoners, McShane and Williams (1990) found that when older inmates were disciplined it was most often for failure or refusing to obey an order. They also found that the inmates who had disciplinary troubles had been in prison longer, had longer sentences to serve and had been incarcerated before. They also had fewer visits than non disciplinary older inmates.

In a report by Wooden and Parker (1980), it is explained that most elderly are involved in friendship networks within the prison and that their primary group affiliations are based on ethnicity. The older inmate is relatively inactive sexually, for only 25 percent reported having at least one sexual encounter in prison while the general prison population

Issues in Medical Care

average rate was 65 percent. To these authors, the elderly seemed more stable and mature and less prone to get into fights or involved with drugs or, in any activity that results in conflicts and trouble. The elderly cooperated with prison staff, maintained low profiles, and related with other inmates. They noted that the elderly were well behaved because as one inmate expressed, "they are too old to compete and they know it." In other words, the physical realities of their age have forced the elderly to "mellow-out" especially in the tougher prisons.

Segregating Older Prisoners: The Controversy

Correctional experts often debate whether older offenders should be separated from younger ones in the prison population. Surveying older prisoners, Kerps & Jolley (2007) found that the elderly often complained about psychological victimization by younger inmates. Forms of intimidation and abuse were things like cutting in line ahead of them, being targeted with insults, fake punches, and threats. Nevertheless, researchers as well as prison administrators appear to be divided on the issue of segregating the elderly in specially designed facilities. Moore (1989) found that older inmates had less safety concerns and were better adjusted when living in special housing units. According to McCreary and Mensh (1977), the older inmate has a greater need for treatment not related to their crime and special rehabilitation programs. However, some prison administrators argue that extending special programming considerations to the elderly is a form of discrimination (Goetting, 1984). At the present time, more than two-thirds of the states have special facilities for the older offender (Morton, 1996).

Against the idea of separate facilities, many argue that there is too much isolation and that the inmate is faced with insufficient programming. In addition, other writers believe that the presence of the older inmate in the general population has a calming, stabilizing effect on the younger inmates. Regarding this, Johnson (1988) warns—be careful! He suspects that prisoners who age while serving long sentences probably differ in their accommodation to prison that those who are incarcerated for the first time at an older age. Thus he argues that not all elderly would have a positive effect on younger inmates or act as a father figure. He suggest that mixing ages would probably be best for 35–60 year old inmates but that those over 65 years are too passive and dependent to influence those younger to any significant degree.

Much of the controversy in the segregation debate focuses on conflicting reports of how the elderly view the prison environment. Some say the older inmate feels defenseless and fears being prey to the younger more violent inmate. For this reason, a number of articles published throughout the 1970s on the issue all advocated separate facilities for the older inmate. There is a consensus that despite the risk of less meaningful activity, the environment would be quieter and less troublesome and would aid them in prison adaptation. It has been argued that even in the general population, the programming is so young people-oriented, older offenders to not participate anyway. The stereotype that "you can't teach an old dog new tricks" has perhaps kept scarce rehabilitation resources focused on the young.

In designing separate programming for the older inmate, recreation activities could include dominoes, card playing tournaments, board games, planting and gardening, and arts and crafts. Diets would include softer foods that are high in fiber, and housing would be on the ground floor—avoiding stairs and providing handrails.

With concerned efforts to meet the special needs of the elderly, there is a good chance for successful adaptation to the prison environment. Many in this group have reported feeling younger than persons of the same age on the outside, and they have claimed that they are interested in politics and able to hold a prison job. Some saw prison has a safe haven from the harsh elements and loneliness of the streets.

SUMMARY

Special needs populations provide challenges for administrators and staff and require many creative adaptations of traditional incarceration. The number of special needs inmates within institutions grows, and we are now able to maintain a variety of once terminal conditions for prolonged periods of time with medical technology and pharmaceutical advancements.

Adjusting to serious medical conditions is a particularly stressful process for anyone, and the difficulties are only exacerbated by incarceration, separation from loved ones and the restrictions of

Issues in Medical Care 191

institutional life. Many inmates faced with paralysis, AIDS and other terminal illnesses, act out, cause disciplinary problems and attempt suicide. Patience and understanding on the part of the staff can make for more positive adjustment for special needs offenders.

Overall, the courts are reluctant to look at individual inmate medical complaints and are more likely to restrict their concerns to the availability of medical care itself or patterns of abuse in the operation of a medical system. Recently, the courts have identified second hand smoke as a significant health issue for inmates (*Helling v. McKinney*) and smoking has been banned in most state and federal facilities for both staff and inmates.

According to Blumberg and Mahaffey-Sapp (1997) challenges for administrators in the future will include containing the cost of care, making ethical and legal decisions about the extent of treatment warranted during incarceration, developing long-term care strategies, dealing with terminally ill inmates and the possibility of inmates' participating in experimental treatments.

Cases

Cordero v. Coughlin, 607 F.Supp 9 (S.D. N.Y., 1984)
Estelle v. Gamble, 429 U.S. 97, 97 S.Ct. 285, 50 L.Ed. 2d 251 (1976)
Hamm v. DeKalb County, 774 F.2d 1567 (11th Cir. 1985)
Helling v. McKinney, 509 U.S. 25, 113 S.Ct. 2475, 125 L. Ed. 2d 22 (1993)
LaRocca v. Dalsheim, 104 A. D. 2nd 445, 479 N.Y. S. 2d 155, 1984
Monmouth County Correctional Institution Inmates v. Lanzaro, 834 F. 2d 326, 1987
Plata v. Schwarzenegger, No. C01-1351, Northern District of CA, 2007
Ruiz v. Estelle 679 F.2d 1115 (5th Cir. 1982), opinion amended in part and vacated in part, 688 F.2d 266 (5th Cir. 1982).
Women Prisoners v. The District of Columbia 899 F. Supp 659 (1995)

References

Adams, K. (1981). Former mental patients in a prison and parole system: A study of socially disruptive behavior. *Criminal Justice and Behavior, 10,* 358–84.

Allen, H., & Simonsen, C. (1989). *Corrections in America.* New York: MacMillan.

Atherton, A. (1987). Journal retrospective: 1845–1986. *The Prison Journal, 67*, 1.

Baum, E. (1984). Handicapped prisoners: An ignored minority? *Columbia Journal of Law and Social Problems, 18*, 3, 349–379.

Blumberg, M., & Mahaffey-Sapp, C. (1997). Health care issues in correctional institutions. In M. Schwartz and L. Travis III, (Eds.) *Corrections: An issues approach* (4th ed.), pp. 333–344. Cincinnati, OH: Anderson.

Cameron, J. (1988, Winter). Balancing the interests: The move towards less restrictive commitment of New York's mentally ill. *New England Journal on Criminal and Civil Confinement, 14*, 1, 91–106.

Camp, G., & Camp, C. (1993). *The corrections yearbook 1993.* South Salem, NY: Criminal Justice Institute.

Dix, D. (1845). *Remarks on prisons and prison discipline in the United States.* Montclair, NJ: Patterson Smith (reprinted, 1967).

Glaser, J. B., & Griefinger, R. B. (1993). Correctional health care: A public health opportunity. *Annals of Internal Medicine, 118*, 2, 139–145.

Goetting, A. (1984). The elderly in prison: A profile. *Criminal Justice Review, 9*, 2, 14–24.

Hassine, V. (1996). *Life without parole: Living in prison today.* Los Angeles: Roxbury.

Hawkins, R., & Alpert, G. (1989). *American prison systems.* Englewood Cliffs, NJ: Prentice Hall.

Hormuth, S., Hood, R., Wicklund, R., Mabli, J., Pribble, M., & Dallas, M. (1977). Freedom in a correctional institution: Relationship between personal variables, expectations and behavioral freedoms. Paper presented at the annual meeting of the Southwest Psychology Association, Fort Worth, TX.

Jensen, G. (1977). Age and rule breaking behavior in prison: A test of socio-cultural interpretations. *Criminology, 14*, 555–568.

Johnson, R. (1987). *Hard time.* Monterey, CA: Brooks Cole.

Johnson, E. (1988). Care for elderly inmates: Conflicting concerns and purposes in prisons. In B. McCarthy & R. Langworthy (Eds.), *Older offenders.* New York: Praeger.

Kay, S., Wolkenfeld, F., & Murrill, L. (1988). Profiles of aggression among psychiatric patients. *The Journal of Nervous and Mental Disease, 176*, 9, 539–548.

Kerps, J., & Jolley, J. (2007) Prison victimization and the elderly. *Crime & Delinquency, 53*, 1, 187–218.

Lachance-McCullough, M., & Tesoriero, J. (1996). In M. D. McShane & F. P. Williams III (Eds.), *Encyclopedia of American prisons*, pp. 12–19. New York: Garland.

Maruschak, L. M. (2006, November). *HIV in prisons, 2004*. Bureau of Justice Statistics Bulletin. Washington, DC: U.S. Department of Justice.

McCreary, C., and Mensh, I. 1977. Personality differences associated with age in law offenders. *Journal of Gerontology, 32*, 2, 164–67.

McShane, M. (1990). The bus stop revisited: Discipline and psychiatric patients in prison. *Journal of Psychiatry and Law, 17*, 3, 413–433.

McShane, M., & Williams, F. P. (1990). Old and ornery: The disciplinary experiences of elderly prisoners. *International Journal of Offender Therapy and Comparative Criminology, 34*, 3, 197–212.

Monahan, J. (1984). The prediction of violent behavior: Toward a second generation of theory and policy. *American Journal of Psychiatry, 141*, 10–15.

Morton, J. (1996). Elderly inmates. In M. D. McShane & F. P. Williams III (Eds.), *Encyclopedia of American prisons*, pp. 190–194. New York: Garland.

Panton, J. (1976–77). Personality characteristics of aged inmates within a state prison population. *Offender Rehabilitation, 2*, 203–208.

Reiterman, T. (2007, September 20). Deadly medical lapses in prison. *Los Angeles Times.* Retrieved September 20, 2007 from www.latimes.com/news/la-me-prisons20sep20,0,5611823.story?coll=la-tot-topstories&track=ntothtml.

Schwartz, G., & Lewis, K. (1987). Effective special education for juveniles. *Corrections Today, 49*, 3, 26.

Sillen, R. (2007, September 26). *Receiver's efforts to improve medical care felt at prisons statewide focus on recruitment and infrastructure.* San Jose, CA: California Prison Health Care Receivership Corp.

Texas Department of Corrections. 1995. *Managing infectious diseases.* Austin, TX: TDC.

Texas Department of Criminal Justice. (2006). *Fiscal Year 2006 Statistical report.* Huntsville, TX: TDCJ.

Toch, H. (1977). *Living in prison: The ecology of survival.* New York: Free Press.

Toch, H., & Adams, K. (1986). Pathology and disruptiveness among prison inmates. *Journal of Research in Crime and Delinquency, 23*, 1, 7–21.

Toch, H., & Adams, K. (1987). The prison as dumping ground: Mainlining disturbed offenders. The *Journal of Psychology and Law, 15*, 4, 539–553.

Wolfgang, M. (1964, July). Age, adjustment, and the treatment process of criminal behavior. *Psychiatric Digest,* 21–35.

Wooden, W., & Parker, J. (1980). Age adjustment and the treatment process of criminal behavior strategies. Paper presented at the annual meeting of the National Gerontology Society, San Diego, CA.

Online Exercise

Death In Prison: go to the website for the National Criminal Justice Reference Service (www.ncjrs.org) and look for a BJS report by Chris Mumola dated January 2007 called Medical Causes of Death in State Prison, 2001–2004.

1. How many prisoner deaths were there between 2001 and 2004? (Not counting Executions)

2. What were the most common causes of death? What were the least common causes?

3. What were the differences between males and females concerning death in prison?

4. What did you find out about death in prison that you did not expect?

Questions for Thought and Discussion

1. What are some of the issues facing prison officials in the management of special medical populations today?

2. What do we know about the AIDS/HIV population and what type of programs and policies would best serve this group?

3. Consider a model that segregates persons with special needs and disabilities over one that integrates them. What are the advantages and disadvantages of each approach?

4. What has case law said about the medical needs of inmates? How would changes in court views over time impact medical care in prison?

Books You May Want to Read

Hornblum, Allen. (1998). *Acres of skin: Human experiments at Holmesburg Prison*. New York: Routledge

Erik Saar and Viveca Novak (2007) *Inside the wire: A military intelligence soldier's eyewitness account of life at Guantanamo*. New York: Simon & Schuster

Movies You May Want to See

Miss Ever's Boys
I Want to Live

CHAPTER 10
Legal Issues in Corrections

Perhaps more than other institutions, correctional facilities require vigorous scrutiny: They are uniquely powerful institutions, depriving millions of people each year of liberty and taking responsibility for their security, yet are walled off from the public. They mainly confine the most powerless groups in America....
　　　　　　Commission on Safety and Abuse in America's Prisons (2006)

INTRODUCTION

There are undoubtedly many areas for dispute between the state and those kept involuntarily within its custody. Although the current "get tough" model demonstrates less public support for inmate rights and privileges, conditions must be constitutional, that is, not amount to cruel and unusual punishment. Historically, the courts seem to swing back and forth between periods where they are more and then less receptive to the plight of incarcerated persons. This is understandable as judges are elected by the public or appointed by political leaders and seem to fall into categories of more conservative or more liberal in their interpretations of the Bill of Rights.

AVENUES FOR INMATE COMPLAINTS

Inmate complaints may take several different forms depending on the type of issue and the availability of potential remedies in any given jurisdiction. Inmates may bring complaints informally to the attention of wardens or administrative officers through letters. Otherwise, a formal grievance may be initiated although the exact procedures vary from state to state. In most instances the written grievance is reviewed at several levels (i.e. unit level then regional level and then, central headquarters level) as are the official responses to those petitions. This process is called the system's **administrative remedies. The 1980 Civil Rights of Institutionalized Person's Act** required that inmates go through this process before they bring any suit to the Federal Courts. To insure uniformity in the way the inmate is handled in the administrative process, the local Federal District Court or the U.S. Department of Justice will certify a state's grievance process. If the state fails to gain certification, inmates from that jurisdiction will be able to petition the Federal Court directly, without going through a grievance procedure.

If an inmate is still dissatisfied with the outcome, he or she may still attempt to notify legislators, lawyers or various inmate rights support groups on the outside. However, only in very specific instances will the complaint be the type of issue that is eligible for review in the courts.

Ways to Reach the Court

A prisoner with a grievance may still approach the courts in any one of four ways. First, an inmate may file a state habeas corpus writ asking for a hearing on the conditions of confinement. When state remedies have been unsuccessfully exhausted, the prisoner may then file a federal habeas corpus writ. Generally, these cases will only decide the status of individual issues and focus on getting that one inmate released with no precedent actually arising from them.

Second, as with an ordinary citizen, a prisoner may file a civil suit or tort action in local courts against a prison employee for damages caused by wanton or gross negligence or some intentional act of harm. Thirdly, an inmate may also seek criminal charges with the state against an employee who has committed a felony—such as assault, theft, or threats to do harm— against him or her. The difficulty in such cases would be the prisoner's ability to find a prosecutor willing to seek an indictment.

The fourth avenue is suit for violations of Section 1983 of the *Civil Rights Act* under which a petitioner may ask for injunctive relief as well as monetary damages. The 1983 suit is the most common action taken by inmates, developed from the original 1871 legislation. As the court expressed in *Preiser v. Rodriguez*, the potential for suits is inherent in the nature of the relationship between inmates and the state.

> For state prisoners, eating, sleeping, dressing, washing, working and playing are all done under the watchful eye of the State.... What for a private citizen would be a dispute with his landlord, his tailor, with his neighbor, or with his banker becomes, for the prisoner, a dispute with the State

HANDS OFF

For approximately the first one hundred and fifty years of their existence, penitentiaries operated outside the protection of the Bill of Rights and beyond the interest of the courts. The most compelling example of the court's reluctance to interfere in prison matters was reflected in *Ruffin v. Commonwealth* in 1871. Here the status of the inmate was defined.

> He has, as a consequence of his crime, not only forfeited his liberty, but all his personal rights except those which the law in its humanity accords to him. He is for the time being, a slave of the State.

According to Hawkins and Alpert (1989, p. 366), this nonperson status also carried the consequences of civil death, meaning that a person convicted of a felony and sent to prison, lost privileges such as voting and holding civic appointments. "These statutes meant the prisoners had no standing in legal action involving their property, marriage, custody of their children or other matters outside the prison." Many of these restrictions are still in effect today.

Another effect of this slave-like status was that inmates were discouraged from addressing complaints about prison conditions through the courts. A **hands-off doctrine** also gave prison officials the green light to administer punishment in whatever fashion they deemed appropriate. As Farrar (1996) reports, this position was easy to maintain because society generally desired retribution and was not sympathetic to the problems of inmates. Also, the political climate was such that judges were not particularly eager to consider inmate problems. Though judicial precedent had stated that "a prisoner retains all the rights of an ordinary citizen except those expressly, or by necessary implication, taken from him by law" (*Coffin v. Reichard*), legal interpretations of this time did not offer them many rights.

The "hands-off" philosophy remained active through the 1950s as decisions continued to reflect that the "courts are without power to supervise prison administration or to interfere with the ordinary prison rules or regulations" (*Banning v. Looney*). As Farrar (1996) explains, this doctrine was not a rule of law but rather a policy of judicial abstention. According to Justice Powell, the Court believed at that time that prison administrators had a tremendous task in maintaining security with the prison and that the courts lacked the expertise to intervene in such matters (*Procunier v. Martinez*).

> There were other reasons that the courts refrained from becoming involved in prison issues. One was the notion of separation of powers, a kind of diplomacy that meant one branch of government did not interfere in another. Because prisons were the responsibility of the executive office, the courts as well as the legislature were unwilling to be critical. Consequently, great administrative discretion was afforded prison officials, and there was little exercise of the power of judicial review (Jones & Rhine, 1985).

This was expressed in *Williams v. Steele* when the court said:

> Since the prison system of the United States is entrusted to the Bureau of Prisons under the discretion of the Attorney General... the courts have no power to supervise the discipline of the prisoners nor to interfere with their discipline.

Another reason cited for the lack of court intervention in prison policy was the federalist principle that certain aspects of state government should not be interfered with by the federal government. As a matter of courtesy, the federal courts were reluctant to stir up any conflict between the two jurisdictions (Jones & Rhine, 1985). The states were very sensitive to the federal government's meddling in "their business."

Finally, the courts were also concerned that if they were regularly involved in cases of prisoner complaints, there would be a flood of litigation on every conceivable issue. To avoid this, they separated themselves from prison matters except in rare cases where they were faced with "exceptional circumstances" in which beatings, torture, and physical abuse would "degrade the individual and destroy the sense of personal honor" (*Cornell v. State*). As stated in one 1949 case (*Siegel v. Ragen*), the court was

> ...prepared to protect state prisoners from death or serious bodily harm in the hands of prison authorities but not prepared to establish itself as "co-administrators" of state prisons along with the duly appointed state officials.

This judicial trend continued until the 1950s when judges began taking a more active role in prison affairs.

HANDS ON

What precipitated the court's intervention in the area of prison rights was the same series of complex social and political changes that characterized other reform movements of the late 1950s through the 1970s. School desegregation, war protest, and women's rights were all part of the fabric of developing humanistic reforms. Simply by being a minority group under the regulation of the state, prisoners, as a class, were swept up in the process of redefining the parameters of rights and the limits of punishment. As Del Carmen explains:

> Prisons had become much more visible to the public. The prison riots and demonstrations, which started in the early seventies..., brought the plight of prisoners dramatically to the attention of the American public.... Secondly, the United States Supreme Court... ushered in what some writers have called the "due process and equal protection revolution." This meant that, more than ever before, equitable treatment and fundamental fairness had become great concerns of the court. They realized that some abuses could only be controlled judicially and not through policy decisions by legislative bodies.

The U. S. Supreme Court paved the way for prisoner litigation when it handed down its 1961 decision in *Monroe v. Pape* ruling that state officials could be sued in federal court on claims that they had abused their authority. This decision is significant because previously inmates had to channel all complaints through the state first, which was often a long and discouraging procedure. The process was further clarified three years later by the court in *Cooper v. Pate*. In this case, inmates alleged that officials at Stateville had unconstitutionally banned the Muslim religion and restricted their right to associate for religious purposes. While the Muslims eventually won limited religious recognition, the most important aspect of the case was the use of Section 1983 suits as an avenue of relief. The opinion held that Section 1983 of the *Civil Rights Act* was an appropriate means for the inmates to come to federal court alleging violations of their constitutional rights.

The spirit of the courts' new role in prison cases is best described in *Wolff v. McDonnell* when it was expressed that "there is no iron curtain drawn between the Constitution and the prisons of this country" and in *Ruiz v. Estelle's* the "court may not take a 'hands off' approach when the constitutional rights of inmates are at risk." In a series of cases, the court attacked the traditional defenses used by the state for restrictive practices and policies and made it clear that such excuses would be of limited utility in the future and subject to critical analysis.

> …only a compelling state interest centering about prison security, or a clear and present danger of a breach of prison discipline or some substantial interference with orderly institutional administration can justify curtailment of a prisoner's constitutional rights.

Though many important decisions of this period were made in the lower courts, judicial activism in the area of prisoner rights is often associated with the U.S. Supreme Court under Chief Justice Earl Warren. Precedent setting cases were handed down by this group in most areas of prison life. Some can be categorized as clarifying fundamental civil rights including rights in the areas of marriage, correspondence, privacy, access to courts, and religion as they apply to prisoners. Others are in areas specific to prison and involve living conditions and policies that inmates allege represent cruel and unusual punishment.

FUNDAMENTAL CIVIL RIGHTS

Though the inmate's right to have access to courts is generally recognized and accepted, just what degree of cooperation and assistance is required to make this right "meaningful" is very controversial. For the average, undereducated and unsophisticated inmate, even the simplest legal correspondence may be beyond their grasp. For example, when officers approached one inmate to take him to the execution chamber, he commented that he wanted to save half of his "last meal" for when he got back to his cell. Reasonable access, therefore, could mean anything from simply not obstructing the inmate's correspondence to helping them prepare legal briefs.

In *Johnson v. Avery*, the Supreme Court held that unless the state provides some reasonable alternative to assist inmates in preparation of postconviction petitions, they may not enforce any regulation that prohibits inmates from furnishing such assistance to each other. While the Court's concern in this case was the high number of illiterate inmates, prison officials considered jailhouse lawyers a nuisance.

Legitimizing of the jailhouse lawyer was seen by many administrators as a potential source of inmate violence, extortion, and manipulation. Some states, such as Texas, moved to initiate alternative legal-aid programs that would minimize the number of inmates setting themselves up in the legal business. Other states, like Louisiana, gave the inmates the full responsibility of assisting each other.

As time went by, other decisions followed, and the mandate was strengthened. Not only were inmates allowed to assist each other, but the burden shifted to the state to furnish additional means through which inmates would be assured meaningful access to courts (*Younger v. Gilmore*). In *Hooks v. Wainwright,* the court even concluded that most jailhouse lawyers were ineffective. The justices held that where more than one-half of the prison population was functionally illiterate, the establishment of law libraries run by inmate "law clerks" and staff librarians did not insure the protection of constitutional rights. Security and cost restraints, however, have made most professional and legal assistance programs appear inefficient and half-hearted. Correctional institutions were simply not able, or willing, to provide enough attorneys to meet the inmates' legal needs (McShane, 1987).

Further clarification came from the Supreme Court in 1974 through *Procunier v. Martinez*. The case struck down a California ban against interviews by law students and paralegals in an attorney-client relationship as this state regulation was found to restrict an inmate's right to access to the courts. The Court's determination to provide prisoners access to either adequate legal materials or legal assistance was also evident in the 1977 decision *Bounds v. Smith*. Here it was held that prisoners have a constitutional right to access to courts, and this cannot be denied by cost. This decision also required that prison authorities assist in the preparation and filing of meaningful legal papers by providing adequate assistance from person trained in the law.

CONSERVATIVE COURTS TODAY

In summary, while there are some instances of specific attempts of judges to improve the rights and status of inmates in prison today, these are usually at the lower court level and these cases are often overturned by the U.S. Supreme Court which has maintained a much more restrictive approach to inmate rights. The high court continues to lend **substantial deference** to the professional judgment of prison administrators in ways that legitimize restrictions and make it very difficult for inmates to challenge policies and conditions of confinement in all constitutionally interpreted areas (Robertson, 2007).

Today there are two reasons to be concerned about inmate access to courts. First, in some high profile cases prisoners have been found not guilty of crimes for which they have already served considerable time. A study by Bedeau and Radelet (1987) determined that prior to 1987 at least 23 persons had been executed in error, another 22 were reprieved within 72 hours of execution, and over 300 others convicted of capital or potentially capital crimes have been found innocent. In Illinois, a review of 285 death penalty convictions found that almost half of the cases had been ordered to conduct a new trial or sentencing phase because of serious problems. Of those, twelve defendants were exonerated and 74 warranted sentence reductions (AP, 1999). More importantly, recent polls show that 95% of Americans believe that innocent people are sometimes convicted of murder, that knowledge of wrongful death penalty convictions has reduced support for the death penalty and that 63% of Americans favor a halt to executions in light of recent exonerations (Miller, 2006).

Another concern is that access to courts and to media are often the only ways the public can find out about serious abuses occurring in prisons. Recently, incidents at the Pelican Bay facility and at the Corcoran Prison, both in California have raised significant legal questions about gross physical abuse and negligence at the hands of the state. This comes at the same time as legislation has made it more difficult for inmates to approach the Federal Courts and the California Department of Corrections has reduced media access to the prisons.

FIRST AMENDMENT CONCERNS

Religion

The freedom to worship according to one's own religion is one of the rights most vigorously attended by the courts. As far back as 1940, inmates have been assured that the constitutional guarantee of freedom in religion is an absolute one (*Cantwell v. Connecticut*). The cases that come to court usually argue infringement of this right for members of non-traditional prison religions as was the case with Muslims and Buddhists in the 1960s. In *Cruz v. Beto,* the Court held that Cruz's First Amendment right had been discriminatingly denied by the state which had a duty to provide reasonable opportunities for him to exercise his faith. The Court suggested that a reasonable opportunity would be "comparable to those afforded fellow prisoners who adhere to conventional religious precepts." The ruling also implied that the state is under no obligation to recognize a religion that appears to be frivolous or insincere in its purpose. Thus requests on behalf of new religions for steaks, wine, and marijuana to conduct their services were appropriately denied by officials.

The free exercise of religion was interpreted for almost two decades by the 1987 court decision in *O'Lone v. Estate of Shabazz*. In this case, Muslims argued for relief from the prison's policy (1) which required inmates in custody class "x" to work outside their housing or religious meeting areas, and (2) prohibited them from returning to the building during the day, and prevented them from attending a Friday afternoon congregational service. The Supreme Court found a rational security purpose in the policies and stated that the state did not have to go to all the trouble of showing that there was not a reasonable way for the group to assemble without causing security violations. Because the prison provided other times and means for religious activity and because giving Muslims special jobs within their work/worship area would be favoritism, the state had not jeopardized the inmates' First Amendment rights.

In a 1992 case, the Sixth Circuit Court of Appeals found that, absent an independent finding that the inmate posed a security risk, a homosexual inmate cannot be banned from attending religious services *(Phelps v. Dunn)*. Over the years, institutions have found ways for Native American prisoners to incorporate elements of rituals involving long hair, sweat lodges, and access to medicine men. And, more recently, administrators have had to develop strategies to accommodate inmates practicing Santeria without causing security and health risks from food/animal sacrifices left at homemade alters.

Grooming restrictions developed by the California Department of Corrections were challenged by inmates in regard to religious freedom. The regulations had been upheld by the court because the grounds the inmates had used to file, **The Religious Freedom Restoration Act of 1993** was struck down by the U.S. Supreme Court in 1997. The CDC argued that the grooming requirements are for hygiene and security purposes and will promote a more uniform appearance among inmates as well as "more discipline and respect for authority" (Detention Reporter, 1998). However, after The *Religious Land Use and Institutionalized Persons Act* **of 2000** was passed, inmates practicing the Islamic faith refiled their request to be allowed to grow short beards, to attend Friday mid-day services without losing good time credit or facing disciplinary charges as well as to have previous disciplinary charges filed over these issues expunged from their records. The Court ruled in their favor. Justices in *Mayweathers v. Terhune* were not impressed by the state's argument that the altering of appearance with even trim beards quickly grown or shaved would enhance escape opportunities. They reminded officials that any interest, such as safety or security must be addressed in ways that would be least restrictive of religious freedom. Thus, even arguments like cost, such as the financial burden of supplying Jewish inmates with kosher meals, would not be considered legitimate by courts such as in Colorado in 2002 (Haynes, 2004).

Association/Marriage

Up until 1987, the courts had maintained a restrictive posture on the right of the inmate to marry while in the custody of the government. In *Turner v. Safley*, however, the U.S. Supreme Court struck down a Missouri regulation that required inmates to receive the approval of the superintendent of the prison before being allowed to marry. This was mainly because the practice seemed to discriminate against women prisoners seeking to marry. According to Krantz (1988, p. 111).

> After determining that the right to marriage was a fundamental right that prisoners retain, the Court did hold that marriage was subject to substantial restrictions as a result of incarceration. The test to be applied was whether a particular restriction was "reasonably related to an articulated rehabilitation goal." The Court found the sweeping Missouri regulation... was not reasonably related to valid goals.

Correspondence

Normally, the courts look for a rational relationship between prison policies and legitimate administrative goals when deciding the constitutionality of penal practices. The courts have also vacillated between making officials prove that certain policies were necessary in order to maintain security (a compelling state interest exists) and placing the burden on inmates to prove that such practices violated constitutional rights. In the area of correspondence, prisons have traditionally limited the type, content, and volume of mail an inmate may send or receive. Censoring the mail that inmates send has been defended by officials as necessary "to protect the public from unlawful schemes or from insulting, obscene or threatening letters; to prevent correspondence which casts the prison in an unfavorable or inaccurate light...." (Krantz, 1988, p. 134).

Mail censorship regulations which are to protect legitimate prison interests (concerns regarding the flow of contraband or the planning of an escape), will not be upheld by the courts if they are stricter than they need to be. Judges are also very sensitive to the special category of legal mail and have generally held that this type, either ingoing or outgoing, may only be inspected in the presence of the inmate. The court is also likely to uphold restrictions on inmate to inmate mail and prohibitions against hardback books which might be hollowed out and used to smuggle contraband. For example, in a 1992 case, the court found that the administration acted properly when they revoked a male inmate's correspondence privileges with a female inmate in another facility after he made specific threats to staff who he perceived of as giving her a difficult time (*Purnell v. Lord*). Courts have varied on the rationale for allowing the state to prohibit the subscription of certain types of magazines and to be more restrictive with some inmates who appear particularly recalcitrant or difficult. Some use the standard that a magazine must represent a clear and present danger to security before it can be banned; others have adopted an approach that says magazines may be restricted if they are judged by officials to be inflammatory, obscene, racist, or promote criminal or other unacceptable (particularly homosexual) conduct (Krantz, 1988; Robertson, 2003).

Recognizing that censorship restrictions may be arbitrary and vague, and may jeopardize First Amendment rights, the Court in *Procunier v. Martinez* established some procedural safeguards. These included notifying inmates of all letters either addressed to them or written by them that have been rejected. The author of the correspondence must then be given a reasonable opportunity to refute that decision, and a review process using officials other than the mail censors should be available.

FOURTH AMENDMENT: PRIVACY AND PROPERTY

In some recent decisions, the courts have made clear that an inmate has little expectation of privacy in terms of their cells or bodies when officials can justify intrusive searches in the name of security and deterrence. Body cavity searches for contraband have been upheld even without probable cause. In *Jordan v. Gardner* the Court reiterated that cross sex pat searches were acceptable as long as they were conducted for security purposes, on fully clothed inmates, by trained correctional staff acting in a professional manner. The state has traditionally argued that staffing would be too difficult if male and female officers were not similarly able to perform these security measures.

Cell searches were also found to be outside the scope of the Fourth Amendment's protection from unreasonable search and seizure. In addition, authorities may limit the amount of possessions an inmate may have in his cell. In *Cosco v. Uphoff,* the court held that policies that allow officials to limit without hearings, the amount of property a prisoner could keep with him did not violate due process. In this case, confiscated excess materials are held for 90 days during which inmates are given the opportunity to ship the materials to family or friends. Depending on how this procedure is carried out, inmates without the means to fund the shipping, may be at a disadvantage. While security concerns mean that Fourth Amendment protections in prison are few, the Court has cautioned that prison officials would not be able to "ride rough shod over inmates' property rights without impunity" (*Hudson v. Palmer*).

EIGHTH AMENDMENT: CRUEL AND UNUSUAL PUNISHMENT

The prohibition against cruel and unusual punishment was first documented by Americans in the Virginia Declaration of Rights of 1776. Fifteen years later, it was incorporated into the Constitution as the Eighth Amendment (Albany Law Review, 1972). Though the original intent was to ban unusually barbaric punishments such as pillaring, disemboweling, branding and drawing and quartering, its meaning has been reinterpreted over the years. In 1980, the Supreme Court commented that there is no single test to determine whether conditions of confinement are cruel and unusual. The judgment will, instead, be drawn from objective factors when compared to the "**evolving standards of decency**" that indicate the progress of a maturing society (*Rummel v. Estelle).*

In case law, the courts have recognized two major themes in the Eighth Amendment. In one, the concept of cruel and unusual punishment usually involves the infliction of unnecessary or wanton pain and suffering. The courts generally require a pattern of such abuse stemming perhaps from a policy or practice, or they look for an incident so unreasonable or deliberate that it is easily recognized as a constitutional violation.

Responding to prisoners' Eighth Amendment claims, the courts have used a three part test for determining whether the administration was "deliberately indifferent" to an inmate's situation. The criteria are that there is first, an objectively strong likelihood of harm. Each of the terms; objectively, strong and likelihood are subject to interpretation. Next, the court weighs administrators' or staff members' actual knowledge of the high risk of harm and finally, judges will look at whether knowing of the risk, prison officials failed to respond to the harm in an objectively reasonable manner. Over time, the courts have determined that a specific threat, as in a named person or group need not be identified in order for the inmate to posit a claim of being at risk of harm. This means that officials should foresee that a transvestite, transsexual or someone easily targeted for violence would be at risk (Robertson, 2007).

The second theme addressed by the courts is when punishments are found to be excessive, an issue often raised in death penalty cases. Within the context of prison, an inmate may allege that solitary confinement is too excessive a punishment for some minor disciplinary infraction. In one case, a violation of the Eighth was found where an inmate received two years in solitary for participating in an unauthorized religious service (*Fulwood v. Clemmer*).

Traditionally, prisoner suits alleging cruel and unusual punishment focused on particular practices or incidents involving individual inmates. Only since 1970 have the courts considered the cumulative impact of poor conditions to, in their effect, represent a violation of the Eighth Amendment. In *Holt v. Sarver,* the majority held that

> (T)he concept of "cruel and unusual punishment" is not limited to instances in which a particular inmate is subjected to a punishment directed at him as an individual. In the Court's estimation confinement itself within a given institution may amount to a cruel and unusual punishment prohibited by the constitution where the confinement is characterized by conditions and practices so bad as to be shocking to the conscience of reasonably civilized people....

In this case, the brutality of the "trustee system," fear of homosexual attacks, fights and stabbings, and unsanitary and debasing living conditions all contributed to the courts decision. The entire Arkansas prison system was ordered into massive reforms as were the states of Alabama (*Pugh v. Locke)* and Texas *(Ruiz v. Estelle*) in later cases. In *Pugh v. Locke,* the court found the facilities overrun with roaches and other vermin. In one housing area of 200 men, only one toilet functioned. Inmates were not supplied with adequate eating utensils, and some drank from used tin cans. Garbage sat in large open drums throughout the eating area, and there were no opportunities for exercise or recreation. There were not enough guards to prevent outbreaks of violence, and most inmates carried some form of weapon.

While it is unusual for an entire state prison system to be found unconstitutional, it is not so rare that individual state and federal prison facilities are found in their "totality" to represent a violation of the Eighth Amendment. Former Director of the Texas Department of Corrections, George Beto, cites a number of reasons that prisons lose lawsuits in court. One reason is that the state will decide to fight—although many times they have a poor case to start with—because they do not want to admit they were wrong. Another reason, he adds, is that these cases are often poorly defended by the state, as in *Ruiz v. Estelle.* Finally, according to Beto, the administration often fails to anticipate change, and they will defend issues that have outlived their time such as the use of corporal punishment or bread and water diets. In cases like these, the system fails to recognize the evolution of the standards of decency in contemporary society.

In general, prison conditions cannot present a danger to the health of an inmate. Food must be nutritionally adequate and prepared and served under healthy conditions, and often special medical or religious needs in food will be required. Without resorting to the courts, many food-oriented complaints can be handled by internal grievance mechanisms and the enforcement of state institutional health and safety codes. This is also true for conditions related to heating, lighting, ventilation, and plumbing. Serious deficiencies in a number of these areas may contribute to a finding that the totality of conditions within the prison are unconstitutional. Also, it is not a permissible defense for prison authorities to blame the broken down conditions on acts of abuse or misuse by the inmates themselves.

Prisoners may be required to work and may be disciplined for refusal to work. The work assigned must be medically appropriate and within an inmate's physical capabilities. For example, in Texas a special doctor for paraplegics assured that they could fold clothes in the laundry, and classification prohibited Muslims from being forced to slaughter pigs and prepare pork. Most courts have required reasonable access to showers and limited dental care.

Recent "get tough" trends in the courts have made it more difficult for inmates to prevail in 8th Amendment cases. When an Ohio prisoner filed alleging overcrowding, excessive noise, insufficient locker storage, inadequate heating and cooling, improper ventilation, unclean and inadequate restrooms, unsanitary dining facilities and food preparation and housing mixed with mentally- and physically-ill inmates, the plaintiff was required to show that prison officials were deliberately indifferent to the needs of inmates. This requires a finding that the state had a culpable state of mind or intent in order to set up cruel and unusual punishment which many fear will be very difficult to establish since it is seldom clear what state of mind officials are actually operating under.

THE ROLE OF THE COURTS: HANDS-OFF AGAIN

Many critics of judicial activism have blamed the courts for the costly reforms mandated in the prison system and for each institutional problem that has arisen since the courts became involved. However, prison scholars realize that problems such as violence, gangs and recidivism are more complex in their origin and existence than can be explained by constitutional mandates. Another misconception is that the judges eagerly await the chance to intervene in prison matters. As Judge Johnson (1977) (who decided *Pugh v. Locke*) argued,

> I didn't ask for any of these cases…. In an ideal society, all of these judgments and decisions should be made by those whom we have entrusted these responsibilities. But when governmental institutions fail to make these judgments and decisions in a manner which comports with the Constitution, the federal courts have a duty to remedy the violation.

This same feeling was expressed by Judge Justice (1986, p. 2) who heard *Ruiz v. Estelle*. Commenting that the case took over one year of his life just to hear, he stated, "…we federal judges do not grasp for these kinds of cases; they come to us, and it is our constitutional duty to decide them, whatever may be the cost in time and effort."

The public's misconception about the power of judicial intervention has given the courts both undue credit and blame for their role in American corrections (Nathan, 1988). Their services have been, according to Special Master Vince Nathan, "legitimating prisoners' complaints, energizing local reform groups, providing factual information to governors and legislators and, at least in some instances, enlightening prison boards and directors concerning institutional conditions." Nathan also comments that there is much the courts cannot do like make an administration efficient and effective, prevent bad decision making, or choose the best people to run the system.

Over the years, State's Attorneys who had little time to defend prison cases in the 1960s were replaced by prison administration lawyers whose sole mission was to defend the system and its practices in court. Thus throughout the 1980s and 1990s, prisons took an aggressive legal approach to inmate litigation. First, using media campaigns, they promoted the image that inmate lawsuits were out of control, frivolous and consuming outrageous amounts of taxpayer resources. Legislation was passed to restrict the amount and types of complaints inmates could raise and the conditions under which they could file.

Second, attorneys for the departments argued that the policies, conditions and procedures the inmates challenged were indeed essential on the same grounds the courts had given them earlier: a compelling state interest centering about prison security, a clear and present danger of a breach of prison discipline or some substantial interference with orderly institutional administration. In essence, the states became more sophisticated in making their arguments defending the Departments of Corrections and appear to focus on the very legal lines the courts said they would allow.

Both of these approaches were successful because they were consistent with the mood of the country, namely a "get tough" approach to prisoners. This punitive mood also was evidenced in legislation narrowing the scope of prisoner rights.

THE PRISON LITIGATION REFORM ACT

The *Prison Litigation Reform Act* signed in 1996 exemplifies social disinterest in inmate rights, particularly the concern that inmates somehow have too many legal resources available to them. The legislation requires that inmates exhaust all available administrative remedies before they can file a civil rights action suit in Federal Court. This means that the inmate must go through an institutional or state grievance process regardless of whether that process has been certified as constitutional by the Courts. Also, the Act requires that before inmates can receive damages for mental or emotional injury suffered while in custody they must be able to show physical injury.

Another aspect of the *Prison Litigation Reform Act* prohibits prisoners from filing *in forma pauperis* (as an indigent person who has court fees and costs waived) if they have filed three or more actions in Federal court that were dismissed as frivolous or malicious or for failing to state a claim on which relief can be granted. In addition, inmates who do have any assets or funds in their commissary or trust fund accounts must pay filing fees and costs even when approaching the court *in forma pauperis*.

Finally, the Act authorizes sanctions for Federal inmates who are found to abuse the court system. Federal Courts may revoke any unvested good time credit on Federal inmates whose petitions were dismissed because it was filed for malicious purposes, solely to harass the other party, or because the inmate presented false testimony or evidence (Detention Reporter, 1998).

Although these may sound like reasonable terms, meant to single out the truly undeserving for punitive action, civil rights activists worry that the low educated, uninformed or misinformed prisoner may suffer from the harsh effects of this Act. Regardless of the merit of a future claim, an inmate who has made mistakes in the past, but now has competent representation may be excluded from the judicial process. In addition, inmates with potentially meritorious issues may be discouraged from approaching the Federal Courts because of their lack of faith or fear of retaliation from the state system where they must first exhaust their claims.

OTHER LEGISLATIVE INITIATIVES

The *Antiterrorism and Effective Death Penalty Act*, passed in 1996 also places restrictions on inmates' access to court. According to the Act, inmates must exhaust all state remedies on habeas corpus petitions before approaching the Federal Judicial System. The Act also creates a narrow time frame during which inmates will be able to file these conviction appeals. Ironically, while this federal legislation may reduce or simply slow down the caseload of the federal courts, it may actually increase the number of petitions filed in state courts across the country.

What is popularly referred to as the **"No Frills Act"** was passed by Congress in 2003 as an amendment to the *Violent Crime Control and Safe Streets Act of 1994*. This legislation withholds construction funds under the *Truth in Sentencing* Initiative if a prison system does not comply with restrictions such as no televisions, coffee pots or hotplates in cells, access to many legal resources and some AIDS treatments, the loss of programs for literacy, GED, forms of physical education and visitation. Inmates with violent crime convictions face even harsher measures such as less recreation, no access to television and mandatory 9 hour work days. Such requirements may be difficult to fulfill given that officers, who supervise the work, traditionally work 8 hours shifts.

Some states have also passed their own versions of "no frills" legislation dictating very specific policies while other states have left the daily operations of facilities to the management of administrators. Jails appear more vulnerable to public pressures for "no frills" measures but whether these are sustainable is questionable. In his book, *Mudslingers: The Top 25 Negative Political Campaigns of All Time*, Swint (2006) argues that the "no frills" concept was a political idea developed by New Jersey Representative Zimmer in his bid for election to the Senate in an attempt to make his opponent look comparatively soft on crime and criminals.

SUMMARY

Since the passage of the *Prison Litigation Reform Act*, the number of prison lawsuits filed has dramatically decreased. Even though the number of inmates incarcerated has skyrocketed, the number of civil rights cases filed dropped from 40,000 in 1996 to 14,900 in 2005 (Robertson, 2007). Interestingly enough, federal prisoners file and average of two to three times more suits than do state inmates (Thoms, 1988). Government reports indicate that the most frequently raised issues in civil rights cases filed by inmates are: physical security (21%), medical treatment (17%) and due process (13%) (BJS, 1995). Collectively, religious freedom, living conditions and brutality by officers represent only 11% of the petitions.

Thomas suggests a number of solutions to reduce the amount of inmate litigation that moves slowly through the overwhelmed courts. One alternative is to consolidate claims with similar issues into class action suits (as was done with *Ruiz v. Estelle,* which was originally eight separate petitions). This can reduce duplication of effort in addressing problems. Thomas also believes that law clerks, specifically trained in this area, could assist inmates and, at the same time, improve the quality (often meaning readability) of suits. Frivolous or unmeritorious claims could be identified, and inmates could be counseled over the most appropriate uses of the courts.

In addition, alternative dispute resolution programs could be developed where councils or neutral monitors arbitrate grievances, particularly in cases targeting prison conditions and quality of life. Often general improvements can be initiated or individual circumstances or inequities rectified without the intervention of the court. Since 1981, all state prison systems have had an inmate grievance procedure in effect (Bailey, 1985), and there is no doubt that many problems have been solved and expensive time-consuming legal battles avoided. However, if the volume of civil rights suits is to diminish, the grievance system must be perceived of as a credible and effective alternative to litigation. The inmates must see the grievance system as viable—that they are not only listened to, but able to be successful in the process—if they are to use it in place of the courts.

Finally, Thomas (1988), like many others, recommends against the imposition of filing fees to deter frivolous litigation. In fact, the author argues, this would probably not discourage the zealous filers but only penalize the indigent inmate with a potentially meritorious claim. Any remedy that may block access to courts for certain groups of inmates, as in those too poor to afford filing fees is suspected of violating basic constitutional rights.

Cases

Banning v. Looney 213 F.2d 771, 1954
Bounds v. Smith 430 U.S. 817, 97 S.Ct. 1491, 52 L.Ed.2d 72, 1977
Cantell v. Connecticut 310 U.S. 296, 60 S.Ct. 900, 1940
Coffin v. Reichard 143 F.2d 443, 1944
Cooper v. Pate 378 U.S. 546, 1964
Cornell v. State 74 Tenn 624, 1881
Cosco v. Uphoff, 10th Cir, No.99–8036, per curiam, 11/22/99.
Cruz v. Beto 405 U.S. 319, 92 S.Ct. 1079, 31 L.Ed. 2d 263, 1972
Fulwood v. Clemmer 206 F. Supp 370, 1962
Holt v. Sarver 309 F. Supp 362, 1970
Hooks v. Wainwright 536 F.Supp 1330, 1982
Hudson v. Palmer 468 U.S. 517, 104 S.Ct. 3194, 1984
Johnson v. Avery 393 U.S. 483, 89 S.Ct. 747, 21 L.Ed. 2d 718, 1969
Jordan v. Gardner 986 F.2d 1521, 1993
Mayweathers v. Terhune 328 F. Supp 2d 1086, 2004
O'Lone v. Estate of Shabazz 482 U.S. 342, 107 S.Ct. 2400, 96 L.Ed. 2d 282, 1987
Phelps v. Dunn (U.S. Court of Appeals, Sixth Circuit, 1992).
Preiser v. Rodriguez 411 U.S. 475, 1973
Procunier v. Martinez 416 U.S. 396, 94 S.Ct. 1800, 1974
Pugh v. Locke 406 F.Supp 318, 1976
Purnell v. Lord (U.S. Court of Appeals, Second Circuit, 1992)
Ruffin v. Commonwealth 62 Va (21 Gratt.) 790, 1871
Ruiz v. Estelle 679 F.2d 1115 (5th Cir. 1982)
Rummel v. Estelle 445 U.S. 263, 100 S.Ct 1133, 1980
Siegel v. Ragen 88 F.Supp 996, 1949
Turner v. Safley 482 U.S. 78, 107 S.Ct. 2254, 96 L.Ed.2d 65, 1987
Williams v. Steele 194 F.2d 32 (8th Cir. 1952)
Wolff v. McDonnell 418 U.S. 539, 94 S. Ct. 2963, 41 L. Ed. 2d 935, 1974
Younger v. Gilmore 404 U.S. 15, 92 S.Ct. 250, 30 L.Ed.2d 142, 1971

References

Albany Law Review. (1972). Sexual assaults and forced homosexual relationships in prison: Cruel and unusual punishment. *Albany Law Review, 36,* 428–438.

Associated Press. (1999, November 15). Study finds bumbling, bias in Ill. death-penalty cases. *Houston Chronicle,* p. 6A.

Bailey, D. (1985). Citizen involvement in inmate grievance arbitration. Paper presented at the annual meeting of the American Society of Criminology, San Diego, CA.

Bedau, H., & Radelet, M. (1987). Miscarriages of justice in potentially capital cases. *Stanford Law Review, 40,* 21–81.

Del Carmen, R. (1983). *Legal responsibilities of correctional personnel.* Washington, DC: National Institute of Justice, Department of Justice.

Detention Reporter (January 1998). Washington Grove, MD: CRS, Inc.

Farrar, R. J. (1996). Legal issues: Historical background. In M. McShane & F. P. Williams III (Eds.), *Encyclopedia of American Prisons,* pp. 282–284. New York: Garland.

Haynes, C. C. (July 25, 2004) Religious liberty behind bars. Retrieved July 26, 2004 from www.firstamendmentcenter.org/commentary. aspx?id=13763

Jones, D., & Rhine, E. (1985, Winter). Due process and prison disciplinary practices: From *Wolff* to *Hewitt. New England Journal on Criminal and Civil Confinement, 11,* 44–122.

Krantz, S. (1988). *Corrections and prisoners' rights.* St. Paul, MN: West.

McShane, M. (1987). Paralegals in corrections: A proposed model. *Journal of Offenders Counseling Services and Rehabilitation, 11,* 2, 87–92.

Miller, K. S. (2006). *Wrongful capital convictions and the legitimacy of the death penalty.* New York: LFB Scholarly Publishing.

Nathan, V. (1988). Speech presented at the annual meeting of the Southwest Association of Criminal Justice, Corpus Christi, TX.

Robertson, J. E. (2007). Recent legal developments: Correctional case law 2006. *Criminal Justice Review, 32,* 2, 184–204.

Swint, K. (2006). *Mudslingers: The top 25 negative political campaigns of all time.* Westport, CT: Praeger.

Thomas, J. (1988, July). Inmate litigation: Using the courts or abusing them. *Corrections Today, 50,* 4, 124–27.

Online Exercise

Go to the website for the New Mexico Department of Corrections. Look under policies and find their policy on Inmate Grievances.

1. What categories of subjects or types of areas are grievable?

2. Which topics or issues are specifically listed as not grievable? Is it obvious why each of these areas or topics is excluded? If not, which ones and why?

3. What types of remedies are listed as possible outcomes for successful grievances?

Questions for Thought or Discussion

1. Describe the movement from a "hands off" to a "hands on" role for the courts in terms of prison operations. What social forces seemed to guide that transition?

2. What would an ideal grievance process include?

3. How does the court use the concept of "totality of circumstances" when looking at prison conditions?

4. What would you tell someone who thought that inmates should not have any rights?

Books You May Want to Read

Martin, Steve, & Ekland-Olson, Sheldon. (1987). *Texas prisons: The walls came tumbling down.* Austin, TX: Texas Monthly Press.
Sinclair, Billy Wayne, & Sinclair, Jodie. (2001). *A Life in the balance: The Billy Wayne Sinclair Story.* New York: Arcade

Movies You May Want to See

I Am a Fugitive from a Chain Gang
The Hurricane

CHAPTER 11
Recreation, Privileges, Visitation and Family Relations

The two older boys know she's in prison and why she is there. They are sad, but they don't say much. That's how I know they hurt. The little one is hurt the most. He was closest to his mama. He runs to the phone when it rings and asks, 'that you, mommy?'
Guardian of inmate's children (Henriques, 1982, p. 63)

INTRODUCTION

Any prison administrator will tell you that privileges are not only a very important part of inmate rehabilitation and morale, but an essential tool in the control and management of the prison population. As discussed in the chapter on prisoner subculture, the institutional environment is characterized by many life-style deprivations and a lack of opportunities for a normal existence. Consequently, the few privileges and amenities that are available are highly sought after and valued by the inmates who have access to them. Often privileges are the only things lifers and others serving long sentences have to look forward to. Thus behavior is regulated by the need to conform to requirements that will pave the way for such privileges. As privileges are given, they may also be taken away. This consequence is believed to be a significant deterrent against many of the opportunities to violate the rules that the inmate faces every day.

Some privileges may be associated with status or rank, such as the ability to earn good-time credit (actual time that will count towards release from incarceration). Most prison systems have graduating levels of rank where an inmate can work his or her way up into categories that earn more good-time, require less supervision, allow one to live in less restrictive areas, and provide work in more desirable jobs. Since good-time credit is awarded by statute and is contingent upon continued good behavior, it may also be taken away for disciplinary reasons providing the administration follows appropriate due process procedures.

In many instances, housing assignments also represent a privilege. Living within the general population carries the responsibilities of acceptable behavior and emotional control. Punishment for disturbances in the general population could result in the inmate's placement in more restrictive housing, segregation or lock down.

RECREATION

The presence of recreational programs and opportunities to exercise, while not mandated constitutionally, may be one factor that judges weigh when looking at the totality of conditions within a prison. Regular exercise may help inmates reduce stress and contribute to general good health as well as increase opportunities for positive socialization. Involvement in some type of hobby may also prevent mental health problems associated with idleness and boredom.

The American Correctional Association (Kahler, 1999) recommends that prison recreational programs be comparable to those on the outside and include an outdoor recreation area, an auditorium, a music room and weight lifting equipment. The types of recreational programs available vary from facility to facility and by the philosophy of institutional staff. Many states, like California, have banned weightlifting programs believing that it is best not to have the inmates built up and powerful. A weight coach at a Pennsylvania prison disagrees and argues that sports, even weightlifting, is a valuable experience for inmates. "A lot of prisoners start out thinking, 'Its you against the weight,' he says. But it's not. It's you against you. Like life. That's something men must learn." (Telander, 1988).

The National Correctional Recreational Association (NCRA), a nonprofit organization that assists many prison athletic programs, believes that the goal of sports activities is to raise inmate morale through healthy activity and instill socially acceptable attitudes and conduct as well as to develop inmates' interest in recreation so that they will continue this type of activity following their release from prison (Telander, 1988). Athletic activities inside may range from simply walking or jogging around a fenced-in yard to organized teams of football and baseball. Equipment may include basketball hoops, volleyball nets and gyms with fitness equipment. Most recreational funds come from profits generated by inmate canteens or commissaries within the prison and are not, as often believed, supported by taxpayers. All activities: arts, crafts, sports, music and movies must be supported off the same limited, inmate-generated funding source.

Over the past decade, legislative attacks on prison recreation reflect the "get tough" sentiment of lawmakers. **The Zimmer Amendment** attached to the 1996 Department of Justice Appropriations Bill forbid the purchase and replacement of weight lifting equipment and electric or electronic musical instruments. It also banned the showing of R-rated movies in federal prisons (Kahler, 1999).

In a 1993 lawsuit, an inmate alleged that the banning of his cassette music tapes for explicit lyrics violated the equal protection clause because the system appeared to discriminate against rap music and thus imposed the regulations more on African American inmates. The Court found that the policy was not discriminatory in its intent and that administrators had a legitimate purpose of preventing violence by screening out music that explicitly encouraged violence (*Betts v. McCaughtry*)

VISITATION

Visitation is another important privilege, and institutions may have different levels, depending on the status of the inmate. The concept of visitation in the penitentiary dates back to one of the earliest places of confinement, the Walnut Street Jail. As far back as the late 1700s, well-behaved prisoners were allowed to have close family members visit, except that in this case, it was only once every three months for about 15 minutes. Under the watchful eyes of security, relatives were permitted brief conversations through the thick grills.

The exposure of inmates to visitors was not consistent with the isolation philosophy of the Auburn and Pennsylvania systems, and no visitation or correspondence with relatives was allowed. As the chaplains were instructed to explain to the inmates, they were to consider themselves dead to the outside world (Rothman, 1971).

In the mid 1800s, visitors often were those who paid to receive very limited tours of the ominous fortress-like prisons. Charging the usual 25 cents, visitors, at this time generated small amounts of revenue for prisons like Auburn and Sing Sing. These institutions received thousands of visitors (not relatives or friends of the prisoners) per year, and even prisons in smaller states saw five to seven hundred annually. This practice drew the criticism of prison reformer Dorothy Dix (1845, p. 43) as she commented, "It might be supposed that the exposure of the convicts to such larger numbers of spectators would not aid the moral and reforming influences of the prisons. This source of revenue would be better dispensed with." It was.

The prohibitions of contact with the outside world started to relax about the 1850s. As Rothman (1971, p. 95) notes:

> At Sing Sing convicts were then allowed to send one letter every six months—subject of course to the chaplain writing and the warden censoring it. They could also receive a single visit from relatives, in the presence of guards, during the course of their sentence. Throughout these decades the penitentiaries prohibited newspapers and books.... The thick walls that surrounded the penitentiary were not only to keep the inmates in, but the rest of the world out.

The implementation of visitation programs in prisons throughout the country has been realized; however, their existence does not insure that inmates will receive visitors. In a study by McShane and Williams (1988) of young violent offenders, it was found that mothers were more likely to be listed as potential visitors than fathers, and most offenders had averaged 5 months since they last had any visitor. Other studies have indicated that women are less likely to be visited by males than are males to be visited by females.

The Importance of Visitation

In many studies, the maintenance of stable family relations, including the use of visitation privileges, is tied to success in prison adjustment, higher morale, and good conduct while in prison (Fox, 1981). Visitation while incarcerated has also been linked with later favorable parole outcomes and lower rates of recidivism. For these reasons, the Commission on Accreditation for Corrections linked contact visits to accreditation and called for fewer restrictions on visits when possible (Craig, 1996).

Though visitation programs are somewhat expensive and time consuming to operate, their presence gives management an important incentive or reward to offer inmates to cooperate and maintain good behavior. In most state and federal institutions, visitation policies include limitations on visiting times and days, a restricted number of visitors allowed, and provisions for disqualifying anyone undesirable from a visitors list. This could include anyone with a previous incarceration or those who have previously caused a disruption during a visit. Most policies include limitations on the type of contact visitors may have with inmates.

In a study of changes in visitation policies between 1971, 1981 and 1991, it was found that the average number of visits inmates received per month increased, as well as institutional policies on the length of time per visit. However, there are more limitations now on the number of visitors allowed in at a time, and on the number of days the institution has visiting hours. According to the study, inmates are allowed more phone calls, and longer phone calls with less monitoring of conversations than twenty years ago and more mail is sent and received by prisoners than in previous decades (Dickinson & Seaman, 1994).

Contact Visits

Contact visits permit inmates to have some degree of physical contact with a visitor and usually take place out in a yard at picnic tables or in recreation rooms inside the institution. Most visitation areas are overcrowded, and there is no ability to carry on a private conversation. The presence of the guards is overpowering, and many inmates and families are too disconcerted to appreciate the visit. In the state prison in Southern Michigan, for example, maximum security inmates are stripped and searched including anal cavity inspections both before and after having a visit (Kalinich, 1980). In some states, visitors themselves are subject to pat down and even strip searches. Noting the discomfort of the visitation process, many families mutually agree to refrain from visiting.

The plight of the visitor subjected to strip searches was taken up by the Eighth Circuit Court of Appeals in *Smothers v. Gibson*. On an informant's tip that she would be smuggling drugs, 68 year old Smothers was strip searched prior to the visit. The court found that prison officials had improperly relied on an informant's tip without adequate information as to the nature of the tip, the reliability of the informant, or the degree of corroboration and that the plaintiff's Fourth Amendment rights had been violated. While the court recognized the security interest in such searches when appropriate, they felt that as applied here, the search was unreasonable.

According to Seaman and Dickinson (1996), contact visits support the relationships that inmates try to maintain with their family and friends. Positive social roles such as son, husband, father, brother and boyfriend can be strengthened by the close personal aspects of the contact visit. In addition, the contact visit and the support of friends and family further act to insulate the inmate from the stresses and pressures of institutional life. Less prisonization and involvement in the subculture may help the inmate resist criminal associations and activities both inside the prison and once released. In fact, The American Correctional Association's belief in the value of contact visits has led to its inclusion as one of the standards for accreditation.

While there are certainly security concerns about contact visits, particularly the exchange of contraband, supporters argue that the benefits outweigh the possible disadvantages and that effective screening measures should encourage and not detract from the practice. Proponents of increased visitation argue that the schedule for visits should be extended by increasing the number of visits each inmate is allowed per month and the length of those visits. More visitors should be allowed for a greater percentage of inmates and the visiting environment should be enhanced to facilitate relaxed, comfortable interactions (Seaman & Dickinson, 1996).

Conjugal Visits

Historically, conjugal visits or family visits have allowed prisoners to meet privately with spouses or entire nuclear families in a restricted housing area usually for a twenty-four hour period. Philosophically, the idea is to maintain a "normal" type of family interaction that will preserve ties until such time as the inmate is released. It is believed that releasing prisoners back into intact families is the most effective relapse prevention strategy, something that has been supported by parole data over the years. As one person described it, conjugal visits are more important for maintaining a family that is functional than for repairing a dysfunctional family (Carlson & Cevera, 1991). Some institutions provide a broader range of marital counseling and parenting workshops that have contact components for a limited number of participants enrolled in the programs.

While conjugal visits for inmates are common in other countries like Canada, Japan, Mexico, Peru, Sweden, Poland, and in the former Soviet Union (Hopper, 1969), they have not be favored by prison officials in this country. Interestingly enough, conjugal visits have been utilized in Mississippi and South Carolina since the early 1900s because of strong religious preferences for discouraging homosexual relations and encouraging heterosexual activity. Currently, six states have some type of conjugal visiting program (California, Conn, Mississippi, New Mexico, New York, Washington) which is fewer than nine or ten years ago. The practice is prohibited in federal institutions, because of government concerns about potential security issues, negative staff attitudes, lack of equal access for all inmates, particularly long term prisoners and the potential for abuses such as inmates getting married to a friend, just to qualify (Carlson, 1996).

In most states that offer conjugal visits, the programs have shifted to an emphasis on "family reunification" so that a wider range of family members are included and less focus is on maintaining sexual relations and more is placed on maintaining normal patterns of interaction and communication. Most programs are open only to couples legally married although California has recently announced that gay couples would be included (Martin, 2007). Often prisoners must wait a considerable period of time, and meet a number of classification criteria before a visit is designated to them. States may use adjoining houses, efficiency apartments, tents, trailers, and mobile homes to conduct family visits.

The arguments in favor of conjugal visits have been summarized by Goetting (1982). The value of these visits would be in the contribution toward marital stability by continuing, however, intermittently, some normal relations, and the incentive for conformity or good behavior on the part of the inmate that would allow the extension of such a privilege. Maintaining close contact with a spouse would promote ties to the outside that will ease the offender's transition back to the community and enhance their potential for successful reintegration into society. Conjugal visits are also supported for their potential to enhance an inmate's self-esteem and to provide a healthy intimacy for both the offender and the spouse. Some proponents also believe that conjugal visits would reduce tension and hostility between inmates and could reduce homosexual activity. However, there are a variety of theoretical explanations for such behavior, some of which would not be displaced by periodic conjugal visits.

Opponents of conjugal visits contend that such an arrangement places undue emphasis on the sexual aspects of relationships and unfairly recognizes only legal marriages as well as heterosexual couples. Security concerns have traditionally found such visitation policies to be high risk and expensive to offset with all the necessary precautions. Officials are concerned that there might be legal liabilities and ethical dilemmas in arrangements such as the spread of AIDS and other sexually transmitted diseases, and pregnancies for which the inmate could not provide support.

Conjugal visits in California date back to 1968 and a program instituted by then Governor Ronald Reagan to reduce rape in prison. According to a 1995 report, California spent $3.7 million per year on the conjugal visit program that supervised about 25,000 visits annually (Abrahamson & Sneiderman, 1995). Although it is uncertain how the cost is actually calculated, recent negative public attitudes toward such programming has caused administrators to reduce or eliminate the program in many jurisdictions. A national survey of prison wardens found that about 22 percent supported conjugal visits and that those who did not were more concerned about the operational hurdles (cost, space, security) than public opinion (Leone & Kinkade, 1996).

Legal Aspects of Visitation

While there is no absolute right to visitation, existing policies must be applied equally and fairly with a legitimate security reason for distinctions made in the amount and type of access inmates have to visitors within an institution. The Courts have generally upheld prison administrator's limitations on visits as in the finding that relatives of an inmate could be denied visits on the basis of a criminal record (*Walker v. Pate*) or an informant's claim that the relative had previously smuggled contraband into the unit (*Rowland v. Wolff*). The Courts have also held that there is no right to conjugal visits (*Tarlton v. Clark*) and that visitation privileges can be extended to non-family members if officials believe that the friendship is genuine and of value to the inmate (*Lynott v. Henderson*)(Craig, 1996). In agreeing to continued restrictions on non-contact visits including denying visits to inmates with drug violations in prison, requiring children under 18 to be accompanied by a guardian or immediate family member and denying visits with children for whom parental rights had been terminated, the Supreme Court in *Overton v. Bazzetta* (2003) argued that the policies protected children as well as served the security goals of the institution. The Courts have not ruled, as of this date, on the federal prison system's tendency to deny visits from friends made **after** incarceration while favoring friends that the inmate knew **earlier.** It does not seem completely logical that the friends the inmate knew before would be the best role models, while new relationships may be less criminally connected.

FAMILY RELATIONS

According to many experts, parent-child separations appear to be toughest on women. In greater proportions than men, women have been the caretaker parent prior to incarceration. In many instances, women who are incarcerated have not been included in the decision of where the child will be placed during her absence. The small number of potential sites for women assigned to prison usually means that these inmates will be placed further from the family, in a remote location, so it will be difficult for family members to arrange visits. Many families do not have access to a car and must rely on friends or public transportation.

It is estimated that there are over 1.5 million children with an incarcerated parent and that almost 170,000 children have a mother in prison or jail (Bloom, 1996). Statistics indicate that most incarcerated women in the U.S. are of childbearing age and that 70–80 percent of the women are already mothers. With the female inmate population growing at a greater rate than the male, it is expected that the number of potential parent-child relationship problems brought to prison will increase.

Already, over half a million men who are incarcerated, two-thirds of state prisoners and three-quarters of the federal offenders, are fathers (Lanier, 1996). There are many legal, economic, emotional and relationship problems that arise that are unique for incarcerated parents. Issues that cause stress for inmates generally translate into behavior and adjustment problems for prison management.

The stress of separation from spouses and children may be further heightened by formal legal proceedings initiated against the partner or parent while incarcerated. In 28 states, incarceration is grounds for divorce. In 16 jurisdictions, the court may terminate a parent's custodial rights over a child upon conviction of a felony (6 states) or imprisonment (10 states). A conviction may also serve as grounds for a finding of unfitness in a custody or adoption proceeding (Burton et al., 1987). While most children are taken into care by the remaining spouse or a grandparent it is also possible that parental ties may be formally and permanently severed.

The *Adoption and Safe Families Act of 1997* shortened the time children spend in foster care before parental rights are terminated. Female drug offenders in particular have been significantly impacted by this legislation. Courts may use the mother's conviction as automatic grounds for termination and with delays in notification getting to the female prisoner and the lack of official legal representation to assist her, it is often difficult to prevail in such cases.

According to Bloom (1996) studies indicate that children with a parent in prison suffer stress and trauma from that separation and often exhibit symptoms of anxiety, depression, aggression and learning disorders. Many redirect anger and irritability towards school which leads to disruption, truancy and poor performance.

For a number of reasons, the visits of a child to prison are particularly stressful for a mother. Although the mothers strongly desire to see their children, there are possible detrimental effects associated with the visit. First, some parents do not want their children to see the negative aspects of prison. According to Stanton (1980, p. 65), one mother was angered because her ex-husband brought the child to see her in jail, in her mind, as a way to humiliate her in front of the child and to inspire embarrassment towards her because he planned to marry and seek permanent custody of the child.

Secondly, even if they do overcome their reservations about the child visiting prison, often times, the caretakers or guardians of the child will not bring them to prison despite the mother's wishes. Often this is because the visitation experience itself is so frustrating. As one visiting sister explained (Coralia G. in Bloom & Steinhart, 1993):

> The day would begin at 9:00 am and it would take hours to get to the prison and fill out all the papers. Sometimes we wouldn't get into the visiting room until 2:00 pm. Since we couldn't take in any food, we'd have to eat from the vending machines in the prison. Sometimes it cost forty or fifty dollars to visit.

Sometimes guardians who are trying to win the affection of the child encourage the separation (Stanton, 1980, p. 65). Finally, some children react very emotionally when the visit ends and cry and resist leaving their mother, making the visit very traumatic for both parties and difficult for the mother to attempt again. This was more likely the case when visits were short and no contact was allowed (Stanton, 1980). When measuring mothers' reactions to child visits in a jail, Stanton (1980, p. 56) found that 38 percent of the mothers were positive and 36 percent were negative about the visits, the rest were somewhat ambivalent. Women were more likely to be positive about younger children's visits and more apprehensive about the bad example or image it symbolized to older children. All-in-all the author concludes, "visits appear to be more important in reassuring school-age children about their mom's welfare."

Mothers may also keep in touch with their children by writing letters and through phone calls. In a study of incarcerated mothers, letters were identified as the main form of contact, followed by phone calls and only 28 percent said that their main contact was through visits. Over 50 percent said that they never had a visit with their children during their incarceration (Bloom & Steinhart, 1993). The effects of long-term separation are obvious. Jean Harris (1988) explains the watching a small boy in the visiting area.

"Are you my mother?" the little boy asked.
"No, honey" Dorothy said, "Your mother is over there. See the lady in the yellow blouse, smoking the cigarette? That's your mommy."
"Are you my mother?" the child asked another stranger in the visiting room.
"I don't know who your mother is, dear…." Dorothy had forgotten the child might not know what yellow is. She took the six-year-old by the hand and led him to his mother. They hadn't seen one another for four years, and there had been no communication at all. Now mother would be leaving prison soon, and the sister who had been raising the child was ready to "get rid of him." The child was bewildered by the visit and the mother was too.
"What do you do with a kid that age? Jesus, he's runnin' all over the place."
Her answer was to leave him and have a cigarette.

Certainly one of the most painful effects of prison is the loss of contact with family and friends. This separation, however, can also be viewed as an important part of the personal evaluation and change that is critical in rehabilitation. As Baunach (1979, p. 121) concludes, when mothers lose contact with their children through incarceration, it may

> heighten their understanding of heir own behavior and its effects on their children. Especially for mothers who had been involved in drugs or alcohol for prolonged periods, incarceration provided them with a chance to step back and take stock of the experiences their children have endured.

This generalization may have been prophetic since recent statistics show that over the last 10 years, the number of women incarcerated for substance abuse related offenses has increased dramatically. One southern prison reported that the number of women with drug/alcohol related crimes has increased from 5 to 56 percent of all admissions. Another warden cited an increase of 300 percent in the number of drug related offenses among women inmates (DeCostanzo and Scholes, 1988).

According to Stanton (1980), incarcerated mothers often have very unrealistic and ideological perceptions of their roles and exaggerate their maternal anxiety and concern. Many managers do not approve of children spending increased amounts of time with their mothers or having babies live in with them since the prisoners already have enough personal and adjustment problems in prison.

The concept of children being cared for in the prison by the mother is not new. In English prisons of the 1700s, mothers were permitted to keep their children with them. This practice continued until the 1850s when only those actually born in prison were allowed to be raised there. In some cases, these children remained with their mothers until they were as old as six years (Smith, 1962). Though this idea was not adopted by early American prison officials, some states have utilized the concept over the years.

In a Massachusetts institution from 1858 until 1958, women were allowed to keep their children with them. Volunteer nurses helped with the children during the day while the mother worked, and then the mother cared for her own child throughout the evening. Children remained with their mothers up until anywhere from eighteen months to three years (Boudouris, 1985).

Today, New York maintains one of the most innovative prison nursery programs that allow mothers to keep their infants with them for the child's first year. The Bedford Hills Correctional Facility in New York has worked closely with community agencies for many years to provide opportunities for increased contact between incarcerated mothers and their children. Their summer camp program, operating for the last 28 years, has up to 100 children; 6 to 15 years of age spend their evenings with a host family in the area while visiting their mothers every day for two weeks (Farmer, 2007). The Director explains that the experience is often a healing one that helps children reduce the stigma of having a mother in prison by interacting with other children at the unit and with the host families.

The California-based Prison MATCH (Mothers and their Children) Program combines supportive social service assistance for inmates with young children including parent training. Programs like this also exist in Kansas, Georgia, Nebraska, Texas and Missouri. Some states have also pioneered programs to strengthen the bonds between incarcerated fathers and their children. The PACT (Parents and Children Together) program in a federal prison in Texas utilizes inmate leaders, staff members and community volunteers in an effort to prevent criminality in both fathers and their children. A children's center provides a venue for positive father-child interactions, parenting classes as well as sessions on employment, self-esteem, values, family and marriage relationships, social service assistance in family unification efforts and legal assistance for custody issues. New York state prisoners have a similar program called the PPC (Prisoners' Parenting Center) which includes support groups of inmate fathers using a variety of educational and therapeutic resources to build parenting skills (Lanier, 1996).

SUMMARY

Prisons systems today spend on the average, less than 10 percent of their operating budgets on inmate programs which include all treatment and rehabilitation efforts, recreation and educational programs (Senese & Kalinich, 1992). This is unfortunate, as there are many services and programs that the state could develop to facilitate efforts in each of these areas. Changes in policies and the development of new outreach programs could improve visitation and enhance family ties for prisoners. Research seems to indicate that investment in relationships on the outside is one of the best ways to prevent recidivism.

Cases

Betts v. McCaughtry (U.S. District Court, Wisconsin, 1993)
Lynott v. Henderson, 610 F.2d 340, 1980
Overton v. Bazzetta et al., 539 U. S. 126, 2003
Rowland v. Wolff, 336 F. Supp 257, 1971
Smothers v. Gibson, 778 F.2d 470, 1985
Tarlton v. Clark, 441 F.2d 384, 1971
Walker v. Pate, 356 F.2d 502, 1966

References

Abrahamson, A., & Sneiderman, P. (1995, March 1). Inmates strike over bid to curb conjugal visits. *Los Angeles Times,* B1.

Baunach, P. (1979). The families of inmate mothers: Perceptions of separation from their children. Paper presented at the National Institute of Mental Health's Conference on Incarcerated Parents and their Children. Bethesda, MD.

Bloom, B. (1996). Children of prisoners. Mothers' issues. In M. McShane & F. P. Williams III (Eds.), Encyclopedia of American prisons, pp. 75–79. New York: Garland.

Bloom, B., & Steinhart, D. (1993). *Why punish the children?.* San Francisco, CA: National Council on Crime and Delinquency.

Bloom, B. (1996). Imprisoned mothers. In K. Gabel & D. Johnston (Eds.), *Children of incarcerated parents,* pp. 21–30. New York: Lexington Books.

Carlson, B. (1996). Conjugal visits. In M. McShane & F. P. Williams III (Eds.), *Encyclopedia of American prisons*, pp. 105–107. New York: Garland.

Carlson, B., & Cevera, N. (1991). Inmates and their families: Conjugal visits, family contact and family functioning. *Criminal Justice and Behavior, 18*, 318–331.

Craig, H. (1996). Visitation. In M. McShane & F. P. Williams III (Eds.), *Encyclopedia of American prisons*, pp. 475–479. New York: Garland.

Dickinson, G., & Seaman, T. (1994). Communication policy changes from 1971 to 1991 in state correctional facilities for adult males in the United States. *The Prison Journal, 74*, 3, 371–382.

Dix, D. (1845). *Remarks on prisons and prison discipline in the United States.* Montclair, NJ: Patterson Smith, reprinted 1967.

Farmer, A. (2007, Aug 22). Having a summer camp behind a prison's fence. *New York Times*, A19.

Fox, G. (1981). The family and the ex-offender: Potential for rehabilitation. In S. Martin et al. (Eds.), *New Directions in the Rehabilitation of Criminal Offenders*, pp. 406–423. Washington, DC: National Academy Press.

Goetting, A. (1982). Commentary: Conjugal association in prison. *New England Journal on Prison Law*, 8.

Harris, J. (1988). *They always call us ladies.* New York: Kensington.

Henriques, Z. (1982). *Imprisoned mothers and their children.* Lanham, MD: University Press of America.

Hopper, C. (1969). *Sex in prison: The Mississippi experiment with conjugal visiting.* Baton Rouge, LA: LSU Press.

Kahler, H. (1999). Prison recreation. In P. Carlson and J. S. Garrett (Eds.), *Prison and jail administration*, pp. 94–99. Gaithersburg, MD: Aspen.

Lanier, C. (1996). Children of prisoners. Fathers' issues. In M. McShane & F. P. Williams III (Eds.), *Encyclopedia of American prisons*, pp. 79–83. New York: Garland.

Leone, M., & Kinkade, P. (1996). Prison privatization and conjugal visitation: A nexus of opportunity? In G. L. Mays & T. Gray (Eds.), *Privatization and the provision of correctional services: Context and consequences*, pp. 103–117. Cincinnati, OH: Anderson.

Martin, M. (2007, June 1). *San Francisco Chronicle*, A1.

Rothman, D. (1971). *The discovery of the asylum.* Boston: Little, Brown.

Seaman, T., & Dickinson, G. (1996). Contact visits. In M. McShane & F. P. Williams III (Eds.), *Encyclopedia of American prisons*, pp. 107–109. New York: Garland.

Senese, J., & Kalinich, D. (1992). Activities and rehabilitation programs for offenders. In S. Stojkovic and R. Lovell, (Eds.), *Corrections: An introduction*, pp. 213–244. Cincinnati, OH: Anderson.

Stanton, A. M. (1980). *When mothers go to jail.* Lexington, MA: Lexington.

Telander, R. (1988, October). Sports behind the walls. *Sports Illustrated, 69*, 17, 81.

Online Exercise

Look up the Mississippi Department of Corrections Website and on the column to the left, click on the section for "MDOC Inmate Information." Once there, click on "Inmate Family Information" and look up "Visitation." Review the qualifications for visiting, the restrictions and conditions.

1. What are the basic requirements and are they all reasonable?
2. Are there any requirements you would change? How and why?

Questions for Thought or Discussion

1. What are the benefits of visitation to the inmate, his or her family, and to the prison?
2. Considering practical issues like cost, space, staffing and weather, what components would you include in a viable prison recreation program?
3. What are the barriers to increased prison visitation today and what can be done to maximize the benefits of visitation without detracting from security?
4. Programs that allow mothers and their infants to live together for limited times in prison are controversial. How would you go about making the decision about whether to develop and offer one of these programs?

Books You May Want to Read

Braly, Malcolm. (1976). *False starts: Memoir of San Quentin and other prisons.* Boston: Little, Brown.
Solzhenitsyn, Alexander. (1963). *A day in the Life of Ivan Denisovich.* New York: Praeger

Movies You May Want to See

Les Miserables
Life Is Beautiful

CHAPTER 12
Solutions to Overcrowding

The world thinks we're crazy, they think we're on some kind of binge.
Al Bronstein, Director of the National Prisoner Project, ACLU

INTRODUCTION

The tremendous increase in prison populations did not just occur overnight, but has resulted from continued trends over a 25 year period. Prison construction, as well as the availability of bed space to accommodate the growing population has simply not kept pace. It is not surprising that overcrowding has been one of the key issues in prison lawsuits. In one survey, administrators in 48 out of the 50 states acknowledged that they were struggling with serious problems associated with overcrowding (Vaughn, 1993). As of Fall, 2000, 13 entire state corrections systems were under judicial orders to make reforms to bring units into constitutional compliance and 5 were under the supervision of a special master appointed by the courts (ACA, 2001).

CAUSES OF OVERCROWDING

One of the major reasons that prisons have become overcrowded is that crime control strategies and legislative changes have meant longer sentences. These approaches have taken several forms such as mandatory minimum sentences served in their entirety, three strikes meaning more life sentences and statutes prohibiting parole for many types of offenders. Taken collectively, these approaches have incarcerated more people, for longer periods of time, with less possibility of early release. This is obvious because commitments to prison have grown in disproportionately greater numbers than any increases in the population, in the number of crimes, number of arrests or numbers of convictions. In most states, several of the following have been used:

- The creation of NEW OFFENSES that could possibly result in prison terms or revocation of probation and parole that would send offenders from the community to prison. Some examples are the enactment of felony stalking crimes, domestic violence felonies, hate crime laws and the criminal transmission of the AIDS virus.
- Changes in penalties that now make PRISON TERMS MANDATORY for some offenses that before did not result in incarceration such as DWIs and certain drug convictions.
- LENGTHENING THE PRISON TERMS possible for some convictions particularly if certain victims were involved (children, elderly, disabled) or if weapons were used (aggravated felony laws) or certain quantities of drugs were found. These special circumstances are said to "enhance" the seriousness of the crime.
- Passage of HABITUAL FELON OR THREE STRIKES LAWS where life sentences are possible for offenders convicted of a third similar felony, whereas before one could only receive the maximum allowed for that particular offense.
- Passage of laws allowing for felons to be given sentences for certain crimes that contain the specific condition, LIFE WITHOUT PAROLE. Previously all prisoners, after a designated period of time became eligible for parole, regardless of whether or not they were actually granted a parole release.
- Modifying exiting PAROLE ELIGIBILITY REQUIREMENTS so that offenders must serve more time on their sentences before they are eligible for consideration for parole. Some states have switched eligibility for review from after one-fourth of the sentence to one-third or even more.
- Changes in GOOD-TIME EARNING statutes so that prisoners accumulate less time for good behavior on their sentences each month. This has the effect of making it take longer to acquire enough credit towards parole eligibility or towards the actual discharge of a sentence

One example of legislation that increased prison sentences and virtually eliminated probation and parole for drug offenses is the *1986 Anti-Drug Abuse Act*. The 1994 *Three Strikes Law* in California has had a dramatic effect on the California DOC. By 1996 there were 1655 prisoners with two or more prior serious/violent felonies sentenced to terms of 25 years to life or more under the law. Another 17,080 had only two strikes but found their sentences doubled as this legislation allowed (Furillo, 1996, June 21). A RAND Corporation study estimated the cost of the *Three Strikes Law* in California would be $4–6 billion dollars per year, nearly double the current budget (Furillo, 1996, April 1).

THE COSTS OF OVERCROWDING

Although determining the actual costs of overcrowding is complicated and would include different factors depending on who you asked, we can look at present expenses incurred in institutions today and extrapolate the effects of increases in population size. For example, California lists the average cost per inmate per year at $21,000. This cost is usually set for an average inmate and would not include the additional expenses of a special needs offender. Estimates for special needs offenders could increase the costs from $5,000 to $15,000 more per inmate per year.

Understanding Budgets

The fiscal budget of a correctional agency is usually divided into two parts. One is an **operating budget** which includes personnel and staffing as well as the benefits paid to employees, medical care for inmates, administrative costs, food, clothing, basic institutional equipment, utilities, maintenance, etc. The **capital expenditures** budget is kept separate and includes the building and often the start up costs of a new institution. This may include the purchase of land, interest paid on bonds to build, cost of architectural planning, etc.

In California, the combined operating and capitol expenditures budget for 2003 was $5,480,000,000 while state prison expenditures for Texas came in over 3 billion (BJS, 2003). These two states represent the largest spenders in correctional dollars in this country. In California, prison spending has increased 800 percent over the last twenty years and now consumes over 9% of the General Fund. The prisons' share of the entire state budget has doubled over the last six years (Skelton, 1996). When more is spent on corrections, that means less is available for social programming, education, transportation, and other public services.

Understanding Capacity

Capacity is a space limitation usually expressed in terms of a percent, meaning a flexible number that represents a percentage of your total bed spaces. Some jurisdictions make distinctions between the capacity the facility was originally designed to hold, versus the number allowable given certain modifications including the addition of beds in dayrooms and gymnasiums. The capacity often becomes an issue in lawsuits. If an institution is given a ceiling of 95 percent, then they must stop admitting new prisoners when 95 percent of their total beds are filled. If more beds are acquired, then the population may numerically grow; however, they must still adhere to the 95 percent capacity. Upon reaching the established capacity, admissions should, theoretically, stop. Administrators then should resort to a schedule of receiving one new inmate for each one released.

The Federal Bureau of Prisons and many state correctional systems follow the American Correctional Association's standards for space which is 35 unencumbered square feet per inmate and the requirement for sleeping partitions for every four-to-six inmates housed in a dormitory. These very limited specifications represent maximum square footage standards. Fiscal constraints and punitive legislative philosophies often negatively impact the adoption or implementation of even these conservative space allocations. In fact, most prisons operate above capacity. The Bureau of Justice Statistics reports that at the end of 2002, state prisons averaged one to seventeen percent above capacity while the federal prison system was at 33% over capacity (Harrison & Beck, 2003).

An interview with a white-collar criminal who served his sentence at Eglin Federal Prison Camp, a minimum-security facility near Pensacola, Florida describes the lack of privacy and comforts in these facilities that are often criticized for being "country club" prisons.(Salter, 2002, p. 121).

Each dorm had 32 cubicles, and each cubicle contained a narrow bunk bed, a folding chair and a cramped writing desk. The newer roommate was given the least favorite places, which was usually the top bunk in the cubicle closest to the bathroom—what inmates called "waterfront property"... the bed was about half the size of a normal twin bed. I'm six-one, and when I laid down, an inch of each shoulder extended over the mattress and my head or my feet hit the rail.... The first few days you don't sleep. You're too scared... The hardest adjustment was the noise.... Prison is basically a crowded, cramped place. I can't recall a single period of time when I didn't hear someone yelling, talking, snoring, or flushing the toilet. There's never any silence.

Prison facilities house anywhere from hundreds to thousands of prisoners working different shifts, in different locations within the prison around the clock. In addition, staff working different shifts, taking breaks and conducting multiple inmate counts (including bed checks) at different times, add to the constant activity. This activity usually conducted within brick, concrete, and metal environments, results in a noise level that requires extensive adjustment.

Ultimately, prisoners awaiting prison beds create overcrowding in jails which causes considerable friction between the cities or counties and the state. Overcrowded and under funded, local jails simply do not want to support state prisoners. Some have demanded reimbursements and in Texas, the counties sued the state. The state ended up building a number of its own jails to house short term prisoners as a way to resolve the dilemma.

In 1996, the California Department of Corrections was operating at approximately 181 percent of capacity (Furillo, 1996). If capacity is 100 percent—this means that an additional 81 percent of that capacity was also housed in the state's 33 facilities. Pressure from the increased population, in part fueled by "three strikes" legislation meant that 15 new prisons needed to be built by the year 2000. It is estimated that a new facility holding 4,000 inmates costs $300 million to build and another $100 million per year to operate (Furillo, 1996).

Although California has recently experienced a brief decline in the number of inmates, that drop has only been for a couple of months and so far, has not had a significant impact on the system (Morain, 1999). It may however, have provided the justification for cancelling contracts with private prison firms for four new units of 500 beds each. It is hypothesized that the state encountered significant opposition to the private prisons from the correctional officer's union, a very powerful political organization and may have been looking for a reason to abandon the plans.

EFFECTS OF OVERCROWDING

The results of overcrowding are serious deprivations in the quality of life in any corrections institution. According to one author, "Despite the fact that the nation has opened or expanded over a hundred prisons in less than 5 years, the average prison space available for inmates has dropped by over 10 percent" (Allen & Simonsen, 1989). Stretching resources beyond their capacity is something the courts watch carefully when monitoring prison conditions. Overcrowding may be measured in shortages of basic necessities such as space, bedding, clothing and food. Vocational, educational, and recreational programs may become seriously overloaded and result in minimal achievements. Medical services may suffer in quality and in shortages of personnel and supplies. Throughout the system, high inmate to staff ratios mean poor supervision and scheduling difficulties which result in less inmate activity and greater safety risks for both employees and other prisoners.

The nature of a crowded environment may itself have serious effects on the health and well being of inmates. Increases in noise and the lack of privacy associated with densely populated living areas may contribute to emotional stress and the development of mental health problems. Studies have shown that crowding in prison cells has contributed to the spread of colds, sexually transmitted diseases and other infections diseases. Megargee (1977) found that the grater number of inmates confined to a space, the greater the number of disciplinary infractions per inmate. Paulus et al. (1978) found that as you increase the density of prisoners, you increase the rate of mortality in inmates over 45 years of age. Common to overcrowded conditions are the rates of psychiatric commitments and suicides. Farrington and Nuttall (1980) studied the long-term effects of prison crowding and posited that subsequent reconviction rates are higher among inmates from facilities that were overcrowded.

Solutions to Overcrowding

Research has also been conducted on the issue of whether or not crowding leads to increases in violence. Many suspect that overcrowding heightens tempers and aggressive behaviors and even escalates confrontations. Studies by Nacci, Teitelbaum, and Prather (1977), and Jan (1980) found that as institutions became more crowded, the number of staff and inmate assaults increased.

Central to the relationship of overcrowding and violence would be the notion of space. The distances we perceive of as important for maintaining social contact as well as comfort has been designated our "personal space" or "buffer zone." When people position themselves closer than we feel necessary, we might refer to this as a situation where our "space is being invaded." In casual social interactions, Americans normally remain 48–144 inches apart. Persons who have difficulty relating to others may even require more space in order to feel comfortable. Studies seem to indicate that violent inmates have even greater personal space needs than nonviolent offenders.

In most settings, cell mates experience a highly interactive, low privacy life-style that may cause space to become an extension of themselves and their well being. In order to maintain individuality, inmates may delineate mutually acceptable boundaries that will provide them with an imaginary but psychological separateness. In most prisons where there are high rates of inmates with personality disorders and emotional difficulties, crowding may produce symptoms of stress.

Interestingly enough, surveys of inmates have shown that open dorms represent the least desirable housing arrangement. Besides having higher levels of inmate to inmate and inmate to staff aggression, and higher levels of illness complaints, the inmates' perception of crowding increased in open dorms (McCain, 1976; Cox et al., 1984). However, as Paulus et al. indicate (1981, p. 53), modifications can be made to minimize the negative aspects of open dormitories. Suggestions include not stacking bunk beds on top of each other and separating the dormitory into bays or cubicles. Both arrangements will help reduce the negative reactions associated with open dorms. In addition, administration as well as officers should be aware of the problems prisoners face in coping with crowded living conditions. Efforts should be made to minimize the territorial frustration created by reassignment, the displacement of property in cell searches, cell mate changes, as well as any other short-notice changes in living arrangements.

THE CONSTITUTIONALITY OF OVERCROWDED PRISONS

A common consequence of overcrowded conditions is the use of double-celling, or housing two inmates in a space originally designed for one. Lawsuits by inmate protesting this practice consistently raise the question of the constitutionality of double-celling. This issue came before the U.S. Supreme Court in 1979 in *Bell v. Wolfish* after a lower court determined that you could not "double bunk" unless there was a "compelling necessity." The Supreme Court overturned that holding and instead suggested that the idea of double-bunking was not unconstitutional per se. They also indicated that institutional practices would not be disturbed by the court unless they were not rationally related to a penological objective. The task of demonstrating a "rational relationship" to a penological objective is a much easier standard for prison administrators to meet than the tougher criteria of showing a "compelling necessity" for implementing a policy such as double-celling.

Since *Wolfish* originated in a jail, an important due process issue was the risk of punishing pre-trial detainees who remain innocent until proven guilty. However, the Court held that pre-trial detainees would have to show that they were being punished, by proving the officials intended to punish. This would require a showing that overcrowded conditions were not rationally related to some legitimate purpose (other than punishment) or by showing that overcrowded conditions were excessive in comparison to that other legitimate purpose.

This issue of overcrowding in prison was brought before the Supreme Court in 1981 in *Rhodes v. Chapman*. The Court, in this case, looked at the "totality of conditions," finding that the Southern Ohio Correctional Facility was a new, modern facility where the inmates spent most of their time outside their cells in recreation or library areas and classrooms. It was held that the plaintiffs failed to demonstrate that the level of crowding caused any operational difficulties for inmates.

Unlike *Wolfish*, which had a legal argument centered around the due process rights of pre-trial detainees (the right to not be punished), *Rhodes* would be analyzed in terms of whether the convicted inmate would be subject to cruel and unusual punishment in violation of the Eighth Amendment. Since then, many cases have come before the courts arguing the constitutionality of overcrowded conditions. In some, like Pontiac State Prison in Illinois in *Fairman v. Smith*, double-celling was found unconstitutional. Here conditions were so cramped, ill-ventilated, noisy, and antiquated that they resulted in cruel and unusual punishment.

The perception of overcrowding is just one factor that may contribute to the undesirability of institutional life when courts examine the "totality of conditions." Such was the case when the courts found entire prison systems unconstitutional in Arkansas (*Holt v. Sarver*), Alabama (*Pugh v. Locke*), and Texas (*Ruiz v. Estelle*). In a study of 65 lower court decisions on overcrowding since 1981, 74 percent ruled in favor of the inmates. Though the inmates fared better in the trial courts, receiving favorable rulings in 80 percent, they only prevailed in 67 percent of the appeals courts' decisions (Call, 1988).

In examining Tennessee's system in *Grubbs v. Bradley,* the court relied on expert witnesses who testified that overcrowding can lead to depression, stress, increased disciplinary problems, increased suicide, psychiatric problems, illness, hypertension, heart disease, and even death. Specifically, one expert epidemiologist related that overcrowding caused two outbreaks of hepatitis; the Deputy Commissioner of the Department of Corrections testified that overcrowding had been the principle cause of a riot; and a psychological expert identified a direct causal relationship between crowding and inmate psychological problems. As a result, two prisons within a system were deemed unconstitutional.

It is important to note that one could not win a case simply by showing that incidences of disease or assault have increased. There must be some evidence that the physical health of inmates has declined since the overcrowding or that it is the presence of individuals who repeatedly commit assaults and the double-celling of these inmates creates a risk. One must remember that overcrowding, in itself, is not a violation of the Eighth Amendment unless it causes specific effects that result in violations. Some of the effects that are often used include the absence of meaningful programs or activities, a serious reduction in access to meaningful programs, and the absence of reasonable opportunities to exercise.

Though the U.S. Supreme Court has not established any standards for what amount of space is needed per prisoner, the lower courts have set some guidelines for housing. Most courts use 45–60 square feet per inmate in a cell or dorm. In state prisons today, inmates usually occupy an average of 57 square feet which is 11 percent less than in 1979. In

Ruiz v. Estelle, it was determined that there must be a prompt end to triple-celling, that dorms must be depopulated, that double-celling should be eliminated in 45 and 60 square foot cells, but that in 75 square foot cells, it would be appropriate. In West Virginia, prisons must cease confining inmates to cells measuring only 35 square feet. In Utah, the courts found that when filled, the average detainee had 12.2 square feet with no exercise area; the courts deemed this "intolerable." However, perhaps to avoid having to award damages, the court did not call it unconstitutional, and it simply recommended a reallocation of space. Similarly in Idaho, six inmates were confined 22–23 hours per day in what amounted to 16 square feet each (3–4 square feet actually, if you subtracted bunk space). While not calling the situation unreasonable, the appeals court advised officials to reduce crowding by following the remedial orders of the lower court.

While the courts have several options in response to overcrowding, it appears that most simply rule on the constitutionality of existing conditions. As demonstrated by the cases mentioned previously, some of the factors that may be weighed in crowding analyses are the average length of incarceration, square footage per person, privacy, and time spent outside one's cell, including exercise opportunities (National Institute of Justice, 1980). Crowded conditions may also be compounded by deteriorating physical plants and poor plumbing, ventilation and sanitation (Welsh, 1988). Upon finding a facility in violation of the Eighth Amendment, activist judges might do the following: order a ceiling on the population of the institution; limit the number of inmates per cell (to 2); close the institution; order the removal of state prisoners from overcrowded local jails; and/or prohibit some forms of temporary housing such as tents to house overflow.

SOLUTIONS TO CROWDING

There are three basic strategies employed in solutions to overcrowding. One involves reducing the number of people going into prison, another is to increase the number of people coming out of prison, and the third calls for the expansion of bed-capacity or the building of new prisons.

Front-end strategies are attempts to limit the number of people entering prison. One approach to reducing the number of prison-bound offenders is the notion of selective incapacitation. This is based on the premise that a few, serious offenders are responsible for a majority of the crimes. Therefore, it would be most economical and practical for us to allocate the limited bed space to these high-rate offenders. Proponents of selective incapacitation argue that this would probably have the same reduction of crime influence as the rival philosophy of collective incapacitation which advocates incarcerating all offenders, even less serious ones that may not recidivate.

The primary problem with selective incapacitation is that of prediction. Many criminologists assert that it is too difficult and often inaccurate to try and predict who represents a serious offender who needs to be incarcerated. For many theorists, the use of risk prediction tools to assess who should be released is ethically dangerous and potentially unfair.

Along with the notion of selecting only certain offenders for incarceration is the idea of selecting others for diversion. Probation and shock probation are types of sentences that will greatly reduce prison populations. Alternative sentences could also include community service, restitution, education and treatment programs, and electronic monitoring. Certain groups of offenses may be more appropriate for diversion such as drug offenders, DWI offenders, who may be directed to therapeutic centers. There, as inpatients, the offenders could receive treatment for drug and alcohol addiction as well as custodial supervision. Another way to reduce the number of convicted persons entering prison is to enforce population caps or ceilings on the institutions. Many states are already under court orders to maintain a set capacity.

Back-end strategies may also be employed to reduce overcrowding; this involves increasing the number of offenders released from prisons. Halfway houses and other early release programs, such as furloughs and work or education releases, assist the inmate in his/her transition back into society. In a cost/population-cutting measure in Texas, officials decided to reduce the time drug offenders spent in state jails on revocation or relapse terms by three months (Buisch, 2003). Another back-end strategy is the concept of simply increasing the number of paroles issued. Still other approaches include sending inmates with outstanding warrants or pending charges back to the places where those charges originated once they are parole eligible. This may even mean sending incarcerated illegal aliens into the custody of the Immigration and Naturalization Service for deportation hearings.

New construction strategies, the third means of reducing overcrowding, involve either expanding existing facilities or constructing new prisons. In 1986 alone, 38 states added new prison beds, 102 medium to maximum security state prisons were being built, and more were in the planning stages (Carlson, 1988). California, with one of the largest prison populations at 173,000 has the state seeking $11 billion in bonds to add 78,000 more beds to the overcrowded system (Peirce, 2007). The decision to increase available housing through renovation or new construction is controversial not only because of its philosophical implications but because of the expense. Still, proponents of construction always seem to be able to argue that it is cheaper to build it now, then to delay and build it later.

Proponents of new construction argue that incarceration, as punishment, is here to stay. Since there is public support for prison, we have a responsibility to build facilities in proportion to the incarcerated population. This would allow prison administrators to perform their duties in a constitutionally prescribed manner. In addition, they reason, new facilities should be built to replace the old, decayed, and dilapidated relics of the past that do not function efficiently or safely. In 1988, approximately 35 percent of prisoners were living in institutions build more than 50 years ago, and 12 percent were in facilities built before 1888 (Cole, 1989, p. 520). In Texas, twelve of the more than 100 facilities were built prior to 1920. The state's routine maintenance budget tops $100 million per year and construction of new facilities has not kept pace with population demands (Buisch, 2003). Regardless of the growth or decline of the prison population over the next few years, many of the antiquated facilities will have to be replaced by more modern institutions.

Opponents of prison construction also pose some logical arguments. One reason not to build is that we will just fill up any space that is created. In other words, some believe that the availability alone drives up prison sentencing or incarceration rates. Overcrowding today is simply a result of overzealous attempts to warehouse all of our social problems. One earlier study claimed that if present sentencing trends continued, Texas, California, and Florida could build one new 500 bed facility each month and still never reduce their overcrowding (Cory &

Gettinger, 1984). The decade following that prediction was, for the most part, borne out.

PRIVATIZATION

Privatization refers to the process by which the state contracts with private businesses to receive correctional services. These corporations perform various functions in the custody of jail and prison inmates. Their degree of involvement ranges from individual operations such as food preparation or laundry or medical treatment to managing entire prisons.

There is a wide variety of possible economic arrangements to privatization agreements. Many private firms contract to operate the facility or some service at the facility at a set per/inmate per day fee. Those involved with work programs may draw a percent of whatever profits are realized from the goods or services produced within the walls. Another use of private business is simply to provide financing for a prison when the state or federal government needs to build but doesn't have the up-front capital to invest.

Today, there are approximately 64,000 inmates, about 3% of all prisoners, in the roughly 140 private facilities in this country. Revenues from private sector units is near $1 billion. The Federal Bureau of Prisons is the most common user of private incarceration while the states of Texas, Florida, Oklahoma, Louisiana, and Tennessee are also deeply committed to the use of private facilities (McDonald et al., 1998).

One of the most controversial aspects of privatization is that it implies the transfer of management responsibilities to the private business who then provides the daily necessities of programming and services deemed essential by current legal and professional standards. As we will see, this does not release the government from its obligation to insure that constitutional procedures are being followed, nor does it excuse the government from liability when violations do occur.

As explained earlier, American corrections is no stranger to privatization. Leasing entire inmate populations was common in many states like California, Texas, Louisiana, Michigan, and Missouri during the nineteenth and even the early twentieth century. A close analysis of today's prisons might find many problems that are similar to those years ago when overcrowding, understaffing, too little money, rising expenses, and the inability to produce a profit made the prison system a burden the state was desperate to unload. Like today, there was less public concern for how the prisons were run, as long as they ran as economically and securely as possible.

Throughout the correctional system, in institutions, and in the community, private businesses are supplying prison work or industry, educational, vocational, drug treatment, and health programs as well as halfway houses and juvenile detention centers. Private corporations have established facilities to house illegal aliens pending deportation for the U.S. Immigration and Naturalization Service. They also maintain custody of prisoners for the U.S. Marshal's Service and the Federal Bureau of Prisons as well as for local jails.

The Economics of Privatization

Private corrections providers often claim that they can save money by eliminating the traditional "red tape" that accompanies such operations as civil service hiring and costly retirement systems. Corporations may also escape the cumbersome bidding process that is required any time the government purchases goods or services on the open market. The ability to purchase items such as food and clothing quickly results in cost savings.

One early estimate was that private corporations might be able to reduce administrative costs by about one-third of state operated systems. However, critics fear that cost savings will also mean lower paid staff and reduced employee benefits and training which could result in less qualified and more disgruntled workers. It is also feared that state laws that prohibit correctional officers from striking would not apply to private employees. Contractors, on the other hand, argue that they will pay higher wages and offer better benefits than the state and, further, that emergency preparedness agreements with the state will allow for the intervention of the National Guard (Hackett et al., 1987). To date, studies have not really been able to substantiate significant cost savings from the use of private prisons (Pratt et al., 1999). There have also been concerns that some of the positive evaluations of private prison operations that have appeared in the literature have been conducted by persons with financial and professional relationships with private prison corporations.

The Constitutionality of Private Prisons

Current federal law has provided the statutory authority to contract out the management of an entire prison. The Attorney General is empowered to designate as a place of confinement "any available, suitable and appropriate institution or facility whether maintained by the federal government or otherwise." In addition, certain states have enacted legislation, which represents a consensus of elected officials, on how privatization should proceed, Usually prepared by a commission or committee and voted on by state legislators, these acts attempt to clarify how contracts will be prepared and awarded. An example is the *Tennessee Private Prison Act of 1986* which was specifically devised to avoid the costly mistakes of the past. The question that remains open is whether or not the Supreme Court would uphold the constitutionality of such statutes if they were tested with an actual case.

When the delegation question was raised in *Medina v. O'Neill*, the defendant's civil rights attorney charged that the Constitution does not allow the government to "retail out the detention of human beings." However, instead of deciding on whether or not a private company could operate a detention center as delegated by the Immigration and Naturalization Service, the court simply ruled that the contractor was subject to the same constitutional restrictions and standards as the government (Becker and Stanley, 1985). The court also held that the government could not escape its legal responsibility for those held in a privately managed facility under government authority and could be sued for civil rights violation (Logan, 1987).

A strict interpretation of the Constitution might shed doubt on the legitimacy of private industry's involvement in corrections. It is specifically written that "all legislative powers herein granted shall be vested in a Congress of the United States." By that dictum, one could not delegate legislative powers to other institutions. Realistically though the complexity of our modern society has made it impossible to adhere to a doctrine of non-delegation. The authority to delegate may be interpreted in the "necessary and proper" clause of the Constitution that implies that Congress may delegate authority "sufficient to effect its purposes."

According to legal scholar Ira Robins, the Supreme Court has not clearly articulated any standards or tests for determining how government power may be delegated. In fact, the Court has not even dealt with the matter in any substantial way since 1948, so it is difficult to predict how they might rule on a cases involving private prisons (1988, pp. 20–21).

The only two aspects of day to day prison management that seem to require government involvement are classification and discipline. As we discussed earlier, these actions determine level of custody and possible deprivations of liberty that arouse due process concerns. Since these two activities appear to account for less than five percent of current prison administration budgets, Greenwood (1982, p. 41) does not feel that it would burden the state to retain full responsibility for their regulation. Logan (1987), on the other hand, argues that the whole point of developing due process procedures is so that it won't matter who is administering them; the process will be done appropriately.

There is also a middle-of-the-road approach to the debate between the responsibility and the practicality of administering some quasi-judicial prison duties. The government and private contractors might share these two activities in ways that will avoid potential legal conflicts. One way might be to have all disciplinary actions reviewed by or appealed to a neutral government body. Also, the state legislature could constitutionally adopt the disciplinary code used by the private contractor. Greenwood (1982) suggests that if the state does monitor the system of discipline employed by the private contractor, the expense of their efforts should be calculated into the cost of the contract. In any case, Robbins warns that a prison privatization plan should always "take special account of the policy concern that the delegate's private interests will prevail over the interests of both the affected party and the public" (1988, p. 67).

Treatment and Care of Inmates

Constitutional law in the area of privatization and inmate care is extremely vague and for that reason, perhaps dangerous. Private contractors could get by with absolute minimal provisions. Of the American Correctional Association's 495 recommended standards, only 44 are mandated by law. In his report on the legal dimensions of privatization, Robbins suggests that any contract entered into should require the company to comply with not only the mandatory standards but with 90 percent of the non-mandatory standards as well (Criminal Justice Newsletter, November 15, 1988).

Though the American Correctional Association has long been considered an important professional source of standards and policies, its role may need to be reconsidered since a portion of the membership and officers, and even the president have been private correction corporations' executives and consulting representatives, The inevitable influence of a percentage of members with vested interests in easier standards and less costly requirements makes their judgment and objectivity questionable.

Since private operators would be apprehensive about possible negligence suits, there are some people who believe that the quality of the medical care that inmates receive would improve (Kaplan & Skolnick, 1987). It has already been established in the courts that when doctors are under contract with the state to provide medical services, they are acting under state color and are subject to liability for civil rights violations. As Justice Scalia wrote in *West v. Adkins*,

> a physician who acts on behalf of the State to provide needed medical attention to a person involuntarily in state custody (in prison or elsewhere) and prevented from otherwise obtaining it, and who causes physical harm to such a person by deliberate indifference, violates the Fourteenth Amendment's protection against the deprivation of liberty without due process.

Recognizing that both due process and Eighth Amendment rights might be at stake, Justice Blackmun expressed the feelings of the unanimous majority in *West*.

> Contracting out prison medical care does not relieve the State of its constitutional duty to provide adequate medical treatment to those in its custody, and it does not deprive the State's prisoners of the means to vindicate their Eighth Amendment rights.

Advantages of Privatization

Private businesses can mobilize quickly, build rapidly, and become operational in shorter periods of time than the state. With the ability to expeditiously transfer inmates from overcrowded facilities into privately contracted prisons, the state could avoid building costly new institutions that may not always be necessary. If the need for additional space arises, private contracts can be utilized and then terminated when no longer required. This "elasticity" in the supply of imprisonment could enhance efficient management through renewable, adjustable contracts (Logan, 1986).

The private sector could offer temporary relief during peak incarceration periods while the state is either deciding whether to build or in the process of construction. As the city of Atlanta found out, this is important; there, the fact that a new jail was being constructed was no defense to charges that existing conditions of confinement were inadequate, unsanitary and unhealthy. The inmate filing suit in *Goodson v. City of Atlanta* was awarded $45,000 in compensatory damages and $5,000 in punitive damages. The findings were upheld by the Court of Appeals.

Legally mandated changes in corrections policy can also generate the need for rapid capacity expansion capability. In Pennsylvania in 1975, the Attorney General ruled that juveniles could not be incarcerated in adult facilities. Within 10 days, a private company converted state buildings into the Weaversville Intensive Treatment Unit. In another example, a detention center for illegal aliens was privately financed and built within seven months, and it usually takes from two to five years for a state to plan and construct a prison (Clear & Cole, 1986).

In addition to being able to build quickly, the private developer may also be able to select facility sites for economic rather than political reasons. Traditionally, there have been accusations of patronage and lobbying pressure to bring the economically enhancing prison operations to needy or powerful communities. Often these awards did not make good geographic management sense. For example, years ago, Texas officials designated an area in the extreme northwest part of the state for a new prison. While inmate advocates were pleased to see an institution allowing family access to this remote, though largely metropolitan area, its location—almost 700 miles from the department's headquarters—made management challenging. Perhaps the contracting of private management at these facilities would be more practical than long distance supervision.

Another possible advantage to private prisons is in the nature of private enterprise itself. For some reason, the private sector is more likely to experiment, look for creative solutions to problems, and try new methods of achieving desired goals. Although most experimentation is linked to attempts to be more cost efficient, new innovations may also result in improvements in the quality of corrections.

Disadvantages of Privatization

One of the major arguments against private prisons is that private investors would have a monetary incentive to maintain and even increase the number of people imprisoned. As critics Sagarin and Maghan (1986) write:

> ...the Wall Street companies, the architectural firms eager to build new facilities, the contractors who will be paid per prisoner have a vested interest in seeing that the incarcerated population of American increases. Whether that increase should take place is a matter of public policy and should be decided without the propaganda barrage of billion-dollar firms.... They can buy virtually unlimited television and newspaper time and space, reach the highest political levels and unleash upon America a program to convince the public to lock up more and more people for longer and longer periods, carefully concealing that their motive is profit.

It is possible that wealthy companies could pay for substantial political lobbying on "get tough" sentencing laws. Their contributions to election campaigns could buy anti-crime platforms from candidates who create controversy over policies like furloughs and releases that take inmates off the revenue-producing rolls. By instilling in the public fear of drug epidemics and dangerous criminals and by creating the illusion that "locking them up" is the only solution, elected officials and the media have become the unwitting partners in business' struggle for a bigger market share.

A major disadvantage of privatization is the potential for corruption. As we learned with the lessees years ago (McAfee, 1987, p. 864),

The potential for abuse of the political process by those with an economic interest in private prison management suggests that limitations upon the lessee's political activities should be considered in the drafting of any modern contract. While indirect political activities may be unrealistically difficult to control, some background investigation on private contractors might be worthwhile in avoiding scandal.

As Chaneles (1987, p. 3) relates of a New York prison construction project generating valuable benefits,

> it was discovered in the most casual way, that one of the principal contractors was a man accused of racketeering and numerous related crimes; one who had been under investigation for years by federal and state authorities without in any way hindering signing lucrative contracts with the government.

Not long ago, the Director of the Texas Department of Corrections was indicted on 9 felony counts involving bribes and kickbacks in a conspiracy with a private provider of prison goods and services and was forced to leave office.

The development of privatization has drawn sharp criticism from the International Association of Correctional Officers and unions in the various states. The IACO withdrew their affiliation with the American Correctional Association over the ACA's claim that privatization can be consistent with good corrections policy. The IACO has likened private sector employment of security officers to mercenary work. It is not surprising that many public employees see the involvement of the private sector as a threat to their jobs as well as future employment opportunities.

A final moral argument is that it is not right for anyone to make a profit from incarceration. Imprisonment, from this perspective, would be a need of society and not a business. Many feel that the problems of offenders should not be exploited or capitalized on, primarily because they represent the difficulties around us for which we all share responsibility.

Monitoring Private Prison Operations

Scholars writing on privatization all advocate careful monitoring of programs though there is some variation on the degree and type of process necessary. Effective monitoring will insure that the private contractor is fulfilling all designated responsibilities and will prevent managerial abuses. The failure to adequately monitor, according to Robbins (1988, p. 342), could void the contract by causing excessive delegation or by increasing the private company's exposure to liability.

Most state statutes only require private prison operators to be reviewed at most, twice a year and at the least, once every three years. A number of problems have also been uncovered. A private California juvenile facility has been sued for improper strip searches, inadequate recreation, and the lack of visitation and educational/reading materials. A privately operated San Diego Immigration detention center was closed down when the cost-cutting operator failed to provide adequate food, staffing and sanitation. Another private INS facility in Texas was found unconstitutionally harsh when it was discovered that 16 inmates were living in a cell designed for six. Also in Texas, a lawsuit has arisen from an incident where a private guard, untrained in the use of firearms, accidentally shot and killed a detainee and seriously wounded another.

It has been suggested that when private contractors violate their contracts, services should simply be switched to another company. However, the reality is that it often takes time to discover the problems and even more time to get released from one contract and into another. It is also likely that there may not be another provider around when you need them. Still, experts seem to agree that some type of **termination clause** is essential in any contract for private correctional facilities.

It is also recommended that adequate precautions be taken in developing contracts and in the initial phases of the operation of private facilities. Contracts should clearly and specifically define the services to be provided. Expectations and levels of performance should be firmly established, although some areas (such as personnel) may need to remain openly flexible or subject to change. While staff /inmate ratios are the most common way to indicate desired personnel strength, McAfee (1987, p. 864) notes that there is often not enough protection in numerical standards. Legislation in some states has sought to implement standards for private prisons. For example, The Tennessee

Private Prison Act requires that privately run prisons "be equal or superior" to those elsewhere in the state.

Legal experts also recommend that there be regular and frequent inspections by the government. There are two different methods by which this may be achieved. One way is to have a special observer who is in regular continuous attendance in an office on site. This person should have access to all records and books and be able to warn administrators of any potential problems before they become serious. The monitor then serves in a preventive capacity that could avoid costly corrections later. Another method is to have periodic in-depth monitoring by government officials. These usually take the form of inspections and are most often done with previously agreed upon checklists for the proper operational standards.

Finally, there should be a procedure for inmate grievances that the government should also monitor. Care should be taken to insure that inmates filing grievances or giving information to monitors are not retaliated against by the custodial staff. Studies also suggest that inmates leaving these private facilities be surveyed for their input on the quality of food, medical services, and programming. For comparison purposes and to insure fairness, it is recommended that other facilities be surveyed along with the private ones, including those that are government operated.

PUBLIC OPINION AND CORRECTIONS POLICY

Although we have seen many examples of how public opinion has influenced correctional policy, we have also reviewed much evidence that demonstrates that this is not always the case. Some recent research, particularly studies done after September 11, 2001, has indicated that American priorities have changed and choices about the spending of criminal justice dollars have shifted. In a poll taken by Peter Hart it was found that 63 percent of those surveyed felt that prison sentences should be reduced for non violent offenders. Respondents also felt that treatment and restitution were important components of reducing reliance on incarceration. Almost three quarters felt that non violent drug offenders should get treatment rather than prison and other non violent offenders should get probation. Seventy-eight percent believed that low risk prisoners should be released early to participate in rehabilitation programming and more than twice as many favored rehabilitation services over longer sentences (Schiraldi & Greene, 2002).

Cases

Goodson v. City of Atlanta 763 F.2d 1381 (1985)
Medina v. O'Neill 589 F. Supp 1028 (1984)
West v. Atkins 108 S.Ct. 2250 (1988)

References

Allen, H., & Simonsen, C. (1989). *Corrections in America.* New York: MacMillan.
American Correctional Association. (2001). *Directory of juvenile and adult correctional departments, institutions, and paroling authorities.* Lanham, MD: ACA.
Buisch, M.D. (2003, December). Budget cuts present challenge to many state correctional agencies. *Corrections Today,* 65, 7, 102–106.
Chaneles, S. (1987). What do indicators indicate? A statistical lagniappe. *Journal of Offenders Counseling, Services, and Rehabilitation,* 12, 1, 1–5.
Clear, T., & Cole, G. (1986). *American corrections.* Belmont, CA: Brooks Cole.
Farrington, D. P., & Nuttall, C. P. (1980). Prison size, overcrowding, prison violence, and recidivism. *Journal of Criminal Justice, 8,* 4, 221–231.
Furillo, A. (1996, April 1). 'Three strikes'hinges on issue of deterrence. *The Sacramento Bee,* April 1. Retrieved November, 14, 2003 from www.sacbee.com/news/ projects/strikes/future.html.
Furillo, A. (1996, April 2). 'Three strikes' collides with California's bursting prisons. *The Sacramento Bee.* Retrieved November, 14, 2003 from www.sacbee.com/ news/projects/strikes/prisons.html.
Furillo, A. (1996, June 21). Prisoners hope for reductions. *The Sacramento Bee.* Retrieved November, 14, 2003 from www.sacbee.com/news/projects/strikes/cases.html.

Harrison, P., & Beck, A. (2003, July). *Prisoners in 2002*. Bureau of Justice Statistics Bulletin, Washington, DC: U.S. Department of Justice.

Jan, L. (1980). Overcrowding and inmate behavior: Some preliminary findings. *Criminal Justice and Behavior, 7*, 293–301.

Kaplan, J., & Skolnick, J. (1987). *Criminal justice: Introductory cases and materials, (4th ed.)*. Mineola, NY: Foundation Press.

Logan. C. (1986, Jan 23). Private-run prisons are viable. *Houston Chronicle,* Sec. 2, p. 15.

McAfee, W. (1987). Tennessee's *Private Prisons Act of 1986:* A historical perspective with special attention to California's experience. *Vanderbilt Law Review, 40*, 4, 851–865.

McCain, G., V. Cox, & Paulus, P. (1976). The relationship between illness complaints and degree of crowding in a prison environment. *Environmental Behavior, 8,* 283–290.

McDonald, D., et. al. 1998. *Private prisons in the United States: An assessment of current practice.* Cambridge, MA: Abt Associates.

Megargee, E. I. (1977). The association of population density, reduced space, and uncomfortable temperatures with misconduct in a prison community. *American Journal of Community Psychology, 5*, 3, 289–298.

Morain, D. (1999, December 22). State prison rolls drop 2 straight months. *Los Angeles Times*, A3.

Nacci, P., Teitelbaum, H., & Prather, J. (1977). Population density and inmate misconduct rates in the Federal Prison System. *Federal Probation, 41*, 2, 26–31.

Paulus, P. B., G. McCain, & Cox, V. C. (1978). Death rates, psychiatric commitments, blood pressure, and perceived crowding as a function of institutional crowding. *Environmental Psychology & Nonverbal Behavior, 3*, 2, 107–116.

Peirce, N. R. (2007, February 18). *California versus New York: Grappling with the prison dilemma.* Washington Post Writers Group. Retrieved June 2, 2007 from www.napawash.org.

Pratt, T., & Maahs, J. (1999). Are private prisons more cost-effective than public prisons? A meta-analysis of evaluation research studies. *Crime & Delinquency, 45*, 3, 358–371.

Robbins, I. (1988). *The legal dimensions of private incarceration.* Washington, DC: American Bar Association.

Sagarin, E., & Magham, J. (1986, Jan 23). For-profit jails would be a crime. *Houston Chronicle,* Sec. 2, 15.
Schiraldi, V., & Greene, J. (2002). Reducing correctional costs in an era of tightening budgets and shifting public opinion. *Federal Sentencing Reporter, 14,* 6, 332–336.
Vaughn, M. (1993, Spring). Listening to the experts: A national study of correctional administrators' responses to prison overcrowding. *Criminal Justice Review, 18,* 12–25.

Online Exercises

1. Go to the Sourcebook of Criminal Justice Statistics Online (find it at www.albany.edu/sourcebook/. Under the section on prisons/jails, look for the table that has state and federal prisoners housed in private facilities and local jails. In 2005, which state had the largest number of prisoners in private facilities in each of the following regions?
    Northeast
    Midwest
    South
    West

2. Now look for the states that had the largest percent of prisoners in private facilities. Which are these states in the four regions?
    Northeast
    Midwest
    South
    West

Questions for Thought or Discussion

1. What are some of the problems that seem to be related to overcrowding in prisons?

2. What are the possible solutions to overcrowding and what are the advantages and disadvantages of each?

3. Discuss the legal concerns that arise over the use of private prisons and what have the courts said about them to date?

4. How have the courts responded to the issue of crowding in prisons and what might shift this view or change this philosophy in the future?

Books You Might Want to Read

Salzman, Mark. (2003). *True notebooks*: New York: Random House

Mestrovic, S. G. (2005). *The trials of Abu Ghraib: An expert witness account of shame and honor.* Taos, NM: Paradigm.

Movies You Might Want to See

Prison Town, USA
Sleepers

Index

A

Accreditation of prisons, *62, 63*
Administrative segregation, *104, 110-112, 133, 138, 142, 178, 190, 222*
Adoption and Safe Families Act, *230*
AIDS, *71, 105, 176-179, 215, 228, 240*
Alabama, *41, 90, 166, 179, 211*
Alaska, *27, 28*
Alcatraz, *29, 32*
Alcoholics Anonymous, *8, 114*
Almshouses, *9, 19*
American Bar Association, *140*
American Correctional Association, *62, 79, 222, 226, 255, 258*
Americans with Disabilities Act, *79*
Angola prison, *30, 167*
Anti-Drug Abuse Act of 1986, *241*
Antiterrorism and Effective Death Penalty Act, *215*
Arizona, *24, 27-28, 31, 69, 135*

Argot, *131*
Arkansas, *30, 43, 90, 211, 247*
Ashurst-Summers Act, *44*
Assessment process, inmate, *103-108*
Attica prison, *32, 86, 130, 161-164, 167*
Auburn System, *20-22, 24, 35, 83, 223, 224*

B

Banning v. Looney, *200*
Baxter v. Palmigiano, *140*
Beccaria, Cesare, *3, 9*
Bedford Hills Correctional Facility, *233*
Bentham, Jeremy, *3*
Betts v. McCaughtry, *223*
Boot camp, *32*
Bounds v. Smith, *204*
Brockway, Zebulon, *22, 23*
Bureaucratic era, *33*

C

California, *24-25, 29, 30, 41, 43-44, 50, 64-69, 78, 90, 92, 97, 128, 176, 180, 185,*

204-206, 233, 243, 250-252, 259
Capacity, *242*
Capital punishment, *3, 5-6*
Chain gang, *45-46*
Civil Rights, *32, 50, 88-89, 132, 159, 181, 202-203, 214-216, 253, 255*
Civil Rights of Institutionalized Persons Act, 183
Classification, *68, 79, 85, 93, 101-112, 153-154, 227, 254*
Cleavinger v. Saxner, 141
Clemmer, D., *125-127*
Closed system, *57*
Coffin v. Reichard, 200
Cognitive behavioral programs, *7*
Collateral consequences, *5, 139*
Collective incapacitation, *4, 249*
Colorado, *20, 23, 27-28, 47, 67, 105, 207*
Community Mental Health Act, 184
Congregate system, *21-22*
Conjugal visits, *169, 226-229*
Connecticut, *39, 161*
Contact visits, *135, 225-226*
Contraband, *83, 93, 134-136, 156, 166, 207-208, 226, 229*
Cooper v. Pate, 32, 202
Cordero v. Coughlin, 178
Cornell v. State, 201

Corporal punishment, *4, 137-138, 211*
Correctional officers, *13, 32, 47, 77-95, 151, 154-155, 166-167, 187-188, 244, 252, 258*
Stress, *82-83*
Subculture, *83-84*
Turnover, *90-91*
Unions, *91-92*
Cosco v. Uphoff, 209
Cruz v. Beto, 205
Custody levels, *108-109*

D

David K. v. Lane, 157
Death row, *52, 67*
Deinstitutionalization, *32, 184-185*
Deliberate indifference, *178, 181-182, 255*
Deprivation model, *126-128, 156*
Desserts, see Just desserts
Deterrence, *3, 5, 6, 15, 208*
Discipline, *19, 22, 39, 62, 79, 87, 125, 132-141, 166, 178, 188, 200, 202, 211, 213, 254*
Disenfranchisement, *67*
Dix, Dorothy, *22, 79, 184, 224*
Dothard v. Rawlinson, 32
Double-celling, *110, 165, 246-248*
Drug offenders, *249-250, 261*
Drug treatment, *113-115, 252*
Drug War, *33, 66, 70, 77*

Due process, *32, 139-141, 178, 201, 209, 222, 246, 254-255*

E

Eastern Penitentiary, *21*
Education of all Handicapped Children Act, 113
Education programs, (See also GED programs), *22, 47, 101, 103, 112-113, 132, 135, 161, 168, 184, 234*
Eighth Amendment, *86-87, 178, 209-211, 247-248, 255*
Elderly inmates, *52, 67, 175, 187-190*
Elmira Reformatory, *22, 83*
Employer model of prison industry, *49*
Equal protection, *157, 178, 201, 223*
Escape, *20, 25-29, 42, 45, 85, 101, 103, 108, 160*
Estelle v. Gamble, 181

F

Family visits, *108*
Federal Bureau of Prisons, *81, 88 93, 138, 166, 177, 215, 242*
Federal Prison Industry (UNICOR), *50*
Female inmates, *68, 88, 151, 160, 208, 229*
First Amendment, *64-65, 205-208*

Florida, *48, 88, 242, 250-251*
Fourteenth Amendment, *88, 178, 181, 255*
Freedom of Information Act, 58, 64
Fulwood v. Clemmer, 210
Furman v. Georgia, 32

G

Gangs, in prison, *101, 105-107, 110-112, 116, 125, 127-128, 132, 149, 152, 156-158*
Garfinkel, H., *123*
GED programs, *112*
Georgia, *32, 45, 165, 233*
Gill, Howard, *24*
Goffman, E., *123*
Good time policies, *40, 109, 206, 214*
Goodson v. City of Atlanta, 256
Graham v. Willingham, 111
Grievances, inmate, *155, 164, 181, 197-198, 214, 260*
Group therapy, *115*

H

Habitual felon laws, *240*
Halfway houses, *249*
Hamm v. DeKalb County, 182
"Hands Off" doctrine, *199*
Harris, Jean, *231*
Haviland, John, *21, 24*
Hawes-Cooper Act, 44
Health care, *5, 67, 175-184*
Helling v. McKinney, 191

Hepatitis, *247*
High-profile inmates, *104*
HIV-positive inmates, *106, 177-179*
Holt v. Sarver, 210, 247
Hooks v. Wainwright, 203
Hoover, J. Edgar, *29*
Howard, John, *19-20*
Houchins v. KQED, 65
Hudson v. McMillan, 87
Hudson v. Palmer, 209
Hutto v. Finney, 111, 138

I

Idaho, *248*
Illiteracy, *67, 112, 140, 203*
Importation model, *126-128*
In forma pauperis, 214
Incapacitation, *4-5*
Incarceration rates, *29, 151, 251*
Individuals with Disabilities Education Act, 113
Industry, prison, *32, 39-52*
Infectious diseases, *107, 179*
Inmate code, *129-130*
Inmates of Attica Correctional Facility v. Rockefeller, 86
International Association of Correctional Officers, *258*
Inwald Personality Inventory, *78*
Irwin, John, *129*

J

Jackson v. Bishop, 138

Jacksonian Era, *33*
Jail, *6-7, 10, 25*
Jailhouse lawyer, *203*
Johnson v. Avery, 203
Johnson v. Glick, 87
Joliet State Prison, 31, 166
Jordan v. Gardner, 208
Just desserts, *13, 175*
Justice System Improvement Act, *48*
Juveniles, in prison, *22, 113, 133, 256*

K

Kansas, *23, 63, 69, 106*
Kant, Immanuel, *3*
Kentucky, *41*
Knuckles v. Prasse, 111

L

Labor, inmate, 21, 26, 39-52
Lanier v. Fair, 105
LaRocca v. Dalsheim, 178
Lease system, *41-43*
Level of Supervision Inventory, *103*
Life-skills, *7*
Literacy programs, *215*
Louisiana, *30, 42-43, 159, 165, 203, 251*
Luther, Dennis, *92*
Lynott v. Henderson, 229

Index

M

Management, of prisons, *20, 31-34, 40, 57-65, 77-81, 92-94*
Mandatory minimum sentences, *239*
Martinson, Robert, *7, 12-13*
Maryland, *66, 153, 187*
Massachusetts, *9, 23, 90, 233*
Maximum security prisons, *14, 70, 84, 108-110, 141, 225, 250*
Mayweathers v. Terhune, 206
Media access, *58, 63-65, 104, 205*
Medina v. O'Neill, 253
Meachum v. Fanno, 141
Medium security prisons, *70, 109, 250*
Medical care, *167, 175-191*
Medical model, *7, 13, 33*
Mental health, inmate, *5, 101, 132, 152, 244*
Mentally-ill inmates, *68- 69, 184-186, 222*
Mentally retarded inmates, *184, 188*
Mickens v. Winston, 105
Minimum security prisons, *14, 108, 116*
Minnesota, *23, 69*
Minnesota Multiphasic Personality Inventory (MMPI), *78, 103*
Mississippi, *227*
Missouri, *21, 24, 30-31, 41-42, 159, 207, 251, 233*
Modern Era, *33*

Monmouth County Correctional Institution Inmates v. Lanzaro, 182
Montana, *27-28, 41*
Morales v. Thurman, 138
Mortification, *124*
Muehlbronner Act, *43*
Mutilation (see self-mutilation)

N

Narcotic Addict Rehabilitation Act, 32, 114
Narcotics Anonymous, *8, 114*
National Advisory Commission on Criminal Justice Standards and Goals, *140*
National Commission on Correctional Health Care, *177*
Needs assessment, *103*
New-Gate Prison, *39*
New Mexico prison riot, *32, 130, 162-164, 167*
No Frills Act, 215
North Carolina, *45*

O

Ohio, *23, 69, 166, 212, 246*
Oklahoma, *63, 251*
O'Lone v. Estate of Shabazz, 205
Open systems, *57-60, 63*
Opportunity costs, *70*
Oregon, *41, 47*
Osborne, Thomas Mott, *24, 31*
Overcrowding, *29*

Causes, *239-241*
Effects, *33, 116, 241-246*
Legal Aspects, *212, 241 246*
Solutions, *249-251*

P

Pains of imprisonment, *126-127*
Parole, *7-8, 15, 23, 33, 65, 105 132, 139, 188, 239-240*
Pelican Bay prison, *92, 205*
Pell v. Procunier, 57, 64
Pennsylvania System, *20-24*
People v. Lovercamp, 160
Phelps v. Dunn, 206
Philadelphia Society, *9*
Plata v. Schwarzenegger, 180
Prison Litigation Reform Act, 214
Political patronage, *31-32*
Preiser v. Rodriguez, 199
Pregnant inmates, *182-183*
President's Commission on Law Enforcement and the Administration of Justice, *137*
PRIDE, *49*
Prison Industry Enhancement Act, 32
Prison Industry Enhancement Certification Program, *48*
Prison Inmate Work Initiative, 50
Prison Rape Elimination Act, 160-161

Prison Reform and Inmate Work Act of 1994, 47
Prisoner Rehabilitation Act, 32
Prisoners
  Data on, *65-70*
  Rights, *132, 197-213*
  Subculture, *124, 127-130*
Prisonization, *124-126*
Private prisons, *251-260*
Procunier v. Martinez, 200, 204, 208
Progressive Era, *33*
Public relations, *63-64*
Punishment, *1-11*
Pugh v. Locke, 211-212
Purnell v. Lord, 208

Q

Quakers, *9, 21*
Quay, Herbert, *109*

R

Race, of employees, *80*
  Of prisoners, *67, 105-106, 131-132*
Ragen, Joseph, *59, 201*
Ramos v. Lamm, 105
Rape, in prison, *158-161*
Reformatory, *22-23*
Rehabilitation, *6-8, 112-116*
Rehabilitation Act of 1973, 32, 183
Religion programs, *5, 202, 205-206*
Restitution, *3, 47, 249*
Retaliation, *111, 151*

Retribution, *2-3*
Rhode Island, *21, 45*
Riots, *57, 85-87, 130, 150, 153, 161-166*
Risk assessment, *108-110*
Role dispossession, *124*
Rothman, David, *9, 22-23, 40*
Rowland v. Wolff, 229
Ruffin v. Commonwealth, 199
Ruiz v. Estelle, 155, 179, 202, 211-212, 216, 247-248
Rummel v. Estelle, 209
Rules, prison, *25, 62, 79, 124, 132-142*

S

Sampley v. Ruettgers, 87
San Quentin, *26-27, 44-45, 83*
Sawyer, Kathleen Hawk, *81*
Schrag, C., *129*
Searches, *109, 135, 209*
Segregation, *71, 85, 104-106, 110*
Selective incapacitation, *4, 249*
Sex offenders, *15, 69, 115, 185*
Shifts, *82-83*
Siegel v. Ragen, 201
Silent system, *21*
Sing Sing, *22, 31, 83, 137, 224*
Smith v. Wade, 159
Smothers v. Gibson, 226
Solitary confinement, *9, 21, 33, 109-110, 138-139, 210*
Solitary system, 21
South Carolina, *63, 116, 153, 166, 227*
Special-needs inmates, *116*
"Square John," *129*

Stateville Prison, *31, 59, 134, 202*
Status degradation ceremony, *123*
Stephany v. Wagner, 105
Stigma, *115, 123-124, 233*
Stokes v. Delcambre, 159
Stress, correctional officer, *82-83*
Strip search, *109, 135, 225-226*
Structural accommodation, *127*
Subculture, inmate, *124, 127-130*
Subculture, officer, *83-84*
Suicide, *132, 191, 244, 247*
Sykes, Gresham, *77, 126, 129-130*

T

Tarlton v. Clark, 229
Tennessee, *247, 251, 253, 259*
Texas, *28, 40, 42-43, 52, 60, 67, 90, 109, 133, 151, 155, 179, 211, 233, 241, 249*
Three-strikes laws, *4, 239-240*
Total institution, *124, 157*
Training, officer, *25, 30, 79, 89*
Truth in sentencing laws, *215*
Turner v. Safley, 207

U

UNICOR, see Federal Prison Industry
Unions, correctional officer, *88, 91-92, 244, 258*

U. S. v. Wyandotte County, Kansas, *106*
Use of force, *84-86*
Utah, *27, 67, 248*
Utilitarianism, *3, 9, 13*

V

Vengeance, *1-2*
Violence, *69, 103, 149-169*
Violent Crime Control and Safe Streets Act, 215
Visitation, *23, 62, 109, 221-234*
Vocational education, *4, 7, 22, 32, 47, 52, 101, 107, 132, 164*
Vocational Rehabilitation Act, 32

W

Walker v. Lockhart, 111
Walker v. Pate, 229
Wallace v. Robinson, 105
Walnut Street Jail, *10, 39, 223*
War on Drugs, *66, 68, 77*
Washington, *64, 69, 125, 227*

West v. Adkins, 255
West Virginia, *248*
Wheeler's U-shaped curve, *125*

Wickersham Commission, *137*
Williams v. Steele, 200
Wilson v. Kelley, 106
Wisconsin, 69
Wolff v. McDonnell, 130, 139-141
Women, prisoners, *67-68*
Women, officers, *80*
Women Prisoners v. The District of Columbia, 176
Work programs, *48, 51-53*
Workhouses, *19*
Wright v. Enomoto, 141

Y

Younger v. Gilmore, 203

Z

Zimmer Amendment, 223